The Public Clash of Private Values

The Public Clash of Private Values
The Politics of Morality Policy

Edited by Christopher Z. Mooney
University of Illinois at Springfield

CHATHAM HOUSE PUBLISHERS
SEVEN BRIDGES PRESS, LLC
NEW YORK • LONDON

Seven Bridges Press, LLC
135 Fifth Avenue
New York, NY 10010-7101

Publisher: Ted L. Bolen
Managing editor: Katharine Miller
Cover design: Stefan Killen Design
Cover art: © PhotoDisc, Inc., 2000
Composition: Linda B. Pawelchak/Lori Clinton
Printing and binding: Victor Graphics

Library of Congress Cataloging-in-Publication Data

The public clash of private values : the politics of morality policy /
edited by Christopher Z. Mooney.
    p.   cm
  Includes bibliographical references and index.
  ISBN 1-889119-40-7 (pbk.)
  1. Policy sciences.   2. Policy sciences—Moral and ethical aspects.
3. Social values.   I. Mooney, Christopher Z.   II. Title.

H97.P776   2001
320′.6—dc21

                                              99-050743

Manufactured in the United States of America
10 9 8 7 6 5 4 3 2 1

Contents

Preface

THE POLITICS SURROUNDING morality policy in Western democracies appears to pose a number of contradictions. Relative to other public policies, morality policy can be at once symbolically important and economically insignificant. It can raise some of the most profound questions of right and wrong and the role of the state in society, yet it has been, until very recently, rarely studied as a class by political scientists. Morality policies are intensely worried about and debated by citizens, groups, and politicians, yet they are rarely resolved. In short, morality policy and its unique politics raise many important questions about the democratic policymaking process, and its study may reveal much about how policy decisions are made; how government functions; and the relationship between a government, its citizens, and the values that the latter hold.

The fifteen chapters in this book tackle a variety of substantive aspects of morality policy politics with a variety of methodologies as well as work in areas with different levels of theoretical development. Each chapter deals with the same basic question, however: How do the unique characteristics of morality policy affect the policymaking process? The chapters are organized around significant aspects of that process, each contributing to the state of knowledge on a specific subject within its respective field, both theoretically and (in most cases) empirically. Just as important, each chapter also suggests directions for future research in these fields.

I begin the book with a chapter that surveys the literature in the field, staking out the general issues under consideration: What is morality policy? What are the politics of morality policy? In Part I, definitional and theoretical questions are discussed. Meier's theoretical analysis of morality policy implementation and definition generates hypotheses that should prove seminal. His distinction between "sin" and "redistributive" morality policy is particularly important in that it clarifies a definitional question that has had researchers talking past each other for several years. Studlar brings a comparative perspective to bear on the definition of morality policy, looking at both the differences in what is treated as morality policy among countries and the way that individual countries frequently deal with morality policy. He finds that Anglo-American democracies, especially that of the United States, are particularly preoccupied with morality policy, arguing that this is in large part due to institutional arrangements that give access to disgruntled losers in morality policy debates.

Part II contains one of the very few published studies of an extremely important phase of morality policymaking—agenda setting. Since, as many of the chapters in this book argue, what makes an issue a "morality" issue is the definition of the problem and policy, the agenda-setting phase is central to understanding how morality policy politics arises in the first place. Glick and Hutchinson's findings suggest that morality policy has a distinctive agenda-setting pattern, with mass media reporting preceding that of the professional media, thereby allowing the mass media to set the tone for the debate.

Part III examines the role of interest groups in morality policy, with both chapters focusing at least in part on the Roman Catholic Church. Fabrizio analyzes the 200-year development of the interest group activity of U.S. Catholic bishops. He finds that the bishops initially shunned political action, fearing reprisals from the non-Catholic majority. Their initial forays into politics were solely in pursuit of their church's economic interests, as is typical of interest groups. The bishops slowly became active on morality policy as the twentieth century progressed, however, with abortion politics mobilizing them into a powerful and well-organized participant. Brisbin takes a careful look at the quasi-governmental censorship of the movies in the United States in the mid-twentieth century. He finds that morality policy can become a bargaining game between public and private actors and that both economic and moral values can be at stake in the process. More important, Brisbin finds that synoptic morality policy change is possible, especially when there is a change in the values of the political elites involved.

Part IV examines how individual-level political behavior is affected when morality policy is under consideration. Both of these chapters examine the behavior of members of the U.S. Congress. Haider-Markel examines roll call voting in the U.S. House, using a creative method of comparing the influence of interest groups and constituency opinion. He demonstrates that even on the same substantive issue, the level of salience of specific votes can have a systematic impact on the balance of these influences. Through interviews with information sources of congressional subcommittee members and their staff, Goggin and Mooney find evidence that when they develop morality policy, legislators solicit less information, listen to and learn from this information more selectively, and use information that is less analytical than when they are developing nonmorality policy.

The chapters in Part V follow the most well-trodden path in the study of morality policy—patterns of aggregate policy behavior in the U.S. states. Norrander and Wilcox try to differentiate between the influence of public opinion and interest groups on morality policy adoption with a creative use of data. They also raise an intriguing point about how the specificity of opinion and policy can change the balance of these forces. Pierce and Miller show that issue definition is central to determining the politics of the policymaking process. Even a small change in this definition can affect the extent to which the process is driven by morality-based concerns. Mooney and Lee demonstrate that the temporal diffusion of morality policy among the U.S. states varies systematically with changes in public opinion and policy definition. They find that the social learning process, which has been shown to drive policy adoption under a wide variety of circumstances, is nullified by the conflict of first principles that characterizes morality policy debate.

Part VI focuses on the implementation of morality policy. Smith looks at both state pornography policy adoption and implementation, showing that values dominate both processes more consistently than do factors related to the stated policy justifications. He also finds that for "sin" policy, the visibility of and demand for the sin in question may well lead not to acceptance and reduced regulation but to more restrictive policy, demonstrating the effect of differences between publically stated and privately held values that Meier suggests in his chapter. Vergari explores the local and state implementation of a federal abstinence-only sex education policy. She provides evidence of policy compromise occurring on this morality policy and attributes it to bureaucratic discretion, federalism, and the fact that the values expressed in the policy were not held by the majority of citizens.

Finally, Part VII explores how morality policies are dealt with in two other English-speaking countries. Both studies find that strong political parties and closed institutions make it easier for policymakers to keep these "troublesome" policies off the political agenda. Cowley finds that even though British parliamentary policymaking appears to put the responsibility for morality policy (or "conscience issues," as they are called there) squarely into the hands of members of Parliament, free of party constraints, the habits of party and majority government policymaking die hard. This "free vote" facade allows the parties to take no official responsibility for morality policy, thereby taking it out of the political arena. Mylchreest describes how successive Australian governments of both major parties virtually ignored the abortion issue, even though the de jure law starkly contrasted with the de facto policy, due to creative judicial reasoning.

The studies in this book are certainly closer to the first word than the last word on their respective subjects. They identify important questions and demonstrate some of the unique qualities of morality policy and its politics. They lay down markers for the study of morality policy politics that should stimulate research in the area for some time to come.

Editor's Acknowledgments

There are many people to whom I would like to express my deepest thanks for their help with this volume. Dozens of people served as referees for the papers submitted for this book. Among those I imposed on to read more than one manuscript were Ken Meier, Don Studlar, Kevin Smith, Ray Tatalovich, and George Krause. Ray Tatalovich was dogged in his support for, and constructive criticism of, these papers and this project and provided thorough comments on the entire manuscript. Several of these chapters first appeared in a symposium on morality politics published in *Policy Studies Journal*. Don Hadwiger originally encouraged the idea for the symposium, and after Don's untimely death, the task of working with me to completion fell into the capable hands of Dave Feldman. Bob Gormley of Chatham House strongly supported the project from the time he first heard about it, and he was a great help in seeing that this volume was completed. Ruth Walsh and Lorrie Farrington provided excellent editorial assistance in the final phases of preparing this book. Finally, I would like to express my gratitude to and admiration of Allan S. Hammock, my former department chair at West Virginia University, for establishing a wonderful working environment in which this and many other interesting works have been nurtured and have grown over the past decade.

Dedication

To Laura, Allison, and Charlie—my first principles.

Introduction

CHAPTER ONE

The Public Clash of Private Values

Christopher Z. Mooney

ABORTION, CAPITAL PUNISHMENT, gambling, homosexual rights, pornography, physician-assisted suicide, sex education—these are among the most controversial and widely discussed issues facing public policymakers today. At first blush, they appear to have little in common. Some are criminal justice issues; some are health care issues; some have to do with civil liberties. What ties these issues together is that each involves a controversial question of first principle, when does life begin? Does the state have the right to take a life? Is gambling inherently evil? Should homosexuality be on a moral and legal par with heterosexuality? Public policies in these areas are, therefore, no less than legal sanctions of right and wrong, validations of particular sets of fundamental values. Such policy helps define the official morality of a polity and as such is *morality policy.*

In this chapter, I survey the literature on morality policy to understand what we know and what we do not know about two basic questions: (1) What are the characteristics of morality policy? and (2) What are the politics of morality policy?

What Is Morality Policy?

Morality policy and its politics are characterized, first and foremost, by debate over first principles, in which "at least one advocacy coalition . . . portray[s] the issue as one of morality or sin and use[s] moral arguments in its policy advocacy" (Haider-Markel and Meier 1996, 333; see also Meier 1994, 4; Mooney and Lee 1995). Such arguments are presented as "self-evident and morally compelling" (Bowers 1984, xxiii), leading to "ultimate clashes of values that cannot be resolved by argument" (Black 1974, 23).

Therefore, the definition of morality policy lies not in any intrinsic, objective characteristic of a policy or the substantive topic. A policy dealing with sexual behavior need not necessarily be morality policy, just as a policy dealing with economic regulation might well be a morality policy. A policy is classified as a morality policy based on the *perceptions* of the actors involved and the terms of the debate among them. Perceptions of issues drive political behavior, and since it is the unique political behavior surrounding morality policy that scholars in this area are trying to explain, it is these perceptions that we should be concerned with when defining this policy category. If at least one advocacy coalition involved in the debate defines the issue as threatening one of its core values, its first principles, we have a morality policy. More important, in these cases, we have a policy debate and a process that will have the characteristics of morality politics.

The core values that stimulate morality policy debate are rooted deeply in a person's belief system, determining how he or she defines himself or herself and his or her place in society (Tatalovich, Smith, and Bobic 1994). These are the values of primary identity: race, gender, sexuality, and especially religion, which is for many people the basis of their most fundamental values (Tatalovich and Daynes 1998; Button, Rienzo, and Wald 1997, 5–6). Unlike more secondary identities, such as class and socioeconomic status, most people never even hope to change these primary identities, even in the socially mobile, optimistic U.S. culture.

In a homogeneous society, in which most people share basic values, rarely are these first principles the subject of political controversy. Only when values are threatened do they need to be codified (Studlar, Chapter 3, this volume). And when threats to basic values do occur, they cut so deeply into the core of a society that their codification appears imperative, literally to "save the world" as it has been known. These values define not only who each individual is and his or her place in society but also society itself. If these values change, then society changes. Nothing is certain anymore. It is as if Newton's third law of motion was suddenly repealed.

While much law codifies right and wrong, morality policy is different in that it reflects values on which there exists no overwhelming consensus in a polity. At least a significant minority of citizens has a fundamental, first-principled conflict with the values embodied in any morality policy.[1] For instance, while almost all people agree that murder and burglary ought to be illegal, there is no such consensus on right-to-die or gambling policy. The degree to which there is public consensus on the values embodied in a morality policy varies among policies and over time and indeed can affect the politics of morality policy (Meier, Chapter 2, this volume; Mooney and Lee, Chapter 11, this volume; 2000). For example, the politics of abortion regulation in the United States, where the public is closely split on competing values, is very different from the politics of the death penalty, for which public opinion and values are more lopsided. But in each morality policy debate at least one faction holds values that are fundamentally in conflict with those of another and wishes to define the debate in absolutist, moralistic terms.

Why Study Morality Policy?

Public policy scholars traditionally have avoided the systematic study of morality policy. Perhaps this is because morality policies often require little public expenditure, especially as compared to the vast sums spent on defense, economic redistribution, and development, and therefore appear somehow less important. Furthermore, the dominant theories of political behavior in the nineteenth and twentieth centuries have emphasized economic class conflict and the pursuit of economic self-interest. While people's positions on morality policy may at times be correlated with socioeconomic status, these correlations are theoretically indirect and empirically weaker than those with their positions on economically based policy (Fairbanks 1977; Cook, Jelen, and Wilcox 1992). Because the political behavior that morality policy generates is not explained easily by these dominant theories, it may be written off as mere "flashes of political insanity" (Hunter 1991, 33). Morality policy appears to move us out of the realm of facts and reason, where social scientists and especially policy scholars feel comfortable, and into the realm of values. And as one eminent policy scholar warns, "Policy analysis is not capable of resolving value conflicts" (Dye 1984, 14). Since "moral judgement . . . is guided more by feeling than by reason" (Smith 1997, 1), it is hard to explain, and so it has been avoided by policy scholars.

To understand policymaking at the turn of the millennium (at least in the United States and other Western democracies), however, one must understand the politics of morality policy. Students of Western mass public opinion have for a generation argued that the class-based ideological cleavages upon which much of our traditional political analysis has been based have been disintegrating (Inglehart 1977). Layman and Carmines (1997) argue that U.S. politics is increasingly value based and that the basic cleavage is between those who follow traditional Christian beliefs and those who do not. The basis of political conflict in this country may be becoming, therefore, not who *gets* what but who *believes* what. And the politics of fundamental, first principle–based conflict is likely to be very different from the politics of the distribution of material benefits.

Morality policies are also the type of persistent and nontechnical issue that can create sustained and systemic changes in a political system (Carmines and

Stimson 1989). Abortion regulation, the quintessential morality policy, had precisely this effect in realigning U.S. political party politics in the 1970s and 1980s (Adams 1997). The basic values that drive opinion on morality policy are typically more fundamental to the average citizen's worldview than the values that drive even his or her political party identification (Layman and Carsey 1998). Therefore, a conflict between these basic moral values and party identification may well be resolved in favor of the former, changing how people view the parties and their relationship to them.

Perhaps the most important practical reason that political scientists need to examine morality policy more closely is that while risk-averse incumbent politicians may do their best to avoid these issues, they are so seductive to citizens, activists, campaigning politicians, and the media that they will undoubtedly drive our politics for some time to come. With clear limits on the financial capacity of government, especially at the national level, U.S. politicians need "cheap" policies with which to appeal to voters (Meier, Chapter 2, this volume). Therefore, morality policies have been and will be invoked with increasing frequency and effect in election campaigns.

What is the utility of studying morality policy as a unique phenomenon from a broader theoretical perspective? Clearly, this is a far less general approach to the study of politics than the general policy frameworks of rational choice, advocacy coalitions, or even punctuated equilibria (Sabatier 1997). Rather, the study of morality policy follows in the tradition of developing typologies and studying the political differences of various policy types. Two such approaches have been common in policy studies in the past. The first is the classification of policy by substantive topic, such as health policy, transportation policy, criminal justice policy, and so forth. This approach has journalistic and prima facie appeal and is used in many textbooks, but it is not helpful theoretically. For example, what do abortion regulation and Medicaid have in common other than that they relate to health care? What is the connection that makes an explanation of political behavior on one useful in understanding political behavior on the other?

The second approach to policy categorization is based on a consideration of the politics surrounding policy in order to enhance generality and theoretical usefulness. Authors of these typologies generally attempt an exhaustiveness to which the substantive typologies do not aspire (Wilson 1989, 76–78; Lowi 1998; Sharp 1994), thus providing an admirable level of explanation and connectivity. Lowi's (1972) well-known two-by-two policy typology is the classic example of this approach. The problem here, however, is that as with most rich theoretical concepts, applying them in the empirical world is often difficult.

Those who study morality policy take a middle-ground approach by identifying a subset of public policies with certain common characteristics that could have impacts on political behavior. This class of policy is particularly interesting theoretically both because (1) we can explain political behavior regarding this class of intrinsically interesting policy more fully and (2) we can assess the robustness of broader policymaking theories developed largely through the study of other types of policy. In one of the seminal arguments in the study of public policy, Lowi (1972, 1998) posited that different types of policy spawn different types of political activity. Most of our theories of policymaking come from the study of policy that deals with the distribution and redistribution of wealth and the regulation of business activity. But, as Tatalovich, Smith, and Bobic (1994, 2) put it, "Issues of moral conflict are not easily assimilated into theories and models based upon economic and class interests." Incrementalism (Lindblom 1959; Simon 1958), the impact of socioeconomic and political factors on state policy adoption (Dye 1966; Hwang and Gray 1991; Hill, Leighley, and Hinton-Andersson 1995), and the inordinate power of interest groups (Olson 1965) are just a few of the dominant lines of thought about policymaking that are based on analyses of economic policy. The literature on morality policy seeks to expand and test the generalizability of our understanding of policymaking by identifying whether or not, and in what ways, morality policy politics differs from that of nonmorality policy.

What Are the Politically Relevant Characteristics of Morality Policy?

To understand the unique politics of a class of policy, we must first define the politically relevant characteristics that set that class of policy apart from others. Early consideration of this question for morality policy (Tatalovich and Daynes 1988; Meier 1994; Nice 1992; Smith 1975, 90–126; Mooney and Lee 1995; Haider-Markel and Meier 1996) has yielded a degree of consensus on a few simple characteristics. These characteristics are closely related to each other and follow from the fact that at the heart of morality policy debate is conflict over first principles.

First, morality policy is technically simpler than most nonmorality policy. Because the debate is about first principles, not instrumental policy impact, almost anyone can legitimately claim to be well informed. These are "easy issues" (Carmines and Stimson 1980), and technicalities and information barriers do not limit who can be informed about them (Emery and Stiles 1998; Arnold 1990). Banning the death penalty, for example, validates a certain value regarding the sanctity of human life. There is little gainsaying this. Some of the points of debate on the death penalty are technical and instrumental, to be sure: Is there a deterrent effect? Are there bias and mistakes in its implementation? But these technical issues are largely secondary to the basic question of values that must be addressed by a polity considering the death penalty (Berns 1979, 8–9): Is it morally permissible for a government to kill a person? All morality policies have certain technical and instrumental questions associated with them, but the distinction is that nontechnical, controversial moral questions are far more prominent and primary in the debate over them than they are in the debate over nonmorality policy.

Second, because morality policy debate is characterized by conflicts of first principle, it can be highly salient to the general public (Haider-Markel and Meier 1996; Mooney and Lee 1995; Gormley 1986). These are clear and simple statements about a polity's values, not arcane policy instruments. It is often more meaningful to many people if their state decides to execute criminals or ban abortions than, for example, whether the state dramatically modifies its income tax code. In the latter case, the impact on their financial well-being is often tenuous and hard to understand, leading citizens to turn off to the debate. In the former cases, however, the debate over basic values is exciting and meaningful and so can grab citizen attention.

The third politically relevant characteristic of morality policy flows from all of these other characteristics—morality policy politics has a higher than normal level of citizen participation (Gormley 1986; Carmines and Stimson 1980; Haider-Markel 1998). With little technical information needed to participate and high salience, citizen involvement will be increased in all phases, from their paying more attention to the debate, to having informed opinions, to actually speaking out and participating actively in the policymaking process. Citizens have a great incentive to become involved because their basic values are being threatened, and the information barriers that usually limit citizen involvement do not exist. If widespread citizen participation is going to occur in the policymaking process for any policy, it will occur for morality policy.

These politically relevant characteristics of morality policy and its politics—that it involves clashes of first principle on technically simple and salient public policy with high citizen participation—are only the most agreed upon in the literature. Other definitional points are not so settled. One of these, to which several of the chapters in this book speak, has to do with differentiation among types of morality policy. An important distinction drawn by several scholars has to do with the level of public and elite consensus on the values at stake. When opinion is split on the issue, we have what Mooney and Lee (2000) call "contentious" morality policy or what Meier (Chapter 2, this volume) refers to as "redistributive" morality policy. In such a circumstance, there are at least two legitimate and supported policy alternatives, and value redistribution occurs when one side has its values validated and the other side does not.

Alternatively, there are situations in which the values represented by a particular morality policy are in line with a clear majority or minority of a polity. If one advocacy coalition succeeds in defining the opposing view as "sinful" for the majority of citizens, the politics that ensues will likely be different than when there are two legitimate opposing positions (Pierce and Miller, Chapter 10, this volume; Haider-Markel, Chapter 7, this volume; Mooney and Lee, Chapter 11, this volume, 2000). Mooney and Lee (2000) call this "consensus" morality policy. Furthermore, when there is institutional congruence of opinion on an issue— that is, when all or most of the elites controlling the relevant policy institutions are in agreement—the politics of morality policy may be nonconflictual regard- less of the distribution of values in the population (Culver and Smailes 1999; Mylchreest, Chapter 15, this volume; Cowley, Chapter 14, this volume). Clearly, the context of public values on a morality policy will have an important impact in determining its politics.

Another important question is whether and how policy can change from morality to nonmorality policy (or vice versa) and from one type of morality policy to another (Meier, Chapter 2, this volume; Pierce and Miller, Chapter 10, this volume). Again, the driving force is policy definition and citizens' percep- tion of the impact of policy on their basic values. If an issue is redefined and these perceptions altered, either purposefully by an advocacy coalition or by some external event, its status as a morality policy or as a specific type of morality policy may change. Lowi (1998, xxiv) argues that any policy can be "radicalized" by injecting a moral dimension into the debate. Court decisions, natural disas- ters, or even the media may change the terms of the debate (Baumgartner and Jones 1993; Bruce and Wilcox 1998, 11; Mooney and Lee, Chapter 11, this volume). Since the definitions of this policy type and subtypes are based largely on the perceptions of the impact of a policy on deeply held personal values, changes in the values of elites and citizens may also change a policy's classifica- tion (Brisbin, Chapter 6, this volume; Mooney and Lee 2000).

What Differences Do These Differences Make?

Beyond these questions of definition, the central question in the morality policy literature is, how do the unique characteristics of morality policy affect its poli- tics? Much theoretical and empirical headway has been made on this question, and the chapters in this book go a long way toward both consolidating what is known and staking out new territory for study.

The Influence of Public and Elite Opinion

The most strongly supported general conclusion in the morality policy literature is that policymakers are more responsive to citizen values on morality policy than on nonmorality policy (Mooney and Lee 1995, 2000; Haider-Markel and

Meier 1996; Fairbanks 1977). These simple and salient policies on basic values create "ideal conditions for democratic responsiveness" (Mooney and Lee 2000). Since morality is a political or social construct, both democratic and elite theory hold that morality policies ought to be shaped at least in part by the preferences and values of the citizens and policymakers involved (Brisbin, Chapter 6, this volume). When there is a strong, clear signal from citizens, policymakers in democracies—who by and large are elected or respond to someone who is—will do their best to reflect the desires of their constituents (Norrander and Wilcox, Chapter 9, this volume). Given the high salience and technical simplicity of morality policy, policymakers cannot rely on technical obfuscation and lack of interest to hide their actions from public view. They must pay close attention to what the public wants, be it out of a sense of democratic duty or electoral self-interest. Whereas on typical nonsalient and technical policy, there can be slippage between citizen values and public policy (Erikson, Wright, and McIver 1993, 252), on morality policy there is a much stronger and more direct correspondence (Mooney and Lee 2000).

Most research on democratic responsiveness has focused on the factors influencing the adoption of morality policy, especially in the tradition of comparative U.S. state policy studies (Fairbanks 1977; Meier and McFarlane 1992; Mooney and Lee 1995, 2000). These studies have examined the differences between the socioeconomic and political factors found widely to influence the adoption of nonmorality policy (e.g., Dye 1966; Hwang and Gray 1991; Hill, Leighley, and Hinton-Andersson 1995) and those factors found to influence morality policy adoption. Indicators of citizens' values, such as aggregate measures of religious affiliation and public opinion, have been used frequently in empirical models of state morality policy adoption, indicating that moral, rather than or in addition to economic, values tend to drive morality policy adoption (Mooney and Lee 1995, 2000; Berry and Berry 1990; Fairbanks 1977; Nice 1992).

A more subtle question that has begun to be explored along these lines is, what is the relative influence of elite and mass values on morality policy adoption? In nonmorality policy, the lack of attention paid to the policymaking process by the average citizen allows, or even forces, policymakers trying to represent the values of their constituents to listen to middlepersons—interest groups, bureaucrats, and other attentive political elites. On morality policy, however, elites should have less influence than on nonmorality policy for the reasons outlined earlier. A variety of studies makes clear, however, that elites' values do still have an impact on morality policy. Sometimes this influence is on little more than the extent and timing of the adoption of a policy that the majority of the public favors (Mooney and Lee 2000), but sometimes elite values can be determinative and antimajoritarian (Van Dunk 1998; Brisbin, Chapter 6, this volume;

Culver and Smailes 1999). Adams (1997) goes so far as to argue that elite values on abortion regulation led to a major realignment of the political parties in the United States in the 1970s and 1980s. A variety of studies suggest that both mass and elite values have an influence on the adoption of morality policy (Norrander and Wilcox, Chapter 9, this volume; Mooney and Lee 1995; Schroedel and Fiber 1998; Patton 1998). An important task for future research is to sort out these effects and compare them to their effects on nonmorality policy.

It has also been suggested that public opinion and citizen values may have an inordinate impact on other phases of the morality policy–making process. For example, Syzmanski (1997) argues that in the nineteenth century United States, even though elites managed to pass laws banning alcohol and prostitution in many states and communities, the laws often could not be implemented due to their unpopularity among the masses. Mooney and Lee (Chapter 11, this volume) found that the social learning process driving diffusion of public policies among the U.S. states is of less importance for morality policy than is public opinion. Other phases of the morality policy–making process are also likely to be affected especially strongly by public opinion.

Interest Group Activity and Influence

A question related to that of democratic influence on morality policy is the difference between the influence of interest groups and citizen values (Haider-Markel and Meier 1996; Meier and Johnson 1990; Mooney and Lee 1995). Interest groups can advocate successfully for nonmorality policy supported by only a minority of citizens when the majority is apathetic (Olson 1965). Interest groups have the advantage of being active and concerned and possessing the technical information that policymakers need to make decisions. With simple and salient morality policy, however, these advantages are lost, suggesting that majority public opinion trumps interest group power on morality policy (Mooney and Lee 2000; Haider-Markel, Chapter 7, this volume; Haider-Markel and Meier 1996). Of course, a significant problem with testing this hypothesis is the strong correlation that often exists between interest group strength and citizen values in a polity. Two chapters in this book (Haider-Markel, Chapter 7; and Norrander and Wilcox, Chapter 9) address this question with the creative use of opinion and interest group influence measures, but this remains an important area for study.

Another important question is whether the interest groups active on morality policy are systematically different from those groups that are active on nonmorality policy. For example, Tatalovich and Daynes (1998, xxix) argue that these issues are dominated by single-issue groups. But perhaps of more theoretical interest, Studlar (Chapter 3, this volume) suggests that morality policy interest groups are more altruistic than the typical materially oriented interest group. These groups fight not for what they may get for themselves but for some broader good or value that they think ought to be reflected in public policy, regardless of their personal gain. For example, death penalty opponents do not expect to be convicted of murder some day, and antiabortion advocates have no fear that they themselves will be aborted. Do groups whose goals are altruistic behave differently from those that strive to achieve material benefits for themselves? Groups that offer different membership incentives at the individual level exhibit different political behavior, and it is likely that these macrolevel goals would likewise affect behavior. Consider two competing hypotheses. First, if economic and material motivations dominate political behavior, as existing political theory suggests, morality policy groups would be weak, unstable, and easily co-opted or destroyed by parallel or crosscutting material interests, respectively. For example, religiously based antigambling groups in southern U.S. states are being marginalized in the debate over the lottery there as economically driven groups set the public agenda (Hochberg 1999). Second, if religious and other core values are more important than material benefits (at least for some people), these morality policy interest groups may exhibit a cohesion and fanaticism not seen in economically based groups. Witness the extremes to which antiabortion advocates go to achieve their goals (Adler 1998; Stefanovic and Strickland 1998). While there is anecdotal support for each of these hypotheses, systematic study of them has yet to be carried out.

Religious organizations have a special place in the discussion of morality policy politics. Since the basis of many of the fundamental values at stake in morality policy debate is religious belief, these groups often play an important role in the process, either as an organized force or merely through moral guidance and the shared values of members. Fabrizio (Chapter 5, this volume) documents the 200-year development of the Roman Catholic Church into an active and powerful morality policy interest group in the United States. Although it began its political activity very timidly, pursuing only its own economic interests, the Catholic Church is now involved in a variety of morality policy issues with a high degree of effort and organization. The Christian right has also developed a highly organized strategy to influence public policy in the United States (Wilcox 1992).

How are the behavior and organization of religiously based interest groups different from those of economically based interest groups? One hypothesis is that these groups use grassroots advocacy to capitalize on the moral indignation and fervor of their members and the ability of their leaders to make authoritative pronouncements on morality. But Brisbin (Chapter 6, this volume) demonstrates that the Catholic Church had great success in controlling movie censorship in the United States in the mid-twentieth century by adopting an insider role. Haider-Markel and Meier (1996) and Haider-Markel (Chapter 7, this volume) argue that on minority-favored morality policy, interest groups are more successful if they pursue an insider strategy. How these groups tailor their activities to the political situation at hand is an area ripe for study.

Implementation

There is good reason to believe that policy implementation is especially problematic for morality policy. First, Goggin and Mooney (Chapter 8, this volume) find that legislators use less formal policy analysis in developing morality policy than in forming nonmorality policy, and Meier (1994, 4) argues that this lack of empirical policy analysis leads to policies that are "extremely popular but rarely effective." Perhaps more important, the first principle–based, noncompromising, and highly salient nature of morality policy and politics may also lead to significant noncompliance by those affected, including passive resistance and even political violence (Tatalovich, Smith, and Bobic 1994; Szymanski 1997; Doan and Meier 1998; Sharp 1997; Stefanovic and Strickland 1998). Smith (Chapter 12, this volume) and Haider-Markel (1998) find that citizen and interest group values systematically influence the extent to which a polity enforces its morality policies, again indicating the special importance of values in the morality policy–making process. Noncompliance may even be seen as a positive moral statement by those who believe that the very basis of their identity and their most fundamental values are threatened by a law. For example, antiabortion activists may choose to be arrested for demonstrating too near an abortion clinic rather than give up their mission to stop abortions. When faced with a choice between "man-made" and "god-made" law, many will choose the latter.

A less extreme form of opposition is demonstrated by people who just quietly disregard a morality policy that imposes a moral restriction not in line with their values. Such policy is sometimes called "unenforceable" because many citizens, even those charged with enforcing it, may ignore it (Mylchreest, Chapter 15, this volume; Szymanski 1997). This overly restrictive morality imposed on a polity is often seen in so-called sin policies, where policymakers' misperceptions of citizen values are caused by people's unwillingness to express their true values (Meier, Chapter 2, this volume). For example, while certain people want to view pornography, drink alcohol, use recreational drugs, or engage in homosexual activity and prostitution, they may be reluctant to say so in public due to the social (and legal) stigma sometimes associated with these behaviors. Consequently, at various times and in various places, these acts have been illegal. Meier's

(Chapter 2, this volume) insightful analysis of this problem suggests many hypotheses that need to be fleshed out and tested empirically.

Other important topics for future study in this area include the behavior of those charged with implementing morality policy. What is the role of the high-level bureaucracy in forming and implementing morality policy? What are street-level bureaucratic responses to morality policy, and how does this vary between policies that clash with the values these bureaucrats hold and policies in which they believe? What is the role of an agency's culture in its approach to morality policy? If we are to understand the true impact of morality policy, these questions need to be addressed.

Failure to Reach Policy Equilibrium

Since morality policy debate focuses on first principles, it is notoriously difficult to resolve. As Tatalovich, Smith, and Bobic (1994, 3) put it:

> Since morality conflicts are perceived as zero-sum games by those involved, settlements are not resolutions, and opponents may not accept the democratic verdict. . . . Because values are the defining core of one's status in society, being a good loser may not be acceptable.

The losers retain their values and continue to seek their validation, whether in the same or other venues (Epstein and Kobylka 1992). Indeed, losers may actually be inspired to heightened political action by their defeats (Zimring and Hawkins 1986, 41–46). They may pursue their causes in the courts, hoping to overturn democratic decisions through appeal to higher authority, or, conversely, they may appeal directly to citizens through direct democracy mechanisms when available (Studlar, Chapter 3, this volume). Indeed, if advocates receive no satisfaction through normal political channels, they may even resort to extreme measures, such as political violence (Stefanovic and Strickland 1998; Doan and Meier 1998; Adler 1998). As soon as a morality policy is changed, the new losers, who also refuse to give up their values, begin the process again. In short, equilibrium is hard to come by.

In addition to the central conflict of basic values, the characteristic of morality policy that drives this process of disequilibrium is political salience. Since these are high-profile issues and compromise is not possible on basic values, any policy change is "in the face" of the losing side. Such an obvious affront to core values must be addressed. Indeed, there is some suggestion that these conflicts may be settled and equilibrium reached if salience can be reduced, perhaps by bureaucrats in the implementation phase (Vergari, Chapter 13, this volume).

Two other conditions may also allow for the resolution of morality policy conflict. First, advocates of a minority-held value may attempt to reform a policy that they find abhorrent with an incremental approach, dealing with the most objectionable parts of the policy one at a time. For example, death penalty opponents in the United States had little success in banning executions completely, and therefore tried to fix what they saw as the worst problems with it, such as by allowing mitigation for murder convictions and using more humane methods of execution. Advocates found it easier to gain political support for these incremental, less salient changes in policy (Mooney and Lee 1999; Bedau 1977). Another example of this approach was right-to-die advocates' redefinition of "brain death" and other moderate policy changes that helped move policy closer to their ultimate position (Boggan 1998). Ironically, however, while incremental changes may move the issue toward equilibrium, when the majority of the public believes that the worst problems with a policy have been solved, reform efforts may stop short of the ultimate goals of staunch moralist advocates (Bedau 1977).

The other condition that scholars have suggested could lead to equilibrium on morality policy is the existence of strong and unified political institutions. In a political environment in which all of the major actors agree on the values represented by a morality policy (or agree not to deal with the issue at all), equilibrium can be enforced from above. Risk-averse incumbent policymakers are usually happy to keep these issues off the agenda if they can. In political systems with many points of access for groups and advocates, such as that of the United States, it is harder to keep these issue suppressed. Mylchreest (Chapter 15, this volume) and Cowley (Chapter 14, this volume) demonstrate how, in a parliamentary system with a small number of parties, leading policymakers can agree to ignore an issue even if they do not agree on the values the current policy represents. This is particularly important in Australia, for example, where parliamentary leaders fear that these values could cut across the traditional party cleavages and therefore disrupt politics as usual. Culver and Smailes (1999) demonstrate, however, that political leaders putting up a unified front can come to morality policy equilibrium even in a system as porous as that in the United States and even in perhaps the most polarized political environment in the country, California.

Cross-National Differences

An important part of understanding morality policy politics is understanding the conditions that foster them. Unfortunately, most studies of morality policy politics have examined them in only one country—the United States. But there is evidence that the United States may be unique in its handling of these issues. Studlar (Chapter 3, this volume) finds that the United States has more issues that can be classified as morality policy than other Western democracies have. Given the pluralistic culture of the United States and its stated values (perhaps not always practiced) of liberalism and religious tolerance, this may be an unexpected result. Three factors may help explain why the United States is so preoccupied with morality policy, and these factors may in turn help us understand morality policy politics in general.

First, the United States is perhaps the most religious Western democracy today in terms of adherence and attendance (Wald 1992; Hunter 1983). With so many people holding authoritative religious values, the chances for a fundamental clash of first principles increase. Furthermore, religion has become the central political cleavage in the United States in the past few decades (Layman and Carmines 1997). Morality policy politics may be more prevalent where fundamental religious principles are the foundation for political debate.

Second, the growing heterogeneity of U.S. society increases the number of potentially conflicting sets of fundamental religious values held by citizens. A set of values needs to be codified only when it is threatened; in a homogenous society, social constraints and traditions are usually enough to sustain value systems intact (Studlar, Chapter 3, this volume). For example, morality policies prohibiting alcohol and narcotics in the United States in the early twentieth century were in large part a response of the dominant Anglo-American culture to waves of immigrants from Eastern Europe, Latin America, and Asia (Meier 1994). Heterogenous societies may generate more clashes of first principle and, therefore, more morality policy politics.

The third possible reason that morality policy politics is more prevalent in the United States than in other countries has to do with political structure rather than values. In parliamentary systems with strong political parties and limited points of access to the political system, there is little recourse for those who lose in a political fight. In the United Kingdom, political party voting is so ingrained in parliamentarians that even when given a "free" vote (which is traditional for morality issues), the overwhelming majority of them vote with their copartisans (Cowley and Stuart 1997; Cowley, Chapter 14, this volume). In Australia, with its strong, economically based political parties, governments of both major parties have for a generation been able to endure the ambiguity of a de facto abortion policy that was de jure illegal, simply because the leaders of neither party wanted to address the issue (Mylchreest, Chapter 15, this volume). In the United States, in contrast, there is a seemingly endless array of alternative venues in which morality policy advocates can pursue political satisfaction. The defining characteristics of the U.S. political system—federalism, weak political parties, autonomous and entrepreneurial legislators, judicial review, separation of powers, direct democracy mechanisms—work against the possibility of there being closure and equilibrium on morality policy. The more open the system, the more likely a morality policy debate will never be resolved, and so the more likely a polity will have a variety of ongoing morality policy debates at any one time.

Of course, with only one case (the United States) and three potential causal variables (religiosity, heterogeneity, and open political structure), it is impossible to determine which, if any, of these is the key to generating morality policy politics in a polity. Future study of these and other variables at the aggregate level, in both cross-national and cross-regional studies, may shed more light on the nature and genesis of morality policy politics.

Other Questions

These lines of inquiry into the politics of morality policy are but the most developed to date. A few isolated studies have also examined the effect of the unique characteristics of morality policy on other aspects of the policymaking process. There have been suggestions about morality policy politics having special impacts on judicial decision making and policymaking (Epstein and Kobylka 1992), enhancing the role of political entrepreneurs (Haider-Markel and Meier 1996; Meier 1994; Sharp 1997; Brisbin, Chapter 6, this volume), affecting policy reinvention (Mooney and Lee 1995; 1999), failing to diffuse as other policies do (Haider-Markel and Doan 1998; Mooney and Lee, Chapter 11, this volume), and having unique agenda-setting politics (Glick and Hutchinson, Chapter 4, this volume). Each of these suggests a fertile avenue for future research.

Conclusion

This survey of the existing research on morality policy suggests that this unique type of policy does indeed have a unique politics. The goal for future studies in this area is to map out the differences between morality and nonmorality policy politics and establish their causes more clearly in order to generalize our understanding of the policymaking process. This book presents a research agenda for future work on this subject. At this point, we have more hypotheses than evidence (although this appears to be changing rapidly). These hypotheses suggest a coherent set of relationships and effects that set morality policy politics apart. Further study will help us understand the often puzzling politics of these difficult and important issues in the twenty-first century. More important, what we learn about morality policy politics will also help us understand the general policymaking process more thoroughly.

Note

An earlier version of this chapter was presented at the 1999 meeting of the Midwest Political Science Association, Chicago.

1. Whether or not both sides of the debate need to adopt this first principled position and to what extent the debate on values must dominate the political atmosphere for the characteristics of morality policy politics to appear are points that are unsettled and that are taken up in this book (see chaps. 10 and 11).

PART ONE

Theoretical and Definitional Perspectives on Morality Policy

CHAPTER TWO

Drugs, Sex, and Rock and Roll: A Theory of Morality Politics

Kenneth J. Meier

IN TODAY'S NEOCONSERVATIVE political environment, traditional redistributive policies are passé. Welfare reform means eliminating welfare; health care reform has stepped back from its grandiose plans and now seeks merely to provide insurance for children but only if cigarette companies can be forced to pay for it. Using the power of government to redistribute income from one class of persons to another in an open manner[1] no longer seems politically feasible in the United States. Even with this decline in traditional redistributive policy, morality politics has flourished and has become the last stronghold of those who would use the power of government to redistribute. Rather than redistributing income, however, morality politics seeks to redistribute values and to put the government's stamp of approval on one set of values and to abase another.

The rise in morality politics and policy in recent years has been accompanied by a modest growth in scholarship. The literature now contains studies of pornography (Smith, Chapter 12, this volume), the death penalty (Mooney and Lee 1996, 1997), abortion (Mooney and Lee 1995; Meier and McFarlane 1993), alcohol and illicit drugs (Meier 1994), gay rights (Haider-Markel and Meier 1996), and cigarettes (Licari 1997), among others. This chapter takes a step back from the empirical studies and offers theoretical answers to three questions about morality politics: Why does morality politics generate the type of policies that it does? How can morality politics be transformed into a more open form of redistributive politics? Why are morality policies destined to fail? In a break with traditional theories of morality politics, this chapter does not generalize from past research but attempts to deduce propositions logically based on a few simple assumptions.

Why We Do It

Morality politics deals with values, specifically those values that are accepted by the state and those values that are defined by the state as perverse. State acceptance of values enhances the social status of some groups and reduces that of others (Gusfield 1963). These values are related to the demand for, or desire to consume, what some people think of as sin. While thinking of sin as just another commodity (see Posner 1992; Becker 1996) has some theoretical payoff, preferences for sin actually have some unique characteristics that make them different from preferences for potatoes, baloney, or Republicans.

Legislative Adoptions

Assumption 1. The demand for sin is characterized by heterogeneous preferences; that is, it varies greatly across individuals. Theoretically, the density of demand for sin probably forms a distribution similar to that shown in Figure 2.1.[2] At the extreme left of the curve are individuals with virtually no interest in sin. I label these individuals nerds. To nerds, the accessibility of a sinful product or its cost is not an issue since they would not normally partake of it even if offered without cost or consequences. Toward the middle of the distribution are the vicarious sinners, those who might gamble if in Las Vegas, catch a dirty movie in a hotel room, or sample drugs if offered. To the far right of the distribution are those individuals with a high demand for sin. Some of these might be addicts; others might simply enjoy their sins immeasurably. I label these individuals perverts.[3]

The lessons of Figure 2.1 are twofold. First, for some people, sin is fun. If it were the equivalent of poking one's eye with a stick, laws against it would be

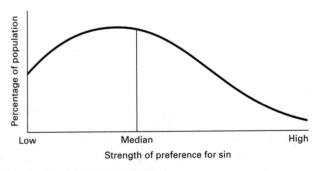

FIGURE 2.1   THE TRUE DEMAND FOR SIN

unnecessary. People sin because they get substantial utility from doing so.[4] Second, *the demand for sin varies greatly across individuals.* For perverts, the benefits so outweigh the costs that laws may be only minor obstacles; for nerds, the benefits are so low that laws against sin are unnecessary for deterrence.

Assumption 2. In terms of sin, the correlation between public behavior and private behavior is less than 1.0. A striking phenomenon of morality politics is that no one is willing to stand up for sin. Legislators do not rise and recite the joys of drunk driving, the pleasures of prostitution, or the thrill they get from serial killings. If one graphed the density of demand for sin based on the public statements of politicians and others, the graph would resemble that of Figure 2.2, a skewed distribution with a much smaller mean than the distribution in Figure 2.1. (Although these figures are drawn in a way to show stark differences, the perceptions figure needs only to have a lower mean than the real demand figure for the model to work.)

This mismatch between the pronounced and actual demand for sin structures the policy debate and the politics of policy adoption in morality politics. If politicians correctly perceived the demand for sin (Figure 2.1), they would seek moderate policies designed to appeal to the median voter (e.g., substance X would be available to adults under controlled circumstances). Because politicians perceive the distribution of preferences based on public expressions (Figure 2.2), they rationally move policy to the left of the graph in their quest to satisfy their (erroneous) perceptions of the voters' preferences. Politicians, therefore, always perceive that support for being tougher on sin is greater than it really is—nothing could be worse than being labeled "soft" on drugs, sex, or even rock and roll. The structure of perceived preferences, therefore, leaves no room for reasoned debate. Policies are adopted with little discussion and in an environment that rewards extreme anti-sin positions.

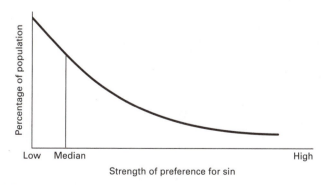

FIGURE 2.2   **PRONOUNCED DEMAND FOR SIN**

Bureaucratic Behavior

Bureaucracies are mission-oriented collectivities; over time, every bureau becomes an advocate for the policy it implements (Downs 1967; Wilson 1989). The bureaucracies involved in sin policy are law enforcement bureaucracies. They are characterized by low levels of technology, personnel-intensive processes, and an output (but not outcome) orientation. Morality bureaucracies produce arrests and expect to be rewarded on the basis of the volume of arrests made (rather than on the level of sin committed). Bureaucrats, like politicians, generalize from the persons with whom they come into contact. Unlike politicians, bureaucrats primarily come into contact with perverts, those they arrest for violating the laws against sin. As a result, bureaucracies see the demand for sin as depicted in Figure 2.3 rather than Figure 2.1. Bureaucracies, therefore, will overestimate the danger of any sin and continually seek greater resources. Even if the agency heavily discounts the preferences of the perverts and incorporates other information, it is still likely to overestimate the demand for sin.

Because law enforcement agencies generally lack policy analysis capabilities, their bureaucratic role is reduced from one of equal participation in the policy process to that of a cheerleader. Bureaucracies will favor more extreme policies because such policies will create a climate that supports more resources for the bureaucracy. Because their mission is law enforcement, the policy instruments prescribed will be those of command and control (more arrests) rather than alternative solutions to the problem (reduction of demand, reduction of transaction costs, treatment, etc.).

Together, these factors create the environment that generates the politics of sin. Bureaucracies lack policy-relevant information, so expertise plays no role in the process. Public support for stronger laws is perceived as overwhelming, so entre-

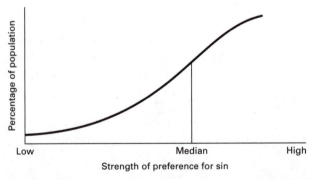

FIGURE 2.3   THE DEMAND FOR SIN AS PERCEIVED BY THE BUREAUCRACY

preneurial politicians seek innovation at the expense of deliberation. The lack of expertise and deliberation then leads to the enactment of policies that resemble current policies except that the penalties are greater and enforcement is increased.

Transforming the Politics of Sin into Redistributive Policy

The sin politics scenario is one of two possible paths for morality politics. The logic holds if one side succeeds in setting the agenda by defining a behavior as "sin." Within that social construction, opposition is the equivalent of joining the other side at Armageddon. The only possible option is to change the social construction of the debate from sin to some other dimension, that is, to frame the issue in such a manner that opposition becomes legitimate and the redistributive nature of the policy becomes open and acknowledged.[5] In this second form of morality politics, the underlying value conflict is exposed and the politics is openly redistributive with a focus on key values.

Most issues have the potential to be transformed from the politics of sin to the politics of redistribution simply because most policy issues are multidimensional. Even on a "sin" issue, a person could oppose the sin but believe that government should not be involved in regulating it or that the costs of regulating are far too high. Many other morality issues are complex and inherently multidimensional; abortion, for example, involves such dimensions as the sanctity of life, fetal health, maternal health, the status of women, medical research, and countless others. In addition, sin issues such as gambling can be linked to other issues by simply earmarking funds for education, senior citizens, or some other positively valued policy. The key issue is framing and whether or not one group is successful in framing the issue as one of sin.

The contemporary abortion issue best illustrates the transformation of an issue from one framed as sin to one for which alternative frames exist and the redistributive nature of the policy is open and visible. Figure 2.4 (p. 26) shows the general distribution of attitudes toward abortion for both the general public and the activists.[6] Clearly the pro-life activists have tried to define abortion as a sin—the killing of innocent babies. The pro-choice strategy has been to construe abortion as a woman's right and a part of the control over reproductive processes, linked to the changing status of women in society (Luker 1984). Activists' opinions thus form a classic U-shape distribution of highly salient, redistributive issues (Doan 1998). In such redistributive situations, citizen forces and political forces will dominate in the policy process (Mooney and Lee 1995; Meier and McFarlane 1993).

Alternative frames of issues clearly have policy implications. Viewing alcoholism as a disease suggests that treatment is the preferred policy option. Viewing alcoholism as a moral failing implies that law enforcement should be used to discipline the individual drinker (see Beauchamp 1980).

The deconstruction of a sin issue occurs periodically in our political history. The antiprohibition movement was able to redefine prohibition as an issue of government revenues and political corruption (Meier 1994, 150–55). The short-lived marijuana decriminalization movement owed a great deal to conservative Republicans who "constructed" the issue as one of government interfering in the private lives of citizens (Meier 1994, 64). Debates over the death penalty, while colored by religious arguments, turn on two distinct sets of polar values (the sanctity of life and "an eye for an eye") that are both accepted as legitimate. At times, issues are deconstructed and transferred to more favorable settings. The gay rights movement has had success by keeping the issue nonsalient and using inside-the-system lobby tactics. The Christian right has been moderately successful in expanding the scope of the conflict via referenda and raising the sin issue again (Haider-Markel and Meier 1996).

The key to transforming morality politics from sin to redistribution is the ability to establish a credible case for opposing a policy presented as sin. Explaining this politics of ideas (Derthick and Quirk 1985) and when it is successful should be a major priority for scholars of morality politics.[7]

The logic of both types of morality politics explains the common patterns found in a variety of empirical studies. Citizen forces with links to religion as a source of values are active and influential. Policymaking, especially in the redistributive form, is partisan with greater party competition raising the stakes for proposing and passing morality policy laws (Mooney and Lee 1995). If the sin in question is legal, the industry has some modest influence but little compared

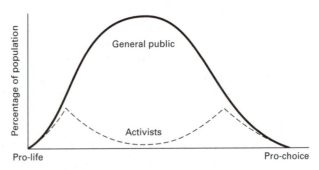

FIGURE 2.4 **DISTRIBUTION OF ABORTION ATTITUDES: GENERAL PUBLIC AND ACTIVISTS**

to that of industries that are merely regulated. Bureaucracy, while exercising a great deal of discretion in the enforcement of policy, has virtually no influence in the policy adoption process (Meier 1994).

These forces interact to generate a policy process with distinct characteristics. Compromise is not a viable strategy because that implies compromising one's deeply held values and because support is often perceived to be greater than it actually is. This suggests that policy failures will be expensive failures because the moderating influence of incrementalism will be absent in policy design. Expertise has no value because the issues grow out of conflict between core values; salience and simplicity trump expertise in such situations. Framing, therefore, is crucial because it has the potential to generate legitimate opposition and thus a redistributive pattern of politics. Such redistributive policies will be no better informed by expertise, but opposition may prevent the rapid escalation of policy in a direction with little prospect of success.

Why Sin Policies Fail

Sin in Theory

Sin policies are poorly designed because they do not notice the misperceived preferences, the lack of expertise and analysis, and the failure to compromise that characterize the politics of sin. Even if these problems can be avoided, however, sin policies are still likely to fail. The underlying causal theory behind all sin policies is that government will increase the costs (broadly defined) of sin through law enforcement. Even if such policy were effective in influencing the cost of sin, it will fail because the policy does not consider the implications of the heterogeneity of demand for sin.

The three archetypes of consumers, the nerds (n), the vicarious sinners (vs), and the perverts (p), will serve to illustrate the problem. Figure 2.5 (p. 28) graphs the likely individual demand curves for each of these archetypes (note that I have reversed the axes so that demand, the dependent variable, is on the y-axis). Nerds (or perhaps proto-nerds, since the nerds have already quit sinning) have a steep demand curve, one that is highly elastic. Even a modest rise in cost will cause proto-nerds to forgo sin. Vicarious sinners have a moderate demand curve. Perverts, the key category, have generally flat demand curves; they enjoy sin (or are addicted to it), and thus increases in price will have only minimal effects on their demand for a product (Meier and Licari 1997). Examining what occurs when a new policy is adopted will illustrate why sin policies fail to achieve their goals.

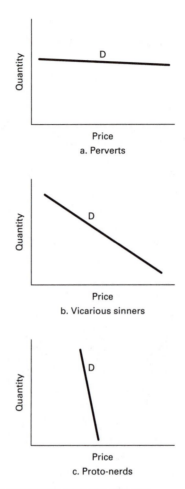

FIGURE 2.5   TYPES OF CONSUMER DEMAND FOR SIN

Assumption 3. All costs associated with sin are fungible in that they are incorporated into the price of the sin in question.[8] The quantity (Q) of any sin consumed, therefore, is merely a function of its price (p):

$$Q = f(p) \qquad [1]$$

The slope of the demand curve on a log graph is the elasticity of demand relative to price.[9] Elasticity (E) at time $t = 1$ is merely the partial first derivative of quantity with respect to price.

$$E_1 = \frac{\delta Q_1}{\delta p_1} < 0 \qquad [2]$$

The aggregate demand curve for any product is by definition the sum of the individual demand curves for each of the types of consumer. Hence, at time 1 before the adoption of a new policy:

$$Q_1 = \Sigma Q_i = \Sigma Q_n + \Sigma Q_{vs} + \Sigma Q_p \qquad [3]$$

The reactions of the individual types of consumer to a price increase given their present elasticities will then determine how the aggregate demand curve will shift. Figure 2.6 (p. 30) shows the impact of a one-unit shift in price (from p_1 before the new policy to p_2 after). For the perverts, with their highly inelastic demand curves, the additional increment in price has little consequence. The overall level of demand drops only slightly if at all.[10] For the vicarious sinner, who has a moderately elastic demand curve, consumption will drop by a moderate amount; the sinner will sin only when it is easy to do with few consequences. Finally, for the nerd or the proto-nerd with a highly elastic demand curve, consumption will drop sharply to zero. (Graphically, the new price would intersect the demand curve below the x-axis, but since consumption cannot be negative, the amount demanded is zero). These curves suggest for each type of sinner that they will consume less at time 2 after a new policy is adopted:

$$\Sigma Q_{1p} > \Sigma Q_{2p}$$

$$\Sigma Q_{1vs} > \Sigma Q_{2vs}$$

$$\Sigma Q_{1n} > \Sigma Q_{2n} \text{ and } \Sigma Q_{2n} \to 0 \qquad [4]$$

Therefore, given Equation [3], it follows that total demand after the new policy has to be less than total demand before the policy:

$$\Sigma Q_1 > \Sigma Q_2 \qquad [5]$$

Recall from Equation [2] that elasticity

$$E = \frac{\delta Q}{\delta p} < 0 \qquad [6]$$

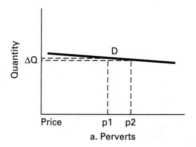

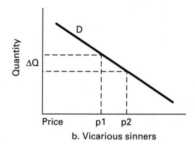

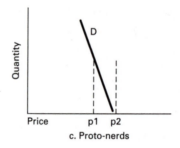

FIGURE 2.6 **CONSUMER RESPONSE TO A NEW POLICY THAT INCREASES THE PRICE OF SIN**

and that elasticities are negative. The aggregate demand curve, however, is merely the sum of individual demand curves. Because, after a new law, the group of active consumers contains all perverts consuming at nearly the same level as before, all vicarious sinners consuming less than before, and no proto-nerds consuming, the following is true:

$$\frac{\Sigma\delta Q_{1p}}{\delta p_1} + \frac{\Sigma\delta Q_{1vs}}{\delta p_1} + \frac{\Sigma\delta Q_{1n}}{\delta p_1} < \frac{\Sigma\delta Q_{2p}}{\delta p_2} + \frac{\Sigma\delta Q_{2vs}}{\delta p_2} \qquad [7]$$

or for the aggregate demand curves,

$$E_1 < E_2 \qquad\qquad [8]$$

In short, after the adoption of a new policy, because the aggregate demand curve is composed of proportionately more individuals with inelastic demand curves (than before the new policy), the consumption of sin will become more inelastic (Meier and Licari 1997). In other words, the new policy operates on a universe of consumers that is less sensitive to cost (law enforcement, penalties, etc.) than the universe of consumers before the new policy. New enforcement policies, therefore, will have to spend far more money for each unit of gain because they are trying to influence individuals who are less and less susceptible to that influence.[11]

The logic of sin policies is such that some individuals will refrain from sin relatively cheaply. Many citizens obey laws simply because they are laws; "Thou shalt not commit adultery" works for a portion of the population. Others will refrain only when they must pay some costs for that sin. Still others will continue to sin with little attention to the costs. This explains why prohibitions have some relatively quick gains but ultimately fail.[12] Because morality politics seeks a total vindication of values, advocates cannot be satisfied with marginal reductions in sin (unlike other regulatory policies); thus, advocates will continue to press for more stringent policies long after any large reductions in sin are possible. If sin issues in such circumstances are not reframed as questions of cost or on some other dimension, a downward spiral of policy failure is inevitable.

Sin in Practice

The preceding model is in my opinion the best-case presentation for a morality policy that has evolved into a sin scenario; that is, it is as effective as a sin policy can be. Morality policies also have three inherent characteristics so that they operate even less well in practice than this model does in the abstract.

First, morality policies are inefficient. The logic of morality policy is that it increases the price of sin and thus reduces demand for it. In practice, this suggests that the most efficient morality policy is a sin tax since it directly affects the price of the sin consumed (Meier and Licari 1997). In most cases, however, the sin is not legal, which means that the government cannot tax it directly.[13] Prices are affected only indirectly; much of the cost of public policy is eaten up by law enforcement salaries, courtrooms, and prison space. In some cases, agencies will make only token efforts to enforce the law.[14] Penalties for sale or use create some additional risk, but they do not directly and efficiently add a specified cost to the sin in question. To the extent that morality policies are inefficient, morality policies will work even less well than the theory predicts.

Second, morality politics, despite lip service to the contrary, appears only to recognize the demand side of the equation. If a morality policy increases price, especially if it increases price relative to risk, an incentive is created for individuals to supply that sin. As the leading symbol of market capitalism, the United States seems to have no shortage of individual entrepreneurs willing to take risks to supply a product with a strong demand. Rural southern moonshiners, for example, were quite willing to shift their business to marijuana when demand for it soared (Meier 1994, 160). While penalties for supplying sin are often very high, entrepreneurs understand that the probability of apprehension is relatively low so that the actual utility (benefits minus costs, where costs include the penalties times the probability of apprehension) is little affected.

Third, the market price for sin does not reflect the full price of the commodity so that sin may well be perceived to be cheaper than it is. The difference between the market price and the social price to the individual can be thought of in terms of indirect costs. The embarrassment of being arrested for soliciting an undercover police officer, the social cost of being named a drunk driver in the local newspaper, and the potential loss of income while sitting in jail (or for a prominent athlete from commercial endorsements) are some of the indirect costs. Because indirect costs are not so visible, individuals may underestimate the cost of sin and thus rationally consume at higher rates.[15]

Other Factors Affecting Morality Politics

Starting from an assumption of heterogeneous preferences and the misperception of those preferences, this model of morality politics attempts to predict why sin policies fail when sin policies are transformed into distributive versions of morality politics and why sin policies that seek a total vindication of values are inherently flawed. I perceive that this base model of morality politics is robust and that any omitted factors are nuances that flavor specific policies. The goal is a parsimonious theoretical core. The other factors that likely influence some morality policies can be divided into endogenous influences, exogenous influences, and the need to incorporate the supply side of the equation.

Endogenous Factors

Three endogenous factors—visibility, rarity, and worst-case scenarios—merit comment. First, the visibility of the sin is probably an important factor in the politics of its regulation. While nerds, to paraphrase, might live in the constant fear that somewhere someone is enjoying himself, visibility is what calls values into question. The presence of a dirty bookstore in town may motivate opposition more than the knowledge that anyone in town can get pornography delivered to his or her home by a variety of parcel services. Prostitutes walking the streets offend people (especially in residential neighborhoods), but public denouncements of the more discreet call girls are rarely heard. People live in like-minded communities and are likely to believe that most people share their values. Visible demonstrations to the contrary imply that one's values are threatened. The perception of sin, rather than sin itself, triggers morality politics.

Second, the rarity of the sin in question probably does not matter. Many people drive while drunk, but it took what are relatively rare events—drunk drivers killing unrelated children—to trigger the formation of Mothers Against Driving Drunk (MADD) and the drunk driving efforts of the 1980s (Meier 1994, 167). What is important is the degree to which values are violated rather than how frequently they might be violated. Despite no evidence that abortions were performed simply for the purpose of obtaining fetal material to do research, the specter of researchers paying women to become pregnant and abort was prominent in retarding policy in this area (Maynard-Moody 1995).

Third, the worst-case scenario often dominates the policy debate. Marijuana is portrayed as the first step to heroin and an inevitable drug addiction or overdose. Children are often prominent in such worst-case scenarios; the emotional appeal of children killed by drunk drivers has been especially effective. The Nixon war on drugs was portrayed as an effort to save children. Recent studies of the Drug Abuse Resistance Education (DARE) program's lack of effectiveness have been widely denounced by the program participants. Several Web browsers make money offering filtering software to let parents view porn but to lock their children out from such sites. Children are a positive social construction; dangers to children, however rare, can often justify extreme policies.

Exogenous Factors

Exogenous factors are those forces that shift the demand curves for sin. These shifts differ from the movement along a given curve as illustrated in this chapter. As an illustration, the introduction of health warnings by the U.S. government shifted the entire demand curve for cigarettes (Meier and Licari 1997). One fruitful theoretical inquiry might address whether framing a morality issue is the equivalent of shifting the demand curve for sin. In recent years, we have witnessed some declines in risk-seeking behavior that could be the result of shifts in the demand curves; these include the decline in driving under the influence, the dramatic decline in smoking, and the rise in the use of seat belts. Morality policies that rely on information (antismoking campaigns, etc.) might fundamentally shift demand curves without any changes in regulatory policies. A full theory of morality politics needs to incorporate these demand shifts.

The Question of Supply

The present theory generally ignores the supply side of sin. Some individuals cannot sin simply because no one is willing to provide the product in question (Morgan and Meier 1980).[16] Sinning is obviously easier in San Francisco than in Sisseton, South Dakota. Many Sisseton residents never get the opportunity to try heroin or purchase sexual services. A complete theory of morality politics needs to incorporate the supply side of sin and derive equilibrium models of the policy process.

Conclusion

This chapter addressed three questions: Why are morality policies adopted? Why do they sometimes change into redistributive policies? Why do morality policies fail? A great deal of empirical work has addressed these questions and has built a large collection of findings. Quite clearly, morality politics generates two sets of relatively unique patterns of politics—sin politics and redistributive politics— that produce policies with a given set of characteristics. These consistencies were the logical result of a few simple assumptions about sin and the people who sin.

At the same time, the unique patterns of morality politics should not blind one to the commonalities that they have with other types of public policy. My belief is that the relatively parsimonious models here can be applied to other forms of policy so that this chapter can serve as the first step in using morality policy as a stepping stone (gateway drug?) to a general reformulation of the study of public policy. The basic concepts used here apply equally well to distributive policies, regulatory policies, and other redistributive policies.

To illustrate briefly, I note how three main types of policies can be generally fit into this framework. In regulatory policies that do not attempt to regulate sin (e.g, environmental regulation, utility regulation), full information often exists so that the perception of demand accurately reflects actual demand. The result should be median voter policies that respond to the relative influence of advocacy coalitions. Distributive policies simply reframe the density of demand distributions as a free lunch rather than as sin. These are policies using the frame that everyone is thus better off generating the politics of pork and inclusion. A key variable is whether bureaucracy possesses policy-relevant expertise and, thus, actually allocates the pork. Redistributive policies are much the same as they are in this chapter, but the basis for redistribution is economics rather than values.

Economic benefits are easier to compromise than basic values, so the actual policies are more moderate. In all three areas, policy is driven by heterogeneous preferences and the perception of these preferences (that is, information). These factors structure how various forces interact to produce public policy.

Following this general outline, I am optimistic that a general framework can be constructed that is a good, parsimonious explanation of the policy process. From that general framework, the nuances of different public policies can be detailed. The result is a theory that should be parsimonious yet at the same time is capable of explaining a wide range of phenomena and can be subjected to empirical tests.

Notes

An earlier version of this paper was presented at the 1997 meeting of the American Political Science Association. I would like to thank George Rabinowitz for triggering the idea behind this paper and Mike Licari, Chris Mooney, Jim Rogers, LeeAnn Krause, three anonymous reviewers, and seminar participants at the University of Kansas and the University of Houston for helpful comments.

1. Redistribution is still possible through subsidies and tax credits; see the 1997 balanced budget legislation. What appears to be unacceptable is redistributing income from haves to have nots.
2. The form of the density is not crucial to the theory as long as it is single peaked. The theory is driven by the heterogeneity of preferences, not the exact form of the density.
3. Some individuals might not partake of the sin themselves but believe that government has no right to restrict others from doing so. These individuals see the issue as having more than one dimension and may be influential in reframing the issue into one in which the redistributive aspects of the issue are clear. See the following discussion on transformation of sin politics into redistributive politics.
4. I am quite willing to defend the proposition that sin policies either attempt to restrict access to utility or alternatively generate a great deal of utility by imposing values. The death penalty gains support in part because some individuals gain great utility from it.
5. The budgeting process has the potential to force trade-offs and moderate policy by limiting resources for enforcement in some cases because the total size of the budget is finite (see the drop in drunk-driving enforcement in recent years). The demands to fight sin could be directly confronted by the need to fund other programs. In the worst-case scenario (e.g., drug wars), however, even budgeting will not moderate sin policies (Meier 1994).
6. For the most part, the general public is centrist because it identifies with both poles of the continuum (Alvarez and Brehm 1995).
7. One hypothesis is that when such values correspond to partisan distributions (e.g., abortion, the death penalty), the transformation of a sin issue into a redistributive one is easier. Explaining when such transformations occur is simi-

lar to the problem of specifying when an agenda change occurs (Baumgartner and Jones 1993) or when an advocacy coalition forms (Sabatier and Jenkins-Smith 1993). In each case, these are rare events. The most promising techniques are those of event history (see Berry and Berry 1992; Mooney and Lee 1995).

8. I envision price in this case as the social price rather than the market price. The difference between the social price and the market price for sin has some interesting ramifications. See the following discussion.

9. The demand curves are shown as linear, but this is not necessary for the logic to hold.

10. For a true addict, the demand curve would be perfectly inelastic. In no case has applied economics ever revealed a perfectly inelastic demand curve, so some modest reduction in consumption is likely.

11. This suggests that the methods of analysis normally used to assess such policies would be inappropriate because they do not recognize the heterogeneity of preferences. Recently developed methods that can deal with such situations are substantively weighted analytical techniques. Several papers on this topic can be found at www.calpoly.edu/~jgill.

12. In *The Politics of Sin* (1994), I argued that these policies failed because they were not informed by policy knowledge and thus were badly designed. The current argument goes beyond that contention and suggests that these policies are inherently flawed. The possibility for good policy appears to be limited to structuring the incentives of sin to minimize the harmful effects or efforts to change values directly via persuasion.

13. There is the example of futile state drug tax stamps in recent years. For some reason, individuals who sell illegal drugs seem unwilling to go to a state agency and pay for a stamp that must be used when selling illegal drugs.

14. My hypothesis is that if the implementing agency has general enforcement powers, that is, responsibility for a wide range of crimes, the agency will put a low priority on sin violations unless money is specifically allocated for such enforcement. Agencies with narrow enforcement powers will become advocates for increased enforcement and greater funding and thus will make more than token efforts to enforce the law.

15. Individuals' responsiveness to these indirect costs varies a great deal. For an individual who has frequently been arrested, the stigma of an arrest is far less than it is for an established scion of middle-class society. On the varied impact of an arrest per se, see the literature on the impact of mandatory arrests in cases of domestic violence (Zorza 1992).

16. An interesting question is whether sins are generally substitutes for one another. Different forms of alcohol are definitely substitutes for one another, as are illicit drugs and alcohol. More work on this question is needed.

CHAPTER THREE

What Constitutes Morality Policy?
A Cross-National Analysis

Donley T. Studlar

Man does not live on bread alone but on every word that comes from the mouth of the Lord. (Deuteronomy 8:3)

What is vice today may be virtue tomorrow. (Chinese proverb)

WHAT IS "MORALITY POLICY"? Does it constitute a distinctive policy area? If so, on what theoretically relevant criteria of content and process can we expect similarities within this policy area and distinctiveness from other areas? This chapter addresses this issue from the perspective of comparative public policy in advanced industrial democracies. Despite the varying views of morality held in different political jurisdictions around the globe, and even within a particular country, is there a core of similar content to these public policy controversies, and do they generate particular patterns of relationships among actors within the political processes of different regimes?[1]

Morality policy stems from mores, which are commonly held beliefs among communities derived from cultural norms. As long as mores are almost uniformly observed, no political controversies occur. The mores are largely self-enforcing; when violations occur, violators are punished socially but not politically. A stronger enforcement mechanism would be to enshrine the mores into laws. When these mores are widely accepted in a polity, such codification is either unnecessary or noncontroversial. A problem arises, however, when there is sufficient questioning of these mores to make laws enforcing them controversial. One way out of this dilemma is to have a certain morality policy but simply not enforce it, as with the Dutch treatment of drugs and euthanasia (Gould, Shaw, and Ahrendt 1996) and the Australian treatment of abortion (Mylchreest, Chapter 15, this volume). But such subterfuges are always subject to challenge by those who want the state to enforce their view of proper human behavior or by those who consider that having a two-faced de facto policy is not as advantageous to their position as a clear de jure policy change would be.

This chapter begins by developing a working concept of morality policy as a distinctive area from previous theoretical and empirical research in policy studies. Dimensions and problems in categorizing morality policy are discussed and prima facie morality policy issues are identified. Preliminary qualitative assessments of the comparability of morality policy across countries are offered for twenty-two advanced industrial democracies. Consideration is then given to how one prominent morality policy, abortion, affects political institutions in these countries. The chapter concludes with a discussion of how well the category of morality policy coheres and what steps need to be taken to improve its empirical study.

The Characteristics of Morality Policy

Since morality policy is about validating values, it must be culturally defined, at least in part. First, morality policy conflicts are principally about values, not the economics on which most nonmorality policy centers. This distinction parallels that between "material" and "promotional" interests and the groups that pursue them (Birch 1973). Material interest groups are devoted to seeking economic advantages for their own members, however much they may couch their arguments in terms of general concerns. Promotional groups, on the other hand, are concerned with general social and state-enforced morality. Their goals are primarily ideal ones, not necessarily benefiting their members' pocketbooks, even indirectly. For example, advocates supporting or opposing capital punishment are not likely to be personally affected by the outcome of the debate (i.e., they will not be executed or spared); the same is true for groups on both sides of the abortion dispute. In short, even though there may be economic aspects to these issues (e.g., the relative costs of incarceration versus execution, or whether the state should pay for legal abortions), the major lines of controversy are about moral values, not economics.

Economic policy disputes are more easily resolved in compromise than those couched in terms of moral values because money is fungible (Rose and Urwin 1969). Justice Harry Blackmun's majority opinion in *Roe* v. *Wade* (410 U.S. 113 [1973]) attempted to justify a right to abortion for women on the basis that pregnancy was a fungible condition depending on the age of the fetus. As the subsequent uproar showed, for many people abortion is a zero-sum issue.

Interest groups involved with morality issues often raise the classic "intensity problem" in democratic theory (Dahl 1956). That is, while morality issues may involve only a minority of people, activists are often strongly committed to their cause and are quite willing to carry the fight to a larger audience. Since morality issues are—at least on the surface—relatively easy to understand, activists can often involve a broader public as sympathizers. With activists committed to moral principles on each side, it becomes difficult to settle these issues on a permanent basis.

Morality policies, even if they do involve life, death, and sexuality, are primarily ideal rather than material and therefore may sometimes be seen as "merely" symbolic (Edelman 1964). But does this mean that they are in some way less important than social or economic policies? Despite what materially minded political analysts might say, those who analyze such policies argue that they actually affect more people, at least in perception, than do other policies (Smith 1975; Cowley 1998). Morality policy can have a major impact on political identity and, therefore, the activism of citizens and the mobilization of interest groups. These policies can in fact even lead to material consequences.

What, then, is *morality policy*? Its debate is framed in terms of fundamental rights and values, often stemming from religious imperatives, by competing promotional groups whose members have little or no direct economic interest in the outcome (Mooney and Lee 1995). Advocates invest considerable emotional capital in the values that they want their society and government to promote or protect. These issues are nontechnical in the sense that they do not require specialized expertise to hold an "informed" opinion (Haider-Markel and Meier 1996). For these reasons, most morality policy issues also have relatively high public visibility. Conflict of basic identities *(gemeinschaft)*, including nationality, race, religion, language, ethnicity, gender, and sexual identity, are likely to lead to morality politics, while conflicts over secondary identities *(gesellschaft)* such as social class and economic sector are less likely to lead to such disputes, at least without the added impetus of one or more of the basic identities (Studlar 1996).

If morality policy is a distinct category of policy, it should have a distinct pattern of policymaking. Countries will attempt to settle their morality policy conflicts, however, through different means, depending on their institutional configurations. The availability of certain nonstandard institutional venues, such as the capacity to introduce legislation by backbench legislators, a willingness to suspend party discipline and allow free votes, the referendum and initiative, and judicial review may encourage the increased political expression of morality policy concerns. The politics of morality policy are based on uncompromising values and as such scare risk-averse elected politicians into ignoring them (Haider-Markel and Meier 1996; Mooney and Lee 1997). Therefore, advocates may need to pursue these nonstandard policymaking processes to achieve their goals.

Some political jurisdictions, for instance Switzerland and certain parts of the United States, have broad provisions not only for referenda but also for initiative petitions whereby an organized public can put issues on the ballot. Moral issues are one of the major categories of issues subjected to initiatives and referenda where they are available (Butler and Ranney 1994; Boyer 1992; Magleby 1984; Gamble 1997). In Butler and Ranney's (1978) comparative study, only the "constitutional" and "territorial" categories of issues exceeded morality policies as referendum subjects. Where the judiciary has the power of judicial review and/or strong interpretive power over a bill of rights, morality policy is also likely to be addressed in this venue. In such countries, the courts may be petitioned to render decisions on morality policy that parties and elected officials would rather avoid (Tatalovich and Daynes 1988, 1998; Scheppele 1996; Mylchreest, Chapter 15, this volume). Countries such as the United Kingdom that lack a justiciable bill of rights have fewer venues for morality policy controversy (Cohan 1986). Furthermore, even in strong parliamentary systems, morality policy may escape the control of parties through private members' bills and free votes (Christoph 1962; Smith 1975; Outshoorn 1986, 1996; Marsh and Read 1988; Cowley 1998). The normal politics of party manifesto and government responsibility for the maintenance of party cohesion in the legislature is less likely for morality policy issues.

Morality Policy Issues

Given these general characteristics of morality policy, what specific issues fall into this category, and how does this specification of issues as morality policy vary across countries? Despite the characterization of some issues, usually ad hoc, as morality policy in various countries, there have been few attempts to answer this question systematically. Furthermore, these few attempts have largely been based on the experience of the United States or Britain in the late twentieth century (Hunter 1991; Meier 1994; Tatalovich, Smith, and Bobic 1994; Tatalovich and Daynes 1998).

The possibilities and limitations of a systematic study based on one country are well demonstrated by the work of Emrey, Schneider, and Stiles (1998), who base their study of morality policies across time in U.S. state legislatures on the rise of the Christian right and its concerns. They argue that there are eight categories of issues, some of which parallel ones developed here: education, gay rights, pornography/obscenity, alcohol/gambling, abortion/birth control, women/family, medical ethics, and church/state. Missing from their categorization are the death penalty, any racial or ethnic issues, gun control, and drugs. Cowley (1998) provides a more elite-based conception of British morality issues, arguing that in the final analysis they are "conscience" issues because parliament defines them as such through a distinctive institutional treatment. Included in Cowley's list are corporal and capital punishment, abortion and embryo research, hunting, contraception, the punishment of war criminals, Sunday entertainment and trading, homosexuality, prostitution, euthanasia, censorship, and divorce. While these studies are informative, the problems of generalizing about morality from such a narrow base are self-evident. What issues are potential morality policy across countries, even if they are not treated as such in all countries? This section discusses several such possibilities.

First, abortion regulation is perhaps the most widely discussed morality issue across Western democracies, despite the fact that in its modern incarnation it emerged mainly from movements to delineate the legal obligations of health care practitioners in light of improved medical technology (Tatalovich 1997). The treatment of abortion regulation is considered in detail here.

While the death penalty clearly has been treated as a morality issue in some countries (Christoph 1962; Mooney and Lee 1997; Chandler 1976), other criminal justice policies are less obviously morality concerns. When criminal justice impinges upon the civil rights of ascriptively distinguishable groups, such as women, ethnic and racial minorities, or homosexuals, morality politics may arise, especially when penalties for similar criminal offenses vary systematically among such groups (Haider-Markel 1998).

Gun control is an issue for which moral arguments are often made, especially where guns have cultural significance and restrictions on their ownership and possession are resented. This is evident in the United States (Spitzer 1995), but proposed restrictions on gun ownership have occasioned populist and parliamentary outcries in other countries as well (Wearing 1998).

The prohibition of alcohol was once a prime moral controversy throughout the United States (Gusfield 1963) and elsewhere (Schwartz 1981). Even after national prohibition was repealed in the United States in 1933, alcohol regulation and prohibition remained a disputed morality policy at the state and local levels, especially in the South where it was often subjected to "local option" referenda (Fairbanks 1977; "Beer Can Be Far Away in Most of West Texas" 1997). This phenomenon also occurs in other countries. For example, Bournville, England, recently had such a local sales referendum ("Village Faces Demon Drink" 1998), and liquor licensing is one of the most frequent subjects of parliamentary free votes in Australian states.

Just as medical technology raised but could not settle the abortion issue in Western democracies in the late 1950s, it has recently raised another concern that is being dealt with in some places as morality policy—the conditions under which life may be ended. The first "living will" legislation in the United States was passed in California in 1976, followed by many others elsewhere. Subsequently, debate has arisen over voluntary euthanasia as public policy, with Oregon becoming the first U.S. state to adopt a right-to-die policy by referendum in 1994 (Glick 1992; Glick and Hutchinson, Chapter 4, this volume). Australia witnessed a major debate on the subject when the Northern Territory legislated euthanasia through a free vote in 1995 only to be overturned via free votes by the two houses of the federal parliament in 1996 and 1997 ("Euthanasia in Australia" 1996). While the Netherlands and Switzerland already have tolerant policies toward euthanasia through recognized administrative (if not legislated) procedures, one can expect morality policy debates over the right to die to spread across more countries, as occurred in France in 1998 (Donnison and Bryson 1996; "A French Debate about Death" 1998).

Regulation of religiously derived practices, especially in education but also in such matters as limiting commercial activity through Sunday observance legislation (often called "blue laws" in the United States), is likely to result in morality politics, even in countries that have a long tradition of close church-state relations. Religion and education are two major carriers of cultural identity. Religious affiliation and religiosity (amount of religious practice) exercise often surprising influence upon ideological self-conceptions, voting behavior, and public policy debate even in ostensibly secular and "post-Christian" democracies (Rose and Urwin 1969; De Vaus and McAllister 1989; Castles and Flood 1993; Castles 1994a, 1994b). Political conflicts involving religion and education have occurred in the school prayer controversy in the United States (Tatalovich and Daynes 1988), aid to church schools in France (Baumgartner 1989), and the conflict over the placement of crucifixes in state schools in Germany. In no two Western countries is the issue of religion and education so controversial as in those two historic progenitors of the separation of church and state, the United States and France. Public financial support of religiously based education is a perennial flashpoint in both systems. Controversies over curriculum issues, including sex education, in public schools are also likely to arise from religiously based precepts (Page and Clellan 1978; Vergari, Chapter 13, this volume).

Another arena of conflict over value concerns, often based on religious principles, has been the censorship of pornography. Although such campaigns are often viewed as the preserve of intense interest groups, such groups are usually speaking for a wider population, as in other morality conflicts (Zurcher et al. 1971; Smith, Chapter 12, this volume; Marsh and Read 1988; Durham 1998). Often, however, these conflicts do not reach the central level of government.

In recent years, gambling has lost some of its religiously related moral opposition in most advanced industrial democracies. Perhaps most remarkable is that the practice not long ago known as the "numbers game" operated by small-time criminals in working-class urban neighborhoods is now not only embraced but also actively promoted as major sources of revenue for governments in the form of government-run lotteries. Even though gambling has increasingly come to be viewed as an economic policy rather than a morality policy (Berry and Berry 1990), there are still moral qualms about it in many jurisdictions that make it a geographically restricted activity. The recent spread of video gambling outlets has led to calls in a variety of political jurisdictions for its further regulation or abolition (Bragg 1998; Seelig and Seelig 1998). Antigambling forces usually involve religiously committed groups (Pierce and Miller, Chapter 10, this volume).

Treatment of nonnationalistic political minority groups, such as racial, ethnic, gender, or sexual orientation groups, often involves morality policy. The debate is often between groups espousing a traditional view of morality and insurgent minority groups claiming equal rights, with each appealing to basic principles (Smith 1975; Tatalovich 1995; Tatalovich and Daynes 1988, 1998; Studlar 1996). Not all such conflicts become morality issues, but the more sweeping the potential policy change, the more likely such legislation will lead to morality-based conflict. Examples include the battles over the Equal Rights Amendment and affirmative action in the United States, both of which generated great moral conflict (Scott 1985; Gamble 1997).

The question of public policy regarding homosexuals is possibly the moral issue that currently most divides the U.S. population (Wolfe 1998). When homosexuality is a principal component of a public policy issue, whether it be regarding AIDS, military service, domestic partner legal protection, or simply as a legal category for general protection, one can expect moral controversy to occur. One such conflict developed in the 1990s over the prospect that a judicial decision in Hawaii might enshrine the legal rights of homosexuals to marry (Ellis 1998). Since the U.S. states must adhere to the "full faith and credit" provision of the Constitution and therefore recognize the laws of other states, fear developed that the legalization of homosexual marriage in Hawaii would make it legal in all states unless specific restrictive action were taken. Not only did some states pass laws forbidding homosexual marriage, but Congress also legislated and President Clinton signed the Defense of Marriage Act of 1996, defining marriage as limited to heterosexual unions. Lurking behind this extraordinary action was apprehension about the extension of individual rights by the judiciary, often a key element in policymaking over moral issues in those countries in which the judiciary is empowered to play such a role (Tatalovich and Daynes 1988, 1998; Tate and Vallinder 1995). Homosexual marriage has been legalized in a few countries, mainly in Scandinavia where traditional public values about sexual roles are especially pliant, but movements toward legalizing social and employment benefits for "same-sex" household partners are more frequent. Same-sex benefits are, however, more commonly offered to private rather than public employees and often depend more on judicial interpretation than on public support or legislative action (Carter 1998). The issue of homosexual rights, especially enshrining such rights in constitutions, frequently engenders morally based conflict, especially when there are mechanisms such as the referendum or parliamentary free votes available for policy decisions (Haider-Markel and Meier 1996; Wald, Button, and Riesner 1996; Overby 1996).

Divorce, like gambling, is less likely to be treated as a moral issue today than in the past. But where there are stringent religiously based principles against divorce, such as in Ireland and Italy, free votes, referenda, or court action can be required to legitimate the practice. In most Western democracies, divorce has largely been removed from the morality policy arena, often with little fanfare (Glendon 1987; Jacob 1988; but see Cowley 1998). Although there is now some backlash against the ease of divorce, there are few signs that divorce is going to be broadly "remoralized" as a political issue in the near future, except in some parts of the United States, as in the enactment of a covenant marriage law in Louisiana.

The damage done by illegal drugs, as well as the legal drugs of alcohol and tobacco, can be argued to have moral as well as public health dimensions. Proposals for legalization of marijuana in California and Arizona through referenda in 1996 occasioned great public outcry. In 1988, the U.S. Congress passed a law prohibiting the use of public funds for needle exchange programs largely for morality reasons. Increasingly, both public and elite opinion in some countries has begun to question the distinction between legal and illegal drugs and to support policies of decriminalization of soft drugs and "harm reduction" for hard drugs rather than abstention (Gould, Shaw, and Ahrendt 1996; Dyer 1998). This has led to both domestic and international morality policy controversy.

Other issues are currently marginal but may develop into full-fledged morality policy. For instance, the animal rights issue thus far has not aroused sufficient political concern in enough places to be a clear case of morality policy, but it has the potential to develop into a morality issue in the future (Jaspar and Nelkin 1992). As attempts to restrict fox hunting and exporting veal calves demonstrate, animal rights represent a long-standing issue of moral concern in the United Kingdom (Garner 1998).

Preliminary Patterns of Morality Policy across Countries

Of the preceding issues that are treated as morality policy in some places, where are they treated as such and where not? Are there distinguishable patterns by country, groups of countries, or issues? While comprehensive descriptive policy information about the twenty-two established Western democracies in this study is difficult to obtain, some suggestive if tentative patterns can be observed in Table 3.1 (p. 46). Abortion is by far the most pervasive morality policy concern, being treated as such in all twenty-two countries. Alcohol and recreational drug regulation and the rights of homosexuals (in various forms) are the second and third most pervasive morality policy issues, with almost half of these countries treating them as morality policy. Other issues are treated as morality policy more sporadically. There are seven countries each for church-state questions about religious education, ethnicity/race/official language rights, and euthanasia. Gambling (including lotteries), the death penalty, divorce, and gun control were treated as morality policy in four of these countries, pornography and woman's rights in three, and animal rights in two.

Two general conclusions can be drawn from this preliminary survey. First, some morality policies are more pervasive than others across Western polities. These seem to be able to arise in various countries despite institutional and cultural differences. Hence, one might label these "broadly shared" morality concerns, at least for the contemporary period. Others may be either more culturally, institutionally, or elite driven. The latter two possibilities are not to be dismissed, despite the fact that much of the literature on morality politics in the United States finds that public opinion and interest groups are the major forces impelling discussion of these issues (Haider-Markel and Meier 1996; Mooney and Lee 1997).

It is also noteworthy that morality-based controversies over divorce, capital punishment, pornography, and women's rights are not more widespread. Except in the United States, capital punishment is largely a nonissue. Divorce is largely left to judicial determination, and pornography may be subject to nonmorality-based local ordinances. Perhaps the most surprising case here is women's rights, which are no more likely to be a subject of moral policy debate than animal rights.[2] This may be due in part to the complexities and economic basis of the issue. It also suggests the dangers of overgeneralizing from policy debates in the United States without careful examination of other countries (Bashevkin 1994).

Among countries, the United States has the most morality disputes, but this may be an artifact of available information. The United Kingdom and Canada are next, with ten issues each. Outside the Anglo-American "family" (i.e., the United States, the United Kingdom, Australia, New Zealand, and Canada), France appears to be the country with the most morality policy issues, with six (abortion, capital punishment, homosexuality, religious education, drugs, and euthanasia). Since at least the French Revolution, France has had long-standing traditions of both committed Catholicism and aggressive secularism against what is viewed as the privileged Church position in society. But the general conclusion here, without considering the intensity or duration of conflicts, is a prima facie confirmation of Anglo-American moralism and a distinction between

TABLE 3.1   MORALITY POLICIES IN WESTERN DEMOCRACIES

	AUSTRALIA	BELGIUM	CANADA	DENMARK	FINLAND	FRANCE	GERMANY	ICELAND	ITALY	LUXEMBOURG	NETHERLANDS	NEW ZEALAND	NORWAY	PORTUGAL	SPAIN	SWEDEN	SWITZERLAND	UK	USA
Abortion	x	x	x	x	x	x	x	x	x	x	x	x	x	x	x	x	x	x	x
Gambling	x										x								x
Alcohol/drugs	x		x			x					x	x					x		x
Religious education/ Sunday observance	x		x			x	x				x							x	x
Animal rights						x												x	x
Homosexuality	x		x	x		x					x	x	x					x	x
Capital punishment			x	x		x					x							x	x
Pornography			x															x	x
Divorce									x	x									x
Euthanasia	x		x			x					x					x		x	x
Women's rights	x		x															x	x
Ethnic/racial minorities	x		x			x	x										x		x
Gun control	x		x															x	x

Sources: Outshoorn 1996; Mylchreest, Chapter 15, this volume; Tatalovich 1997; Butler and Ranney 1994; Marsh and Read 1988; Boyer 1992; Rolston and Eggert 1994; Gould, Shaw, and Ahrendt 1996; Smith 1975; Glendon 1987; "A French Debate about Death" 1998; Dyer 1998; Jasper and Nelkin 1992; Garner 1998; Cowley 1998; Wolfe 1998; Tate and Vallinder 1995; Scott 1985; Gamble 1997; Hunter 1991; Tatalovich and Daynes 1988, 1998; Pierce and Miller, Chapter 10, this volume; Smith, Chapter 12, this volume; Zurcher et al. 1971; Page and Clellan 1978; Meier 1994; Glick and Hutchinson 1999; "Euthanasia in Australia" 1996; Donnison and Bryson 1996.

continental countries and the English-speaking ones on the amount of moral controversy in their politics.

Pursuing the Anglo-American family of nations' treatment of morality policy further (Castles 1993), it is striking that there are also considerable similarities as to which issues are treated as morality policy in these countries. Several issues (abortion, gambling, alcohol, homosexuality, euthanasia, gun control, and ethnic/racial issues) demonstrate characteristics of morality policy across all or nearly all of these countries. Others, such as women's rights, divorce, and animal rights, show more variation in exhibiting the characteristics of morality policy even across these five polities. A more detailed comparison is needed to verify or modify these tentative conclusions.

A Case Study: Abortion Policy in Comparative Perspective

To see whether a larger group of countries shows morality policy characteristics on a single issue, I focus on abortion regulation, for which considerable information across the twenty-two Western democracies exists. Here I assess whether abortion triggers any of four nonstandard policymaking processes: judicial decisions, free votes, private members' bills, or referenda. Recall that it was earlier hypothesized that morality policy frequently triggers these mechanisms as risk-averse elected politicians fail to pursue them in the standard legislative processes.

Table 3.2 (p. 38) shows that at least one of these nonstandard processes has been used for abortion policymaking in all of these countries except the Netherlands. The most common of these is the use of free votes on such bills, whether initiated by the government or a private member. The use of free votes may be most common because of its near universality as an available parliamentary procedure. Nevertheless, where these nonstandard procedural options exist, they appear to be used widely for this morality policy.

The extant cross-national studies of abortion policy (Field 1979; Norris 1987; Outshoorn 1986, 1996) indicate considerable similarities in how it has been dealt with across Western democracies, even considering institutional, religious, and cultural differences. Outshoorn (1986, 1996) finds that in only two West European countries, Norway and the Netherlands, was the issue decided by normal parliamentary procedures (i.e., a government bill and a "whipped" vote on which party cohesion of the governing parties was maintained in passage of the legislation). On an earlier bill, however, there were party splits in Norway, too (Rolston and Eggert 1994). In other countries, abortion was dealt with through a private member's bill and/or through free votes on government bills. Furthermore, in some countries, settlement of the abortion question has been sought through judicial decisions (Germany, the United States, Canada, Ireland, Australia) and referenda (Italy, Ireland).

TABLE 3.2   ABORTION AND POLITICAL PROCESSES IN WESTERN DEMOCRACIES

	JUDICIALIZATION	PRIVATE MEMBER BILL	FREE VOTE	REFERENDUM
Australia	x	x	x	
Austria	x		x	
Belgium			x	
Canada	x	x	x	x
Denmark			x	
Finland			x	
France			x	
Germany	x	x	x	
Greece			x	
Iceland			x	
Ireland	x			x
Italy		x	x	x
Luxembourg			x	
Netherlands				
New Zealand		x	x	
Norway			x	
Portugal			x	
Spain			x	
Sweden			x	
Switzerland			x	x
United Kingdom		x	x	
United States	x	x	x	x

Sources: Outshoorn 1996; Mylchreest, Chapter 15, this volume; Tatalovich, 1997; Butler and Ranney 1994; Marsh and Read 1988; Boyer 1992; Rolston and Eggert 1994.

What has happened recently to abortion as a policy issue? As abortion has become widely legal and available, has its politics become "normalized"? While Outshoorn (1996) argues that most settlements of the issue in Western Europe in the 1967–85 period have not been disturbed, when the abortion issue arose subsequently, it displayed some unusual political features. When abortion became legal in Belgium in 1990, there was the extraordinary spectacle of the devoutly Roman Catholic king of Belgium "temporarily abdicating" for three days to allow the pertinent legislation to become law without his having to sign the bill. In Canada, after the Supreme Court negated the law on abortion, a bill passed on a partial free vote by the Canadian House of Commons was defeated on a tie vote in the Canadian Senate, the only recorded instance of the Senate defeating a Commons-passed bill since World War II. After German unification, abortion policy proved to be an ongoing quandary for the government because the former East Germany had almost no restriction on abortion while West Germany had one of the more restrictive policies in Western Europe. Initially upon reunification, Germany simply allowed each part of the country to pursue its own abortion policy, but in 1993 when an attempt was made to unify abortion policy, the Constitutional Court overturned it. A more stringent policy using compulsory counseling was finally adopted legislatively. The Roman Catholic Church, however, objected to the use of its government-subsidized counseling services for such purposes, and the heavily Catholic state of Bavaria prevented abortion clinics from opening until the policy was overruled by the German Constitutional Court in 1998. The Irish Supreme Court ruled that even in the face of a referendum law banning abortion in the Republic, the government could not prevent Irish women from traveling the short distance to the United Kingdom to have an abortion. In the United Kingdom, the time period in which abortion was allowed was reduced from twenty-eight to twenty-four weeks upon passage of a private member's bill on a free vote in 1990. Such activities hardly qualify as "normal politics."

Conclusion: Morality Policy across Space and Time

While this analysis has found considerable similarity of content and institutional treatment among morality policies in Western democracies, several questions deserve more careful attention. Why are some issues (e.g., abortion regulation) nearly universally treated as morality policy while others (e.g., alcohol regulation in earlier times and homosexual rights and drug policy more recently) are frequently treated as such, and still others (e.g., divorce, pornography, and women's rights) are rarely treated as such? Do morality policies, both individually and generally, arise more frequently in some countries than in others and, if so, why? Is there more variation on this by policies or by countries (Freeman 1985)?

Countries with large proportions of practicing Catholics and Protestant fundamentalists, especially when faced with challenges from secular, urban-based groups, may be especially prone to morality policy conflict. Similarly, issues that can be defined in religious terms for much of the population may be especially susceptible to becoming morality disputes. The key here may not necessarily be claimed religious affiliation itself but the intensity of the practice. There is already evidence that these variables are important in abortion and divorce (Field 1979; Norris 1987; Castles and Flood 1993; Castles 1994a, 1994b). Yet as several British examples of moral conflict indicate, the religious basis of such conflicts is often attenuated to the point of being hard to discern (Cowley 1998). To investigate general influences across countries and policies, there need to be more comparable, systematic analyses.

Schwartz (1981) contends that the United States tends to be a more moralistic political culture than Canada, and Tatalovich (1997) argues that abortion has been a "more moralistic" issue in the United States than in Canada. Both argue for the importance of institutional factors in allowing morality issues to become politicized. The United States may treat more issues as morality policy than Canada does because the United States has a less deferential, more individualistic political culture and because it has a multiplicity of institutional venues, including all four of the ones discussed earlier (plus federalism), to which groups can appeal with their morality-based views. This suggests the possibility of measuring the degree of moral concern in policy disputes and perhaps developing an overall assessment of countries in terms of their tendency toward emphasizing morality policy.

This analysis suggests that future research also needs to address the issue of how the definition of morality policy changes over time, as with divorce in the United States, gambling in some jurisdictions, and even abortion in several countries (Meier, Chapter 2, this volume). The reform of abortion laws, especially in the United Kingdom, Canada, the United States, and Australia, was begun not by women's advocacy groups looking to expand rights but by medical professionals and lawyers aiming to clarify and modernize regulations in light of improved medical technology (Tatalovich 1997; Mylchreest, Chapter 15, this volume; Marsh and Read 1988; Mooney and Lee 1995). In all of these countries, the professional groups lost control of the issue. Especially in the United States, abortion has become not a health or criminal justice issue but a moral one to many people, and a quarter century of rancorous conflict has occurred as a result.

But what causes perceptions of issues to change? Images are certainly important (Baumgartner and Jones 1993), but how are they created and how do they evolve? Despite predictions that such technical developments as RU 486 (the so-called abortion pill) would lessen the moral conflict over abortion, this has not happened. Instead, RU 486 has encountered drug approval problems and has become entangled in the abortion controversy (Jackman 1997). Is this purely a phenomenon of social structure and value change, perhaps postmaterialism as Tatalovich (1997) suggests, or can political actors, institutions, and even policies exercise some influence on this process?

Finally, more systematic work needs to be done on the central question of this chapter: Why are certain issues considered morality policy in some countries but not in others? From one point of view, the more remarkable finding of this analysis is the degree of consistency found for morality policy across countries. After all, these countries vary considerably in culture. Compared to policy problems generated by similar economic and social phenomena, for instance government deficits or an aging population, policy disputes based on culture might be expected to vary more across countries. Education and arts policies, for instance, are difficult to compare. Rose (1993) argues that cultural issues are especially resistant to lesson drawing from one country to another, although there is some evidence that such borrowing can take place (Studlar 1993). Thus, it is perhaps surprising that such a culturally derived category as morality policy would not have more variation across countries.

What is most striking about this largely impressionistic survey is how frequently the same types of issues are considered morality policy. In short, there is a case for "morality policy" as a distinctive policy area, not only within the United States but across Western democracies.

Notes

Thanks to Christopher Z. Mooney, Willard M. Oliver, Barry Harrison, Sean Levine, and the anonymous reviewers for comments on earlier versions of this chapter.

1. Morality policy here does not deal with the individual ethics of politicians and their violations of the accepted norms of morality in a society but with public policies that sanction near-consensus moral values for the entire polity.
2. Women's rights are often part of economic and social policy discussions rather than part of a separate category.

PART TWO

Agenda Setting on Morality Policy

CHAPTER FOUR

Physician-Assisted Suicide: Agenda Setting and the Elements of Morality Policy

Henry R. Glick and Amy Hutchinson

IN JUNE 1997, the U.S. Supreme Court rejected claims that a constitutional right to physician-assisted suicide (PAS) exists for the terminally ill (*Washington v. Glucksberg* No. 96-110 [117 S. Ct. 2302]; *Vacco v. Quill* No. 95-1858 [117 S. Ct. 2293]). In his majority opinion, however, Chief Justice William Rehnquist recognized that PAS had a prominent and legitimate place on the national political agenda when he referred to the serious and thoughtful discussions occurring in the fifty states. These discussions touch deep-seated personal values and conduct, which places PAS firmly in the realm of morality policies.[1]

We are concerned here with the rise of this policy issue to prominence on the national agenda, but our research also contributes to general theory and explanations for the course that most morality policies travel through the political system. These processes generally are distinctive from the ways in which economic or regulatory policies usually are treated in politics.

Certain familiar patterns surface for PAS. First, like other morality policies, PAS appears easy for most people to understand, and the issue quickly elicits intense personal and group-based sensitivities. Nearly everyone has an opinion, which is seen in the very few "don't know" responses about PAS in polls. Consequently, professionals are not as essential or necessarily heeded in discussing, interpreting, and framing the issue, and the mass media, rather than the professional media, are paramount in moving PAS onto the agenda. Controversial and newsworthy public events also provide many opportunities for the mass media to arouse public interest in PAS. Second, as with other controversial morality policies, the opposition of conservative religious interest groups, the sharply divided public opinion, and the mostly negative tone in early media coverage have made most public officials reluctant to take positions or suggest changes in policy. Legislative and judicial support of the status quo has mobilized new groups that battle the old in alternative populist arenas of policy innovation. Therefore, the politics of moving PAS onto the agenda is similar to political processes found for other morality policies.

What Makes a Morality Policy?

The broad contours of policy adoption are similar for all types of public policies (Mooney and Lee 1995), but morality policies are distinctive in certain ways. Previous research indicates that innovations having economic impact, such as highway and school construction, are affected by basic economic and population characteristics (e.g., wealth, urbanism, population size, education). In contrast, morality policies such as abortion, gambling, and PAS are driven more by public opinion, mass media coverage, the strength of relevant interest groups, the political vulnerability of elected officials, and sometimes ideology (Fairbanks 1977; Morgan and Meier 1980; Meier and Johnson 1990; Glick and Hays 1991; Meier and McFarlane 1993; Glick 1992; Mooney and Lee 1995; Hays and Glick 1997).

The differences between these two types of policies develop from the high salience of morality policies. Unlike many economic and foreign affairs issues, morality policies are relatively easy to understand, and, as a result of fundamental differences in personal experiences and socialization, they are prone to widespread disagreement on core values (Tatalovich and Daynes 1988; Meier 1994; Mooney and Lee 1995).

PAS is the most recent issue in the long-running political conflict over the right to die, which is itself an outgrowth of the ability of modern medicine to prolong life technologically in the face of inevitable death, often accompanied by intense suffering and anguish. Since illness and death touch everyone, many individuals understand why some patients might request a physician's aid in suicide to end or forestall prolonged dying. Like abortion, core values associated with the right to die and PAS are the value and the preservation of life, but a central question concerns who has the right to determine when we may die: *we*, as individuals with control over our own bodies and destiny, or *others*, as the state or federal government that claims a public interest in protecting life.

The moral debate surrounding the right to die has grown in the United States since the mid-1970s, following the landmark New Jersey Supreme Court decision *In Re Quinlan* (355 A.2d 647 [1976]). In this and many later cases, courts have ruled that patients and families have the right to order the removal of life-sustaining treatment, such as ventilators and feeding tubes, from terminally ill and permanently comatose persons.

Living wills and other advance medical directives have been endorsed by most state legislatures and many appellate courts as the means by which individuals may relay their wishes regarding end-of-life treatment decisions. These documents do not cover all circumstances. Research shows that only one third of adults have such directives. Although this figure is remarkably high given the more recent visibility of this issue, fully two-thirds of all adults have not legally recorded their end-of-life preferences. In addition, directives do not apply to the early stages of many debilitating and deadly illnesses, such as AIDS, Alzheimer's disease, Lou Gehrig's disease, or multiple sclerosis—all medical situations that can lead certain people to contemplate assisted suicide. In terms of agenda setting and policymaking, existing policies regarding end-of-life medical treatment decisions have not proved especially useful, leading groups and individuals to seek additional rounds of policy innovations (Yates and Glick 1997) and paving the way for alternatives such as PAS.

PAS and Morality Policy Agenda Setting

To analyze the development of the PAS agenda, we employ several key features of agenda-setting theory (see Bachrach and Baratz 1962; Bachrach 1963; Kingdon 1973, 1995; Schattschneider 1975; Cobb, Ross, and Ross 1976; Nelson 1984; Glick 1992; Baumgartner and Jones 1993). We consider the effects of focusing events, professional and mass media coverage, and government agenda activity in terms of legislation, initiatives, and court cases. Since agenda setting and innovation are linked, agenda setting for morality policy is driven by some of the same variables that correlate with morality policy innovation. Therefore, we also consider the role of public opinion, the tone of media coverage, and interest group activity.

The Rapid Rise of PAS on the Public Agenda[2]

We examine the policy development of PAS by identifying major initial focusing events,[3] the frequency of publications in professional and mass media, and the frequency of public opinion polling. In agenda-setting research, publications in various media are important indicators of the content of the *public agenda*, which may be subdivided into the *professional* (expert) and *mass* (general audience) *agendas* (Nelson 1984; on the links between news coverage and public attention, see Iyengar and Kinder 1987). The frequency of polls over time mainly reveals the period when an issue has captured peak public interest so that polling organizations find it worthwhile to investigate public opinion.

Early focusing events occurred in 1987; the California Bar Association endorsed PAS, and the Hemlock Society began a California campaign for a PAS referendum, which failed in 1988. The Hemlock Society, then based in California and headed by Derek Humphry, has long supported PAS. But an event that received the greatest media attention was Dr. Jack Kevorkian's first assisted suicide, performed on Janet Adkins in June 1990. Other newsworthy events in the early 1990s included an article by Dr. Timothy Quill, the New York physician involved in *Vacco* v. *Quill*, describing his PAS experience with a long-term patient; the publication of *Final Exit*, the best-selling how-to book on suicide by Derek Humphry (1992); and beginning efforts to hold a PAS referendum in Washington State.

The importance of these and other events to media coverage and the mass agenda are difficult to overstate. Beginning in 1990, more than half of all right-to-die coverage in the *New York Times* has focused on assisted suicide. Subsequently, PAS and assisted suicide have commanded more than half, and often between two-thirds and three-quarters, of all right-to-die coverage in all mass media. Percentage increases in medical literature, which is the most active professional agenda, are not as striking, but they also increased from 18 to 29 percent between 1991 and 1992. As discussed later, most media publications experienced peaks in 1993 and 1996, years that coincide with the most assisted suicides performed by Dr. Kevorkian—twelve in 1993 and nineteen in 1996. It is unlikely that PAS would have received so much attention without Dr. Kevorkian's continuous and highly publicized acts.

The frequencies of various professional and mass publications on PAS are presented in Figures 4.1 and 4.2 (p. 60).[4] The general patterns in the two figures are similar. PAS received some attention in the late 1980s, began to accelerate in 1990, and coursed its upward trend in 1991 and beyond. However, there are some important differences in the two figures.

Professional agenda. PAS became an important and permanent item in the medical literature in 1990. Since PAS, like other right-to-die issues, directly involves the medical profession, it is not surprising that the issue has commanded so much medical attention. PAS also is an important religious issue, especially to the Catholic Church, which has demonstrated the strongest opposition to all right-to-die policy innovations in state legislatures and courts. Legal interest has increased recently, but it has been much more gradual and seems largely to be a reaction to events that signaled the possible legalization of PAS in Oregon and to court decisions in Washington State. Compared to medicine and law, the humanities and social sciences pay little attention to this issue, which is about the same level of concern they have historically given to all right-to-die issues.

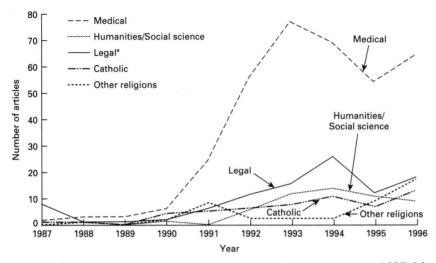

FIGURE 4.1   ASSISTED SUICIDE ARTICLES IN PROFESSIONAL LITERATURE, 1987–96

[a]All legal articles for 1987 are printed in the summer, fall, and winter issues of *Issues in Law and Medicine.*

Mass agenda. Like the medical literature, the mass media began to pay attention to PAS in 1990, but articles in the mass media between 1990 and 1991 actually outstripped reporting in the medical literature by about two articles to one. This is an unusual result in agenda setting. Generally, research on agenda setting has found that professional agendas lead the mass agenda (Nelson 1984; Glick 1992). Experts and professionals become aware of problems first, and their writings gradually are noted by mass media reporters who popularize technical articles for the general public and begin to write about the issue themselves.

Evidence suggests that this heralding pattern for the professional agenda may be more typical of morality policies in general. In the early years of the right-to-die agenda, the medical media surged first in the late 1960s, followed by the mass media several years later. Similarly, the medical profession first addressed abortion reform in the latter part of the eighteenth and early part of the nineteenth centuries. Much later, in 1962, the Sherri Finkbine case, which involved the abortion of a potentially deformed fetus, focused mass media attention on abortion (Mohr 1978; Tatalovich and Daynes 1981; Tatalovich 1997). Likewise, lawyers, judges, and law professors first advocated no-fault divorce reform (Rhode and Minow 1990).

There are two plausible explanations for the appearance of PAS first on the mass agenda. One is that early and greater mass media coverage reflects the continuity between PAS and other recent right-to-die issues that have been reported

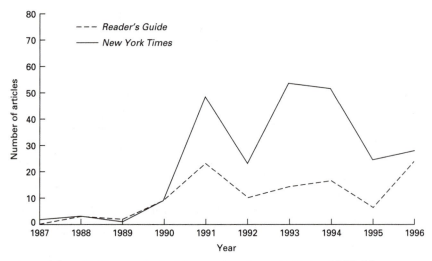

FIGURE 4.2   ASSISTED SUICIDE ARTICLES IN MASS LITERATURE, 1987–96

very heavily in the mass media since the mid-1980s. Thus, PAS is an outgrowth of previous right-to-die issues that already had attracted considerable public attention. Second, Dr. Kevorkian's sensational first and single assisted suicide in 1990 captured enormous news attention, but he was dismissed as an aberration by mainstream medical practice. Therefore, PAS did not explicitly become an issue for the medical community until 1991 when Dr. Timothy Quill sought to cast PAS in a positive way and make assisted suicide an option that reputable physicians needed to discuss and consider.

The continuity of PAS with earlier right-to-die issues suggests that previous agenda setting is a powerful stimulant for gaining attention to new related issues that emerge from experience with the old. In Kingdon's (1995) terms, previous right-to-die innovation had "softened up" the public and made it easier for PAS to win attention. Thus, it appears that the PAS agenda has an advantage that other policies, including other morality policies (e.g., abortion), may not have experienced. The early and rapid ascent of PAS in the mass media also suggests that the mass agenda may be more sensitive than the professional agenda to morality issues. However, further research on agenda setting for morality policies needs to be done to obtain additional evidence regarding this hypothesis.

In addition to tabulating publications, public opinion polls provide additional evidence of the presence of an issue on the mass agenda. We have collected exhaustive polling data from 1987 to 1997 for all right-to-die issues and all polls that were conducted exclusively on assisted suicide.[5] We are interested in the *amount* of polling done on PAS as an indicator of the clear presence of the issue on the mass agenda. Later we examine the content of opinion.

Polls on PAS alone did not appear until 1990, and few broader right-to-die polls included many questions on PAS until 1991. Nearly all questions on PAS were asked during the last three months of 1991, which confirms that new events were necessary to stimulate polling on this issue. However, polling was done quickly once new events attracted media attention. Moreover, 40 percent of all right-to-die questions included polls conducted in the past four years pertaining to PAS. This is huge in comparison to other types of right-to-die questions, for it exceeds the number of questions asked on any right-to-die issue in the previous two decades. Like the sharp increases in news coverage that occurred in 1990, polling on PAS reveals the meteoric rise of this issue on the mass agenda.

Polling in the 1990s also coincides with the frequency of Dr. Kevorkian's assisted suicides, although the novelty of his actions appears to have a shorter shelf life for polling than for publications. Polling increased until 1993, the same year that Dr. Kevorkian sharply increased the number of his assisted suicides to twelve. Continuous legal action in Michigan against Dr. Kevorkian in 1993 also received much more news coverage than his previous behavior. Although legal action continued in 1994, it did not stimulate new or additional interest in PAS among the pollsters. Polling declined in 1995, as did the number of Dr. Kevorkian's assisted suicides. Anecdotal evidence also indicates that while Dr. Kevorkian's later assisted suicides still were reported in the press, the amount of space devoted to these announcements was very small.

Polling reached its peak in 1996, when it increased dramatically. Three new focusing events captured interest that year. First, the New York case of *Vacco* v. *Quill* reached the U.S. Court of Appeals for the Ninth Circuit. Second, the voters of Oregon sustained the 1994 initiative that legalized PAS. Third, Dr. Kevorkian assisted in nineteen suicides, his highest number in a single year. Polling decreased slightly in 1997 but remained high following the U.S. Supreme Court ruling on PAS. The actions of Dr. Kevorkian initially focused attention on PAS. However, by 1994 and 1995, his actions alone were not enough to sustain that attention. New events increased mass attention in 1996 and 1997, suggesting that new focusing events may be just as important as the frequency of these events in keeping an issue before the public.

PAS on the Governmental Agenda

Attempts to put PAS on the governmental agenda have been made since 1987, when the Hemlock Society and others sought to place an initiative on the California ballot the following year. Dr. Kevorkian's activity also moved eleven states to quickly enact antiassisted-suicide laws, joining twenty-five others that had done so previously, often decades earlier. As in other areas of policymaking, such as the early days of civil rights and living wills, supporters of PAS have sought alternative institutions to achieve their goals, notably the popular initiative and the courts. Unlike earlier right-to-die policies, however, legalizing PAS has not been very successful in any forum. In contrast, abortion laws had been liberalized in eighteen states prior to *Roe* v. *Wade* (410 U.S. 113) in 1973 (Tatalovich and Daynes 1981). The U.S. Supreme Court rejected PAS, no state appellate court has approved it, and supporters have had very limited success with the popular initiative. We will discuss specific PAS initiatives and court cases and explain why, unlike previous right-to-die policies, PAS has largely been blocked.

Popular initiative. It is no accident that the initiative for PAS has been tried in California (1988), Washington State (1991), and Oregon (1994, 1997). These states generally are liberal on personal freedom and individual rights, and religious organizations, including the Catholic Church, are less powerful there than in many other states. Voters in these states are less likely to attend church regularly, and religion is not a dominant force in state politics or society (Carson 1992). Also, the Hemlock Society, which is the main supporter of PAS, and its closely related offshoot organizations are located in California and Oregon. Consequently, if supporters of PAS were to have a fighting chance to counter the influence of the Catholic Church and persuade voters to adopt PAS, these states would be the best place to do so.

In the states that have had initiatives, PAS has been vigorously opposed by two prestigious and experienced groups: the Catholic archdiocese and state medical associations. The Washington measure is reported to have originated with grassroots organizations frustrated with the failure of the state legislature to amend its restrictive 1979 living will law (Carson 1992; Gees 1992). Furthermore, in Washington, heavy financial contributions were transferred to the Washington Catholic Church from other dioceses elsewhere in the country, thus indicating the solidarity and purpose of this powerful group.

Initiatives failed in California and Washington by slim majorities of 52 and 54 percent, respectively, but passed in Oregon in 1994 with a 51 percent majority, although a federal court declared the 1994 result unconstitutional. The efforts of the Catholic Church to defeat the measure in Oregon were mitigated by the state medical society's failure to take a clear position on the issue. The Catholic Church failed to influence the outcome of this moral debate in 1997 when the state legislature voted to hold another referendum on PAS (Goldberg 1997), and the voters refused to repeal the 1994 law by a 60 percent majority. The courts have not rejected this vote. Oregon is still the only state to have expressly legalized PAS; very few other states have no legislation on this matter.

Although Oregon's initiative has survived several challenges, its legality is still tenuous. In June 1999, federal legislation was introduced in both houses of Congress that would effectively outlaw PAS. The Pain Relief Promotion Act (S. 1272/H.R. 2260) is a proposed amendment to the Controlled Substances Act. The amendment clarifies the intended use of controlled substances by stating that "nothing in this section authorizes intentionally dispensing, distributing, or administering a controlled substance for the purpose of causing death or assisting another person in causing death." As of September 1999, one House committee had voted favorably on the bill. If the act passes, many physicians probably will be discouraged from prescribing drugs that might be used for committing suicide, although the terms "intentionally" and "for the purpose of" allow discretion in explaining the object of a prescription (i.e., for sleeping, pain relief, or death).

Courts. Until the U.S. Supreme Court's negative PAS decision, the federal courts seemed to be a possible venue for pro PAS litigants. Perhaps since litigants sought to have state laws criminalizing assisted suicide declared unconstitutional, appealing to the federal courts seemed a better option than going to state courts, where many conservative and elected judges would be reluctant to move against state bans. The lessons of most civil rights litigation would support that option.

The two most prominent federal cases involving challenges to state criminal laws are the recent cases from Washington State and New York decided by the U.S. Supreme Court. In 1994, a federal district judge in Seattle declared Washington's law banning assisted suicide unconstitutional. A year later, the U.S. Court of Appeals for the Ninth Circuit endorsed that decision, but only after it decided to rehear the case *en banc,* which is a rare occurrence in which all of the judges in the appellate circuit court, not just the normal three-judge panel, hear a case. In 1996 in New York, Dr. Timothy Quill and other litigants successfully appealed their loss in federal district court to the federal court of appeals. However, the Supreme Court sided with state government in both of these cases.

There have been few recent state court decisions on assisted suicide. After several years of skirmishing on conflicting interpretations of Michigan's law against assisted suicide, the Michigan Supreme Court ruled in 1994 that common law supported a ban. The only case before a state supreme court since the U.S. Supreme Court's assisted-suicide decision in June 1997 was in Florida, where the Florida Supreme Court also upheld the state's criminal law against assisted suicide (Navarro 1997). The case was brought by a terminally ill AIDS patient who sought to persuade the court to apply the state constitution's 1980 privacy clause to his desire to get help in ending his life. The court said the state had a great interest in preserving life, although it invited the legislature to consider PAS. However, the conservative Republican legislature is very unlikely to put the issue on its agenda. Although the Florida Supreme Court in the 1970s followed other courts in endorsing living wills and the withdrawal of treatment, the court generally has not been a leader in creating new judicial doctrines.

Why So Little Support?

We believe that PAS has found little official support because of the content of the mass agenda, particularly the controversial public image of PAS, the generally negative to neutral tone of media coverage, and conflicting public opinion. These three indicators of public sentiment may explain why supporters of PAS have used the popular initiative in a few generally liberal states.

Previous research finds that public opinion is related to morality policy adoption. Therefore, we examine the impact of public opinion on PAS. Since polling is done *after* an issue already has reached the mass agenda, we also examine early images of PAS and the tone of media reporting since they are likely to influence how the public perceives the issue. In a following section, we examine how public opinion, media tone, and interest group activity are related to strategies for enacting PAS and other morality policies.

Image. At the heart of all policy debates are various and often *conflicting images* of a policy. The positive image of PAS links this proposal to earlier and well-established medical and right-to-die policies that emphasize patients' dignity, individual rights, and autonomy. Since physicians have the technological means and power to prolong lives, advocates maintain that physicians also ought to have the power to assist patients who wish to end their lives when living becomes unbearable due to terrible illness or accident. Framing PAS as an extension of individual rights and personal empowerment also ties this new proposal to the primacy of individual rights that has developed in the United States since World War II.

Opponents of PAS frame the issue very negatively. Instead of viewing it as a remedy for the runaway use of medical technology and a way to preserve autonomy, they believe that PAS is contrary to the healing mission of physicians. Since physicians provide the lethal means—even though they do not administer it themselves—opponents associate PAS with murder and involuntary active euthanasia. The negative image is reflected partly by the singular and medically aberrant behavior of Dr. Kevorkian, who used strange-looking homemade devices in nonmedical settings to assist patients he had not known previously. If PAS is portrayed mostly in this way, the negative image may explain why state legislators have refused to legalize the practice.

Tone. Assessing the tone of media reporting is a way to determine which image of PAS is dominant on the mass agenda (Baumgartner and Jones 1993). Figure 4.3 depicts the percentages of *Reader's Guide to Periodical Literature* reporting on PAS from 1990 to 1996 that are positive, negative, and neutral.[6] The data indicate that PAS has a very long way to go before it is portrayed mostly in a positive way. In 1990, PAS received no positive reports. Since 1992, however, PAS has been treated more favorably, and the overall trend is in the positive direction with negative reporting decreasing sharply since 1994 but mostly in favor of neutral tone. These few years constitute a very short time period for reaching reliable conclusions or projections regarding PAS, but the overall pattern in Figure 4.3 suggests that PAS may be gaining ground. If neutral and positive coverage continues to increase at the expense of negative headlines, PAS could gain greater acceptance, and perhaps political institutions will give PAS a more sympathetic hearing.

Public opinion. Public opinion on PAS has followed a pattern similar to that of media tone. Support generally has increased since 1990, but it still is not strongly positive. Assessing public opinion is somewhat difficult, for most questions on this issue are worded differently in various polls. As survey research has shown, different wording may affect responses, which makes comparisons from one year to the next misleading. To minimize these problems, we have compared the most similar questions available.[7]

The responses in Table 4.1 (p. 66) reveal a slight increase in public support for PAS from 1990 to 1997 with a high of 69 percent in 1997. However, support in 1996 was about the same as in 1990. "Don't know" responses (not included in the table) were 6 percent or less of all responses, indicating that most people had an opinion regardless of the way questions were phrased. The lower level of support in 1992 may be due to the blunt wording of the question, but perhaps Dr. Kevorkian's initial involvement with the criminal courts that year also tarnished the image of PAS, at least for a time. The most important information from the sur-

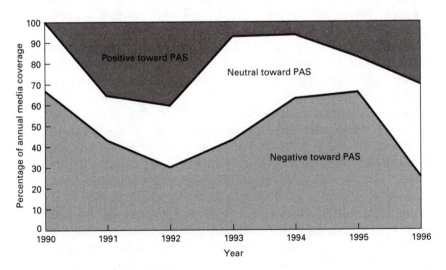

FIGURE 4.3   TONE OF MEDIA COVERAGE

TABLE 4.1   PUBLIC SUPPORT FOR PHYSICIAN-ASSISTED
SUICIDE

YEAR	PERCENTAGE IN SUPPORT
1990	53
1991	53
1992	43
1993	58
1994	57
1995	67
1996	52
1997	69

Source: American Public Opinion Index, various years.

Note: All polls are national, and all questions concern the
legality of physician-assisted suicide.

veys is that there is *much less public support* for PAS than the overwhelming nation-wide support for the withdrawal or withholding of treatment from the terminally ill that existed when most of the states enacted living will laws in the 1980s.[8]

Support for PAS within the medical community is also not strongly positive and has recently been decreasing. A 1996 study drawn from the files of the American Medical Association (AMA) indicates that 36 percent of physician respondents would assist in a suicide if it were legal, and 24 percent would participate in euthanasia (Meier et al. 1998). In studies by Ezekiel J. Emanuel (1999), an oncologist and medical ethicist at the National Institutes of Health, 46 percent of oncologists supported PAS for the terminally ill in 1994, while only 22 percent favored it in 1998. Historically, mass public opinion has taken cues from the medical community. Strong public opinion favoring abortion increased after the reform movement developed within the medical community. By September 1967, seventeen state medical associations had endorsed abortion liberalization, and the AMA endorsed it in June 1967, six years before the Supreme Court decision (Tatalovich and Daynes 1981). In contrast, the AMA is a powerful interest on the opposing side of PAS. Lack of strong support for PAS from the medical community most likely has contributed to fluctuating public opinion.

Lack of cohesive and supportive public opinion within both the general public and the medical community does not encourage legislators, who also face well-organized interest group opposition. It seems unlikely that legislators will support PAS or other controversial morality policy until a large majority of constituents are in favor of it and/or other political venues, particularly courts, have given their assent on the issue.

Future Policy Innovation

Interest Groups

As discussed earlier, the Hemlock Society and related organizations that support PAS were more prominent and active in the policymaking process than were right-to-die interest groups in the past two decades. The increasing activity of these groups supporting PAS suggests that there are parallels between PAS and other morality policies in the ways that agenda setting evolves over time: The experience garnered from previous agenda setting and policy innovation and changes in social contexts encourage the formation and/or development of new advocacy groups.

For example, today the two sides in the battle over abortion are supported by many sophisticated, well-organized, and well-financed groups, including the Catholic Church and the AMA, but that was not always so when abortion policymaking was new (Craig and O'Brien 1993). In the early years of the right-to-die issue (1970s), living will laws usually were put forth by motivated legislators who sometimes were able to take advantage of growing public support, favorable court decisions, and other windows of opportunity, but right-to-die organizations, mainly Choice in Dying, limited themselves to providing information about using living wills, and so on. They rarely lobbied. The Hemlock Society was a new organization, and Derek Humphry did not believe that living wills were sufficient remedies. Although PAS is so controversial that few legislators will support it, the Hemlock Society and similar groups now have more members and are better organized, more successful at fund-raising, and more capable of sustaining a policy battle.

Nevertheless, our analysis of media tone and the content of public opinion reveals that PAS needs much more support to achieve consensus. Until then and/or until other venues adopt favorable policy, the consistent opposition of the powerful Catholic Church and the AMA and its state counterparts will dominate state legislatures. Despite the Hemlock Society's recent political activism, it cannot counter the influence that these prestigious, experienced, and very well-organized and financed organizations have in most state legislatures.

Other Venues

In contrast to the legislature, direct initiatives require government institutions to do little other than comply with formal rules concerning the conduct of elections, and no legislator or other official needs to endorse a measure for it to become law. If proponents can convince a majority of the voters, they can produce a change in policy. However, PAS is so controversial and sensitive that an initiative campaign has been successful only in Oregon. In this sense, PAS exhibits some of the same characteristics of other controversial morality policies for which competing interest groups fight continually for the last word in public policy. This differs from other types of policies, such as economic regulation and foreign affairs, that are much less salient to the public and that few interest groups continually contest.

Unless Congress preempts the states, the history of the right-to-die issue suggests that in addition to the initiative, state courts will be a venue of choice for this controversial new policy, despite limited success thus far, and legislatures may shift. Most courts that have dealt with the right to die have increased patients' rights and autonomy. Therefore, previous state right-to-die decisions and perhaps state constitutions can serve as precedents for expanding patient control to include PAS. More than two decades ago, the New Jersey Supreme Court provided early policy leadership in this area that had enormous influence on other state courts (Glick 1992). The plight of people facing the certainty of an awful death will stimulate more litigation, and if a prominent state supreme court takes the lead on permitting PAS, even more litigation and favorable court decisions may follow. If this trend is accompanied by rising public support, state legislatures also may find PAS acceptable (Glick 1992; Hays and Glick 1997).

Conclusion

We have identified some similarities and differences between PAS and other morality policies. We found that PAS reached the mass agenda before the professional agenda, which is different from previous right-to-die and other morality policies. We believe that this finding is related to the clear linkage between PAS and previous right-to-die policies, as well as the notorious but highly newsworthy events focusing on Dr. Jack Kevorkian's assisted suicides. PAS has received very little official support due, we believe, to its lack of positive image, the negative tone of reporting it, and divided public opinion. These factors are important for any policy, especially for morality policies, which are very salient to the public. Furthermore, the legalization of abortion has led to a bitter and continuing battle between supporters and opponents. The legalization of PAS has the potential to cause a similar conflict. Given U.S. history regarding morality policies, legislators are not likely to endorse PAS until its image and support are clear, consistent, and enduring. Consequently, supporters have tried the popular initiative to overcome legislative and judicial resistance.

Finally, we see some changes in public mobilization on behalf of PAS mainly through local grassroots interest groups. We believe this reflects the maturing of the right-to-die issue, similar to the evolution of other morality issues such as abortion, but the ability of these groups to sway legislatures and courts probably will be severely limited by the greater power of well-established organizations and conservative state political environments. Clearly, well-organized opposition groups have dominated the federal legislature, as indicated by the fact that a result of the pending Pain Relief Promotion Act may be to curtail PAS.

Most previous research on morality policy is concerned with the adoption and/or diffusion of policies, whereas we have focused on the agenda stages of policymaking. Therefore, we have considered issues and variables different from those found in other morality policy research. Too little information is available on morality policy agenda setting over the long term for us to draw firm conclusions about the similarities and differences between PAS and other morality policies, but we believe that our findings suggest some avenues for additional research.

Comparative cross-sectional examinations of additional morality as well as nonmorality policies over time are needed for us to build a more complete theory or model of how the agenda-setting and policy adoption process unfolds. The cross-sectional approach is twofold. First, we need to examine more than single issues, such as PAS or tobacco regulation. Second, studies of policies that largely are the domain of state governments, such as most health policies, need to include all fifty states. This approach will allow us to search for similarities and differences among and between policy types (i.e., morality and nonmorality policies).

Even with this approach, direct comparisons will be very difficult. For example, if we were to compare the few recent years of the PAS agenda to the early period of abortion policies, we could not take account of the enormous political and social changes that have taken place in the United States in this century that would have affected those two policies differently. Probably a better strategy for general theory building is to select policies that are emerging at approximately similar times so that the effects of social and political history can be held constant.

Nevertheless, it is extremely difficult to organize comparative research on the fifty states that includes more than a single issue given the detailed amount of information needed to study agenda setting for several policies at the national level (e.g., Baumgartner and Jones 1993; Kingdon 1995). Perhaps policies could be selected that are the major concern of particular advocacy groups that collect much information on the movement of issues through the state political process. This approach could provide raw data that could be analyzed through the perspective of agenda setting and innovation. Until we can orchestrate research that includes at least several policies that represent both morality and nonmorality policies, we will be limited in the types of generalizations we can make about the agenda-setting process.

Notes

1. We distinguish PAS from voluntary active euthanasia in which the physician, at the patient's request, directly causes the death of a patient (e.g., when the physician injects a lethal dose of morphine into a dying cancer patient). In contrast, PAS implies that the physician only provides the means by which a patient may commit suicide. For example, the physician might write a prescription for a lethal dose of medication, which the patient then administers on his or her own.

2. Data for this research begins with 1987 since previous research has shown that PAS emerged in the 1990s. Backtracking to 1987 provided an empirical check on the currency of PAS.

3. Events were obtained by examining the *New York Times* and the *Los Angeles Times* indexes from 1987 to 1996. Three researchers separately noted major statewide news events and Dr. Jack Kevorkian's assisted suicides that consistently received substantial media attention. Local events and local court cases were not included. The three researchers agreed on what constituted major events in more than 75 percent of the selections. To be included, two researchers had to agree. Complete intercoder reliability did not occur; however, if omissions were made, it is in the direction of eliminating events rather than including local or narrowly reported items that would inflate the number of events included.

4. The sources of data for tracking the mass and professional agendas include counts of articles in *Reader's Guide to Periodical Literature* and *New York Times* (mass media), and *Index Medicus*, the *Religion Index*, the *Catholic Index*, *Index to Legal Periodicals*, the *Humanities Index*, and the *Social Science Index* (professional media) as well as every poll on the right to die. To do an exhaustive search for entries on PAS, we examined all listings under euthanasia, assisted suicide, living wills, right to die, and Kevorkian. In addition, a few articles were found under Cruzan, Quinlan, death with dignity, terminal care, right to refuse treatment, mercy killing, health attitudes, allowing to die, death, suicide, do not resuscitate, and medical ethics. We omitted articles dealing with animals, war, Nazi Germany, and depression.

5. Questions were analyzed from those reported and available in the *American Public Opinion Index*, various years.

6. Following Baumgartner and Jones (1993), we coded story titles according to whether a proponent of PAS would be happy or unhappy with the title of the article.

7. The questions for 1990 and 1993 are identical, as are the questions for 1995 and 1997. All but the question used for 1992 have similar structures (i.e., they contain prologues that introduce the subject before asking respondents for their opinions). The question for 1992 is more blunt and simply asks whether the respondent agrees that doctors should be allowed by law to help terminally ill patients to commit suicide.

8. An additional question asked in 1996, which is worded differently from the others, reveals 68 percent support for PAS. Both questions are from Gallup polls. These varying response rates to different questions underscore the difficulty in discerning public opinion on PAS.

PART THREE

Interest Group Activity on Morality Policy

CHAPTER FIVE

Evolving into Morality Politics: U.S. Catholic Bishops' Statements on U.S. Politics from 1792 to the Present

Paul J. Fabrizio

THE ROMAN CATHOLIC CHURCH, the largest religious group in the United States, is organized in a clear hierarchical structure with parishes at the grass roots tied to dioceses that represent geographic areas (Hanna 1979, 214; Reese 1992, vi–vii). The leaders of the dioceses are bishops appointed by the pope in Rome to be "teachers of doctrine, priests of sacred worship, and ministers of governance" according to the church's *The Code of Canon Law* (Coriden, Green, and Heintschel 1985, Canon 375). The bishops are the "main governing figures" with power over parishes and the priests who staff them. The bishops, in union with the pope, are the final arbiters of Catholic belief; when they teach about church doctrine, they do so authoritatively (Steinfels and Niebuhr 1996, 1).

The bishops as a group are a powerful noneconomic interest group engaged in morality politics. With their hierarchically configured organization, they have the power to define doctrine authoritatively for the 50 to 60 million Catholics in the United States (Morris 1997, 301). When U.S. bishops meet as a group twice a year, they can and do issue pronouncements on such matters of morality as nuclear deterrence, the consequences of economic policy, and most prominently, abortion, that draw widespread attention from policymakers, business leaders, and the news media (McBrien 1987).

Have they always had such power? Perhaps more interesting, have the bishops always taken moral stands on political issues? The study of the political development of this interest group can provide us with insight into how a noneconomic interest group can become powerful in the morality policy arena.

Has the group always spoken out passionately on moral issues? When and under what conditions did it first ask for political action by Catholic citizens? When did it first criticize U.S. policy? In short, how have the bishops' political demands on Catholic citizens and U.S. policymakers evolved?

Previous study of the Catholic Church's political involvement has documented the slow growth of self-confidence among Catholics as they fought anti-immigration prejudices in the nineteenth and early twentieth centuries. Through the sheer force of numbers and avid participation in the nation's great wars they have achieved a place at the political table (Dolan 1978, 1985; Hanna 1979; Hennesey 1981; Ellis 1969). Scholars have noted the importance of popes' social encyclicals and the documents of Vatican Council II in giving bishops the theological underpinnings to enter the political arena on moral questions. Also important to its ability to speak about morals in politics was the U.S. church's own development of a national organization (Dolan 1985; Reese 1992; Hanna 1979). Byrnes has also noted the importance of the partisan political environment to the recent attention that bishops have achieved for their policy pronouncements (Byrnes 1991, 1993).

What is missing from this analysis is a consideration of how the bishops themselves, speaking as a group, developed into the politically powerful interest group that they are today. Previous research has typically focused on the work of individual bishops (Ellis 1969; McBrien 1987; Byrnes 1991; Au 1985). The bishops as a collective, as an interest group, are the subject of study here.

The central political instrument of the bishops as a group has been the open letter to U.S. Catholics. Throughout their history, the bishops have gathered together and issued letters to U.S. Catholics explaining doctrine, exhorting deeper devotion, and explaining to their flock the Catholic understanding of issues facing the country. Using the more than 125 letters written by the bishops to U.S. Catholics since 1792, this chapter demonstrates that just as Catholics slowly developed into a self-confident people with an accepted role in society, the bishops slowly evolved into an important advocacy group on morality policy. Their journey had three steps. First, they expressed concern about Catholic economic interests, most especially property rights and anti-Catholic laws. Second, they spoke directly to policymakers as members of a religious elite. Third, they became political mobilizers, telling U.S. Catholics how to behave politically in the area of morality politics.

Early Insecurity Leads to Search for Acceptance

The first bishops' letter was written in 1792 by the lone U.S. bishop, John Carroll of Baltimore. His effort was strictly religious in nature, speaking about the values of a Christian education and the need for more priests (1792, vol. 1, 16).[1]

The number of bishops grew, but they did not write as a group until 1829 at a gathering in Baltimore. Their concerns in the 1829 letter were strictly spiritual, as were those in the three published after three subsequent meetings. Not until their fifth letter, written in 1837, did they address politics. The tone of this letter was tentative, however; the bishops were concerned with avoiding offense to the Protestant majority, especially in response to contemporary literary and even physical attacks made against Catholics. They explained carefully that "we endeavor to live in peace with our brethren" and "do not aspire to power." Furthermore, they said that they "do not calculate by what processes we should be able . . . to control the councils of the republic." The bishops wrote that Catholics "are comparatively few amongst the millions of our fellow citizens" and most "of our flocks are in humble, laborious, but useful occupations"(1837, vol. 1, 90).

In the most political section of the 1837 letter, the bishops wrote, "We owe no religious allegiance to any State in this Union, nor to its general government. No one of them claims any supremacy or dominion over us in our spiritual or ecclesiastical concerns" (1837, vol. 1, 90). The political import of the 1837 letter was that the bishops had marked their territory. They were telling the government that each had an area of expertise and that in the spiritual world, the Church would teach as it saw fit.

In 1840, the bishops meeting in Baltimore wrote their first letter directly about how Catholics should feel about U.S. politics. They began by saying that they were as divided by the issues of the day as any group of Americans, but that that division could not stop them from speaking out. The bishops said they were speaking because "of the love we bear to our civil and political institutions, and by the obligations of morality." Here the bishops for the first time acknowledge directly a moral component in politics. But then what did the bishops urge their flock to do? They told them to stay away from politics:

> Do then, we entreat you, avoid the contaminating influence of political strife, keep yourselves aloof from the pestilential atmosphere in which honor, virtue, patriotism, and religion perish. . . . Beloved brethren, flee this contamination . . . reflect that you are accountable not only to society but to God. (1840, vol. 1, 134)

The letter mentioned the "meanest passions" and "vile bribery" in politics and asserted that "truth is disregarded" in political campaigns. The bishops concluded their letter by writing, "How often have we had to weep over the havoc of morals, and the wreck of religion which political excitement has produced" (1840, vol. 1, 133–34). Clearly, the bishops were not mobilizing Catholics for a fight on the moral issues of the time.

Twelve years later, again meeting in Baltimore, the bishops were concerned only with the standing of the immigrant church in a Protestant country. "Obey public authorities," they told Catholics:

> Show your attachment to the institutions of our beloved country by prompt compliance with all their requirements. . . . Thus will you refute the idle babbling of foolish men . . . and overcome, by the sure test of practical patriotism, all the prejudices which a misapprehension of your principles but too often produces. (1852, vol. 1, 181)

While the bishops' letters were notable for their concern with getting Catholics to fit in with the rest of society, they make no mention of the central economic and moral issue of the day—slavery. Their 1852 letter would be their last until after the Civil War, and the silence of the bishops on this most critical question is noteworthy. Nolan writes that the bishops saw the problem as a political one, not a moral one, and were more concerned with maintaining peace than in righting wrongs. The bishops were, in essence, apolitical at this critical point in U.S. history. One reason for this apolitical stance was that the bishops were themselves conflicted on slavery and secession. Bishops took active roles for both sides during the war (Nolan 1984a, 167–69). But the bishops were not even functioning as an interest group prior to the Civil War because they expressed no collective interest in the nation's problems. Their concern was only the well-being of their own flock, and to address that issue, they wrote only to their own people. The bishops had no desire to talk to the Protestant majority until Catholics were acceptable to that majority.

After the Civil War, the bishops met as a group to proclaim their unity as a church in the divided land and to consider the evangelization of the newly freed slaves. However, in their letter of 1866, they went beyond those spiritual concerns and reminded civil authorities that "all power is of God" and that governmental authorities' power "must always be exercised agreeably to God's will." This was the first time they quoted from the Bible, specifically Romans 13:1–5, in their discussion of politics. If the authorities did anything contrary to God's will, the bishops warned, then government would have "no claim on the obedience of the citizen." The reason for this comment on the nature of governmental power was the bishops' concern about legal discrimination in some states against the church, whereby its ability to own property was being limited. Missouri was singled out for special attention. The bishops wrote that "this refusal to recognize the church in her corporate capacity" and then passing laws to tax all property not held by corporations is the result of "hostility towards the Catholic Church" (1866, vol. 1, 191–93). The bishops, in an indirect way, were threatening the civil authorities for infringing on their property rights by speaking of the religious foundation of all secular governmental power.

This is the first time the bishops made a comment about the roots of government's authority and had a specific complaint about a government decision. It is also noteworthy that these comments appear together in one letter. Slowly, Catholics and public officials were being set up for the day when the bishops would make moral pronouncements on public issues calling on Catholics to act. In 1866, however, the bishops limited their remarks to a complaint and comment. Catholics were specifically *not* instructed to vote a certain way, and the bishops pointedly noted that all they were doing was formally protesting the state's decision. Still mindful of their minority status in a Protestant country, the bishops took pains to remind Catholics that obedience to government "is a religious duty founded on obedience to God," not merely something to do to ensure peace and security (1866, vol. 1, 191–93).

The timing of this first flexing of political muscle is significant. First, it comes after the Civil War, during which Catholics fought with distinction on both sides. The bishops would make significant political statements after World War I and World War II as well. The loyalty demonstrated by Catholics in those conflicts may have given a boost to the bishops' self-confidence. Second, the bishops were by this time organized at the national level. By the 1830s, the bishops had achieved some measure of organizational unity at the national level through administrative policies and hierarchical rules and were thus better able to stand up to the government, if in a limited way (Dolan 1978, 10, 352). Finally, the Catholics, while still a minority with about 4 million members, were by 1866 the largest religious denomination in the country, further adding to the bishops' social and political confidence (Greeley 1977, 36; Au 1985, ix).

In this 1866 letter, the bishops for the first time acted as an interest group. They were concerned with an economic issue, specifically property rights. They carefully noted the right of the state to decide policy but pointedly noted the error of certain of these decisions. Haider-Markel and Meier (1996) argue that the most effective interest group strategy is one of limiting the scope of the conflict and appealing to elites. That is what the bishops did here. By not threatening Catholic political involvement and staying in the area of minor economic policy, they limited their dispute with the government. The result of such a strategy was that the U.S. Catholic Church found great success in achieving specific economic benefits for itself (Hanna 1979, 208). This 1866 letter was the bishops' initial stab at this strategy.

The bishops next wrote in 1884, returning to the old theme that the country was blessed and that Catholics would defend it from its enemies. In a message to the nation's anti-Catholics, the bishops wrote that Catholics were freedom-loving citizens too, saying, "We believe that our country's heroes were the instruments of the God of nations in establishing this home of freedom." Should that freedom or nation be threatened, Catholics "will be found to stand forward, as one man ready to pledge anew 'their lives, their fortunes, and their sacred honor' " (1884, vol. 1, 215–16). Catholics would demonstrate this further during World War I, when the bishops wrote in 1917 to President Woodrow Wilson pledging Catholic support for the war effort: "Our people, now as ever, will rise as one man to serve the nation. Our priests and consecrated women will once again, as in every former trial in this country, win by their bravery, their heroism, and their service new admiration and approval" (1917, vol. 1, 296). What is striking about this letter is the lack of self-confidence the bishops felt about their church's place in society. Why were Catholics fighting? Not for the defeat of the Germans; not for freedom or democracy; they were fighting, the bishops said, to win "admiration and approval" from other Americans. The bishops were still seeking a place in U.S. society.

Catholic Confidence and General Policy Pronouncements

Catholic bishops' confidence in their church's place in the United States was irretrievably established in their letter written to the general public at the conclusion of World War I. Catholics had died for their country, and by making that sacrifice, the Church now had a place in its affairs. Dolan (1985, 180) writes that Catholics ended the war "confident and optimistic about the future." Just as after the Civil War, when the bishops wrote critically of governmental property policy, Catholic bishops after World War I decided to address serious domestic problems and to state Catholic thinking on those issues. In their 1919 letter, "Program for Social Reconstruction," the bishops moved for the first time into policy politics, discussing specific issues, taking positions, and offering suggestions on rebuilding the country after the war. They wrote explicitly to policymakers from a religious elite perspective. They expressed concern about placing returning veterans in the workforce, especially on farms, and called for equal pay for equal work for both sexes. Wages should not be reduced, they said, even if prices were to fall, and social security insurance should be provided until wages were sufficiently high to pay for old age. Labor unions should exist without question, women workers should quit dangerous occupations in industry, and child labor under the age of sixteen should be so heavily taxed that it would be too burdensome for businesses (1919, vol. 1, 255–71).

The last section of this letter was entitled "A Christian View." Although it acknowledged the necessity of enterprise, it said that the "capitalist must . . . get a new viewpoint." Capitalists must realize that a "laborer is a human being" and that paying a living wage is the "first moral charge on industry." The letter concludes: "This is the human and Christian, in contrast to the purely commercial and pagan, ethics of industry" (1919, vol. 1, 271).

This is a remarkable document for three reasons. First, the bishops made many proposals that Franklin Roosevelt would advocate in his New Deal, more than thirteen years later (Byrnes 1991, 28). Second, during the war, the bishops had institutionalized themselves as a formal group, the National Catholic War Council; at the conclusion of the war, they changed the name to the National Catholic Welfare Council and established the policy of annual meetings. Regular meetings allowed for timely monitoring and response to changing conditions. The 1919 letter, coming at the same time as this institutional change, meant that the bishops as a group were committing themselves for the first time to "social and political action" beyond their own interests (Hennesey 1981, 227). The bishops were no longer a purely economic interest group; they were now interested in the common good. Certainly, their labor proposals benefited Catholic workers, but the bishops were separating themselves from the dominant strains of U.S. business. The bishops had institutionalized themselves by word and deed as a group looking for national consensus on the problems of the day and then writing to Catholics and non-Catholics about their conclusions (Dolan 1985, 352–54).

Finally, after taking the critical steps of challenging U.S. economic and public policy and proposing alternatives for consideration, the bishops stepped back from the fray. Nowhere in the letter were Catholics told to support or vote for certain people or programs. Rather, the bishops merely pointed out social problems and offered solutions. The solutions were proposed as "subject to discussion" as long as the principles of charity and justice taught by the Catholic Church were followed. When it came to talking specifically about Catholic political participation, however, the bishops were silent (1919, vol. 1, 255–71). The closest they came to a call to action was the phrase "it is the obvious duty of Congress to" strengthen the United States Employment Service (1919, vol. 1, 261). The bishops were speaking to policymakers about policy issues.

This is an important step in the bishops' evolution as a morality politics interest group. They were no longer focused on their parochial concerns and were now addressing an elite audience. Getting Catholic voter action would be a step left untaken for fifty years. They chose the middle ground that would present a moral case for changing public policy but would not commit any political muscle to change that policy. The bishops in 1919 were moving beyond advocating particularized benefits for their own members and toward espousing certain values that benefited all. In 1919, however, the bishops did not move beyond the use of moral persuasion to achieve their ends.

The bishops followed this "Program for Social Reconstruction" with a Pastoral Letter specifically addressed to Catholics. This Pastoral Letter congratulated them on their service during World War I and reminded others of Catholic patriotism. The bishops expressed concern about discrimination against religious liberty; to combat it, they reminded Catholics of their duty to obey civil authorities. Quoting from Romans 13, the bishops wrote of "this obedience we are bound to render, not merely on grounds of expediency but as a conscientious duty. 'Be subject of necessity, not only for wrath but also for conscience's sake.' " To end that discrimination, they warned civil authorities that "passing . . . an unjust law is the suicide of authority" (1919, vol. 1, 306, 322). But the bishops continued to offer no threat of Catholic political action even when unjust laws were passed.

In 1922, the bishops wrote one of their shortest and—from a historical perspective—their least diplomatic letter ever. In a two-paragraph "Statement on Federalization and Bureaucracy" without description or analysis, the bishops complained that bureaucratic growth in the United States must be "checked." They warned that

> extreme bureaucracy is foreign to everything American. . . . It means officialism, red tape, and prodigal waste of public money. . . . It would eventually sovietize our form of government. . . . The press, the home, the school, and the Church have no greater enemy at the present time than the paternalistic and bureaucratic government which certain self-seeking elements are attempting to foist upon us. (1922, vol. 1, 334)

Here the bishops were probably harking back to their 1919 letter in which they wrote that the state "is a means to an end, not an end in itself" (1919, vol. 1, 306). Unprecedented growth in the state would mean that unchecked governmental powers could threaten religious liberty. Yet in a pattern noticed earlier, the bishops say nothing about what Catholics should do about it. There is no mention of voting or becoming involved in politics. The bishops seem to have believed that putting their objections on the record for policymakers was enough.

There were good reasons for this restraint on the part of the bishops. First, the church at this time was a church of immigrants. Much of the energy of the bishops was taken up with assimilation of newly arrived Catholics into U.S. Catholic Church life. This was a difficult task, and they were not always successful. In 1907, about 250,000 Polish immigrants had broken off from the church and formed the Polish National Catholic Church, the only enduring schism in U.S. Catholic history. Not until 1921, when the U.S. Congress passed laws limiting European immigration, would the bishops be given enough breathing room to consolidate the church's organizational structure around a stabilizing church membership (Ellis 1969, 129).

Second, the bishops were still feeling their way as church leaders in the worldwide Catholic community. That lack of confidence hindered their U.S. political involvement. Only in 1907 did the pope decide that the U.S. Church produced enough homegrown clergy to declare that it was no longer mission territory and therefore ranked on par with Catholic countries such as France and Italy (Ellis 1969, 124). Only in 1926 would the United States host an international gathering of Catholics, welcoming hundreds of thousands of visitors from all over the world to Chicago for the Twentieth-eighth International Eucharistic Congress (Morris 1997, 135–38). The bishops also had to move tentatively because of the Vatican's opposition to their own National Catholic Welfare Council, which the pope feared would weaken his teaching authority. Some bishops even refused to participate in the organization, further eroding its authority on policy issues (Morris 1997, 135; Reese 1992, 23–26).

Finally, there was the strong anti-Catholic bias present in the United States. This was evident during the 1928 campaign of Al Smith and shown by the fact that as of 1933, only four Catholics had ever served in the president's cabinet and few were in Congress. Catholic leaders were found at local levels, but not many were prominent in the federal government (Ellis 1969, 150–52). In the face of these obstacles, the bishops' reluctance to push a political agenda actively was not surprising.

Following the Mexican Revolution and the suppression of the church there, the bishops in 1926 wrote a long pastoral statement about the Church in Mexico. They examined the abuses against the church there, compared the new Mexican regime with the U.S. Constitution, reiterated their frequently mentioned point that citizens should not follow unjust laws, and called for an end to the new Mexican government. Then, to make it clear to all what they wanted and how they wanted it, the bishops wrote the following:

> What, therefore we have written is no call on the faithful here or elsewhere to purely human action. It is no interposition of our influence either as bishops or as citizens to reach those who possess political power anywhere on earth, and least of all in our own country, to the end that they should intervene with armed force in the internal affairs of Mexico for the protection of the church. . . . Our duty is done when, by telling the story, defending the truth, and emphasizing the principles, we sound a warning to Christian civilization that its foundations are again being undermined. For the rest, God will bring His will to pass in His own time and in His own good way. (1926, vol. 1, 363–64)

In other words, the bishops registered their complaint but did not call for citizen action. Certainly, many other Catholics were calling for intervention, but the bishops themselves, like Pope Pius XI, asked only for prayers (Morris 1997, 230–31; Nolan 1984a, vol. 1, 246). They engaged in classic interest group activity by expressing the concern that their interests were being threatened (Hertzke 1988). In this letter, the bishops reaffirmed the pattern of their political letters for the past 130 years and confirmed it for the next 50 years. They called attention to a situation and prescribed a solution for policymakers but stopped short of advocating any voter response to pursue this prescription.

With the Great Depression, the bishops illustrated this pattern once more. They asked Catholics to give alms and try to help the unemployed find work (1931, vol. 1, 369); they suggested that more governmental help might be needed for those suffering (1930, vol. 1, 366–67); they decried high taxes and their burden on workers (1933, vol. 1, 397); and they encouraged cooperation with President Roosevelt's welfare relief program (1934, vol. 1, 412). They said nothing, however, about voting or being involved in the political process beyond the usual call to obey civil authority. While the bishops were clearly speaking out about societal problems, which were situations far beyond the realm of strictly sacred matters, they were still not acting as leaders in the fight for policy.

Even the rise of Adolf Hitler and fascism did not move the bishops explicitly into the political arena. Instead, in several different letters, they wrote about the need for Christians to be better educated to understand the concepts behind U.S. democracy (1938, vol. 1, 428–29); they asked for a "spirit of calm deliberation" as Catholics watched Germany march across Europe (1939, vol. 1, 433); they renewed U.S. Catholics' devotion to the ideals of the United States and the fight that lay ahead (1940, vol. 1, 454; 1941, vol. 2, 32); and they pleaded as before, for Catholics to obey civil officials (1941, vol. 2, 33). Throughout World War II, the bishops were speaking to the non-Catholics as well as to the Catholics in the United States, just as they had done during World War I. They pledged Catholics' support for the war and Catholics' obedience to the U.S. government.

In one respect, the bishops' statements in this period are not far removed from those of 100 years earlier when the church was struggling for acceptance in a non-Catholic country. As a result of the anti-Catholicism of the 1920s, evident in the rise of the Ku Klux Klan, the campaign against presidential candidate Al Smith, the anti-immigration crusades, and the sensitivity that many immigrant Catholics must have felt with their former countries fighting alongside Hitler against the allied powers (Hennesey 1981, ix; Dolan 1985, 351), the Catholic bishops trod cautiously in policy issues. They seemed to be saying, "Let's win the war first." This period also experienced an increase in political consciousness and debate on the part of the bishops as their self-confidence as U.S.

Catholics improved. They expressed their opinion on policy issues, especially after World War I. They cautioned against the growth of government power. They expressed concern about economic issues that affected non-Catholics as well as Catholics. This period was the precursor to full-fledged political activity.

Injecting Catholic Values into Public Debate

With the end of World War II, the bishops, perhaps more sure of Catholics' position in U.S. life, began to move more forcefully into the political arena. It is interesting to note that after the Civil War, the bishops for the first time criticized a government and after World War I, they first made policy suggestions about economic life. Now, after another war in which Catholics had made great contributions, the bishops took the next step in their evolution as an interest group. They told Catholics to get involved and change the law. Their criticism became more pointed, their analysis of economic and political life became more sophisticated, and they finally began to talk about direct political action, mainly voting. They moved from complainers to mobilizers. In the postwar era, they especially became engaged fully in morality politics, but the politics of interest was still first on their agenda. When their own Catholic education was threatened, the bishops first reached out to Catholic laity, telling them to do something. A direct threat to the bishops' interests spurred action.

In 1948, the Supreme Court ruling in *McCollum* v. *Board of Education* (333 U.S. 203) declared unconstitutional the practice of releasing Illinois public students for religious education. The Court was beginning forcibly to separate church and state in public education, and this early effort drew the ire of the bishops. "Secularism is threatening the religious foundations of our national life," they argued. Catholics were urged to "seek in their faith an inspiration and a guide . . . for good citizenship." Catholic lawyers were asked to get involved in and develop a special competence in the area of law where religion intersects with politics. People must be ready to "avert the impending danger of a judicial 'establishment of secularism' that would ban God from public life." The bishops acted as political elites working for incremental change as they wrote "we shall peacefully, patiently, and perseveringly work" to revise the Supreme Court's decision (1948, vol. 2, 85–89). This is classic interest group behavior; the bishops became most outspoken on the political stage when they perceived that their direct interests were being threatened.

In 1951, they moved beyond their parochial interest to concern for the general good as they commented on the political situation of the day with a letter entitled "God's Law: The Measure of Man's Conduct." The letter began by comparing the problems that faced the Roman Empire near its demise and those facing the postwar era. Calling for "mastery over self," the letter attacked the corruption of political life and spoke against slander and dishonesty in politics. In tones reminiscent of their "weep over the havoc of morals and the wreck of religion" letter written in 1840, the bishops wrote, "in politics the principle of 'anything goes' . . . is grossly wrong. . . . Dishonesty, slander, detraction, and defamation of character are . . . truly transgressions of God's commandments" (1951, vol. 2, 138–45). The letter made no references to anyone, and the bishops urged no action beyond a return to God's laws. Political commentators read it, however, as an assault on both the corruption of the Truman administration and Sen. Joseph McCarthy's relentless campaign against communists. The letter was reprinted in full in major newspapers in both New York and Washington, D.C., and was widely praised as an antidote to the misdeeds of Washington (Reese 1992, 27; Nolan 1984b, vol. 2, 111–12). With this letter, the bishops moved beyond the politics of interest. Their concern was the moral well-being of the country.

In the 1950s, the bishops spoke out on bigotry, the press, communism, education, refugees, and even traffic safety. Other than identifying problems, their concern was for enhancing morality in public behavior, even if only when driving on the nation's highways. They had only praise for the efforts of the nation's chief politician, President Dwight Eisenhower, against communism. It can be argued that they wrote about him for self-interested reasons; after all, communists are atheists, and these statements demonstrated that they were on the side of a popular president. They compared Eisenhower's anticommunist efforts to those of Pope Pius XII and said that the president was "alert to the overriding need of a developed reverence for international law, clearly mindful . . . that without law there can be no peace" (1956, vol. 2, 188).

The Beginning of a New Era as Political Actors

In the 1960s, with the Vietnam War, the civil rights movement, and labor union strife, the bishops became full-fledged political actors. In addition to their detailed social analysis and their nuanced policy prescriptions, they urged specific Catholic action in areas far beyond the self-interest of the Catholic Church. With the election of a Catholic president in John Kennedy and the creation of an administrative structure for all U.S. bishops, the National Conference of Catholic Bishops/United States Catholic Conference (Reese 1992, 28–32), the bishops may finally have felt confident enough about the Catholic place in U.S. life and concerned enough about the issues at hand to call for direct political action. They recommended that certain policies be implemented and that consideration of certain values, such as compassion, be made in policymaking. They were an interest group, stating policy preferences and urging necessary change.

The bishops still would not go all the way, however, and make their pronouncements full-fledged morality issues with the urgency that such issues imply. Consistently throughout the 1960s, the bishops did not ask Catholic voters for political action. Instead they spoke to politicians, functioning more as lobbyists than mobilizers. They did not call for letter-writing campaigns or votes by Catholics in favor of or against certain positions or politicians. They did ask for help from Catholics in nongovernmental areas, specifically the boycott of table grapes and Farah trousers, both the result of labor union action (1973, vol. 3, 404–7), but they never issued guidelines for votes. They asked that politicians heed their calls for reflection on the values that policies represent, but not once did they say to Catholic voters, "Do this!"

On Vietnam, the bishops, and the rest of the country, moved from an early position of support for Johnson administration policy to one advocating peace. While supporting the president, in letters in 1966, 1967, and 1968, they always asked for more peace talks and praised any efforts the United States made toward limiting the war (1966, 1967, 1968, vol. 3, 76, 90, 161). They strongly supported the right of young men to choose to be conscientious objectors to escape the draft. They even offered them the help of their offices and theologians (1971, vol. 3, 283–85). By 1971, however, the bishops called for an immediate end to the war: "[W]e feel a moral obligation to appeal urgently to the leaders of all nations involved in this tragic conflict to bring the war to an end with no further delay" (1971, vol. 3, 289). This letter did not call for political action among Catholic voters, nor did it threaten to withdraw political support. The bishops were interested in individual draftees and individual policymakers. They were religious elites appealing to political elites. They always asked for individual reflection and action based on moral principles. They never called for, nor threatened, group mobilization.

Nor did the bishops mobilize their people against other evils. While they wrote about racism, poverty, welfare, and housing, they did not call on Catholic voters to support any specific legislation, party, or candidates. Rather, the bishops themselves, as spokesmen for the church, supported specific pieces of legislation and urged Congress to pass them (1967, 1970, 1972, vol. 3, 89, 256, 304). For example, in the resolution on welfare, they wrote:

> the Catholic bishops of the United States assembled as the United States
> Catholic Conference urge prompt enactment of the Family Assistance Act
> or some similar family assistance program, at the same time urging that
> the minimum dollar amount of $1,600 for a family of four, be substan-
> tially raised. Strong and clear federal guidelines, to assure equitable
> administration, must be provided. If training for, or acceptance of
> employment by the family head is a condition precedent to the obtaining

of benefits, it is important that such employment be truly suitable. (1970, vol. 3, 256)

Their efforts were those of teacher to legislator; there was no pretext of getting Catholic citizens involved in the political process. They were functioning as lobbyists, providing information and guidance to legislators, letting their opinions be known, but not mobilizing the faithful to action. This was a common tactic among religious groups who lobbied in Washington (Hertzke 1988). Only with abortion would the bishops move toward grassroots political organization and become deeply involved in morality politics.

Abortion and Catholic Mobilization

When the Supreme Court's decision allowing legal abortions was first announced (*Roe* v. *Wade* 410 U.S. 113 [1973]), the president of the bishops' conference, John Cardinal Krol, denounced it as "bad logic and bad law" (1973, vol. 3, 366). Within a month, the bishops issued a more developed statement calling on Catholics to oppose the law and stating that the bishops "reject this decision of the court" (1973, vol. 3, 367–68). In a 1975 letter to Catholics, they called for a "political" effort to *"organize people"* (emphasis in original) to elect pro-life candidates and pass a pro-life constitutional amendment (1975, vol. 4, 89). Here, for the first time, the bishops were fully engaged in politics; significantly, it was on a morality policy issue. Morality politics can be seen in black and white, with little barriers to political participation by citizens (Meier 1994, 4–7). The bishops, in no uncertain terms, told Catholics that abortion was wrong and that they must organize to change the U.S. Constitution to make it illegal. In their 1975 letter "Pastoral Plan for Pro-Life Activities," the bishops discussed the creation of pro-life committees at the parish, diocesan, and congressional district levels, listing who should be on those committees and what they should try to achieve. The bishops wanted action, and they told their flock explicitly how to take it (1975, vol. 4, 88–91).

It was abortion, more specifically *Roe* v. *Wade*, that finally moved the bishops fully and overtly into political action. Their concerns on the subject were not new. They had written about abortion before *Roe* v. *Wade* (see letters in 1968, 1969, 1970, vol. 3, 181, 198–99, 254) and had certainly made no secret of their opposition. In 1969, they entitled one letter "Statement in Protest of U.S. Government Programs against the Right to Life." Again, however, the bishops had stopped short of mobilizing Catholic voters. They concluded that protest by saying merely, "We hope our fellow Americans will appreciate the soundness of our stand" (1969, vol. 3, 213). When the Supreme Court declared abortion a right protected under the Constitution, the bishops moved forcefully to a new level of political activity. In a sense, they were ready for it. They had moved from being apolitical to being an elite interest group, but the Court's ruling made clear that this position was not enough. Appeals to Catholic voters' conscience or politicians' values did not work, so the bishops entered a whole new realm of political activism, grassroots political organizing. This is classic morality politics. The clearly expressed values of the bishops were threatened by governmental action, so they mobilized to reassert those values. This pattern has been noted by scholars in relation to other groups over morality issues such as drugs, pornography, and physician-assisted suicide (Meier 1994; Mooney and Lee 1995; Smith, Chapter 12, this volume; Glick and Hutchinson, Chapter 4, this volume).

The bishops did not stop there. Once their feet were wet, they entered in the political fray with letters that aroused much consternation among policymakers on U.S. nuclear deployment and strategy and the U.S. economy (Nolan 1983, vol. 4, 493–581; 1986, vol. 5, 371–492; McBrien 1987; Au 1985). In 1996, they even coordinated a postcard mailing campaign to the U.S. Senate over partial birth abortions in an effort to overturn President Clinton's veto of a ban on that procedure (Reese 1996). Clearly, the bishops' evolution as an interest group had been completed; from being hesitant to criticize government officials even in the face of state-sanctioned discrimination, they now told Catholics how they should organize so they could change the Constitution. They journeyed from a collection of religious leaders with only joint spiritual concerns through a classic economic interest group into a fully engaged morality politics participant.

Discussion

The bishops' evolution into morality politics went through three phases. First, the bishops of the U.S. Catholic Church worked to bring their "foreign" church into the social and political mainstream by encouraging obedience to secular laws and pledging fidelity to civil authorities. For the first 100 years, only when their property interests or their believers' lives were directly threatened did the bishops mention the religious root of secular power and complain about specific government policies. The complaints had no call to action, however, and were in essence safe ways to become involved in politics because no politicians were threatened by Catholic citizen action.

Second, during the twentieth century, the bishops continued to pledge their patriotism but branched out, functioning as policy entrepreneurs as they sought to introduce Catholic values to public policy discussions. Here the bishops were elites talking to policy elites, and their only requests for action from Catholic voters were for reflection and prayer. This is classic interest group behavior at the policymaker level.

Finally, the full use of the bishops' authority came only with *Roe* v. *Wade*, when the deeply held and publicly expressed values of the church were directly threatened. To reassert their values and have abortions made unconstitutional, the bishops had to become organized at the citizen action level. In this, they fit into the pattern of behavior common in morality politics (see Mooney and Lee 1995). Their interest, after January 1973, was values, not economics. They staked out a position that left little room for compromise. They demanded nonincremental change in policy and laid out a program that extended through congressional districts to dioceses to individual parishes to initiate citizen involvement. Clearly, the bishops evolved slowly into their current position as an important morality policy interest group.

Haider-Markel and Meier (1996) describe the way that the politics of gay and lesbian rights went from being quiet, elite-driven interest group politics to morality policy politics as the issue became widely salient and many people's values were threatened. The civil rights movement and the National Association for the Advancement of Colored People also evolved from an elitist, litigation-intensive strategy to one directed toward such direct action as voter registration drives, mass demonstrations, and direct confrontation of segregation and racism (Garrow 1986; Branch 1988, 1998). The political evolution of the Catholic bishops fits this pattern as well. Until the 1970s, the bishops were mainly discrete lobbyists for public policy change when they lobbied at all. When abortion became a salient issue with *Roe* v. *Wade*, however, the bishops became agents demanding nonincremental change to a pressing problem.

Bishops' Letters Cited (by date of publication)

Pastoral Letter, 28 May 1792

Pastoral Letter, 17 October 1829

Pastoral Letter, 22 April 1837

Pastoral Letter, 23 May 1840

Pastoral Letter, Feast of the Ascension, 1852

Pastoral Letter, 21 October 1866

Pastoral Letter, 7 December 1884

Letter to the President, 18 April 1917

Program of Social Reconstruction, 12 February 1919

Pastoral Letter, 26 September 1919

Statement on Federalization and Bureaucracy, 26 January 1922

Pastoral Letter on Mexico, 12 December 1926

Statement on Unemployment, 12 November 1930

Statement on Economic Crisis, 12 November 1931

Present Crisis, 25 April 1933

Resolution on Cooperation with the National Welfare and Relief Mobilization Committee, 16 November 1934

Statement on Christian Democracy, 14 October 1938

Statement on Peace and War, 16 November 1939

Statement on the American Republic, 13 November 1940

The Crisis of Christianity, 14 November 1941

The Christian in Action, 21 November 1948

God's Law: The Measure of Man's Conduct, 18 November 1951

Peace and Unity: The Hope of Mankind, 15 November 1956

Peace and Vietnam, 18 November 1966

Pastoral Statement on Race Relations and Poverty, 19 November 1966

Resolution on Antipoverty Legislation, 14 November 1967

Resolution on Peace, 16 November 1967

Resolution on Peace, April 1968

Human Life in Our Day, 15 November 1968

Statement on Abortion, 17 April 1969

Statement in Protest of U.S. Government Programs against the Right to Life, 14 November 1969

Statement on Abortion, 22 April 1970

Resolution on Welfare Reform Legislation, 22 April 1970

Declaration on Conscientious Objection and Selective Conscientious Objection, 21 October 1971

Resolution on Southeast Asia, November 1971

Where Shall People Live, November 1972

Statement on Abortion, 22 January 1973

Pastoral Message on Abortion, 13 February 1973

Resolution on Farm Labor, 23 May 1973

Resolution on Farah Manufacturing Company—Amalgamated Clothing Workers of America Labor Dispute, November 1973

Pastoral Plan for Pro-Life Activities, 20 November 1975

The Challenge of Peace: God's Promise and Our Response, 3 May 1983

Economic Justice for All: Pastoral Letter on Catholic Social Teaching and the U.S. Economy, 13 November 1986

Note

1. All letters from the U.S. bishops are cited by the original year of publication, volume number, and page. The letters are all found in Hugh J. Nolan 1983, 1984a, 1984b, 1984c, 1989.

CHAPTER SIX

From Censorship to Ratings: Substantive Rationality, Political Entrepreneurship, and Sex in the Movies

Richard A. Brisbin Jr.

BETWEEN 1966 AND 1971, a remarkable change occurred in the regulation of the moral message of U.S. movies. The long-followed policy of state and local government and industry censorship of sexuality and violence in U.S. general-release movies disappeared. Indeed, in some respects, this change in policy was quite sudden. In 1966, state, local, and industry censorship policies nearly kept actor Elizabeth Taylor from uttering "you son of a bitch" in *Who's Afraid of Virginia Woolf?* By 1971, *A Clockwork Orange* contained scenes of rape, frontal female nudity, and ménage-à-trois. Such change signaled a synoptic shift in the morality policy governing a communications industry with significant influence on public tastes. This chapter explores the reasons for the collapse in the policy of censorship of sexuality in general-release movies.

The chapter first briefly introduces the practice of movie censorship prior to 1968 as a bargaining game with limited information.[1] The censorship bargaining game featured limited information because *preferences* (material or ideological tastes) about displays and discussions of sexuality were restricted by the bargaining game's *substantive bounded rationality*, that is, the rules and ideas about preferences that the collective assumed were rational and normal and that provided opportunities and imposed restrictions on the process of individual choice (Simon 1982, 425–26). The next section of the chapter employs rational choice concepts to describe the collapse of the censorship bargaining game as a *nonmarket failure* (Wolf 1993, 59–64). The path to failure began when avant-garde moral and legal preferences emerged as a resource that entrepreneurs used to dislodge the boundaries of substantive rationality and replace the censorship bargaining game. Existing *opportunities* (institutional rules, procedures, and conditions for action) then allowed policy and economic entrepreneurs to use these avant-garde preferences to achieve their political or economic goals. In the face of entrepreneurial actions, "policy loyalists" could not justify the distribution of economic and political benefits and costs provided by censorship. Stressing the costs of censorship, entrepreneurs forced the loyalists to abandon support for censorship. New leadership within the movie industry then devised a new, "ratings" bargaining game. The final section of the chapter assesses what the entrepreneurs accomplished.

Sexuality in the Movies, 1934–68: The Censorship Bargaining Game

From 1934 to 1968, the regulation of the movies in the United States was a limited information bargaining game with four sets of participants: state and local government censors; the movie studios; the Production Code Administration (PCA), often referred to as the Hays Office after Motion Picture Producers and Dealers Association (MPPDA) administrator Will H. Hays; and the Legion of Decency.

Although not all states and municipalities practiced censorship, between 1911 and 1925, various governments established censorship boards to regulate movie content. The boards' power rested on a 1915 decision of the U.S. Supreme Court that held that movies were not protected by the First Amendment. Therefore, a state's reasonable use of the police or regulatory powers could ensure that movies did not harm public morals (*Mutual Film Corp.* v. *Industrial Commission of Ohio* 236 U.S. 230 [1915]; *Mutual Film Corp. of Missouri* v. *Hodges* 236 U.S. 248 [1915]). Within the next decade, governments established censorship boards in several states and cities geographically situated to affect the national marketing of movies (Kansas, Maryland, New York, Ohio, Pennsylvania, and Virginia, and cities including Atlanta, Chicago, Dallas, Memphis, and Seattle).

The movie studios centered in Hollywood had developed into vertically integrated enterprises by 1930, and they produced more than 90 percent of the movies distributed in the United States. Through ownership of theaters or "block booking" agreements, which required exhibitors to rent several movies from a studio to secure the rental of a desired film, the studios also controlled exhibitions. Almost all U.S. movie studios belonged to the motion picture trade association, MPPDA, which in 1948 was renamed the Motion Picture Association of America (MPAA). It encouraged the studios to practice self-censorship of sexual displays and dialogue through the enforcement of the Production Code, a set of rules on movie content drafted by the studio heads and MPPDA officials in 1930. Initially, the MPPDA enforced the Production Code laxly. However, faced with severe criticism about the moral tone of movies, in 1934 the MPPDA created the PCA (Doherty 1999). Established as a semiautonomous agency, the PCA interpreted and enforced the Production Code for the MPPDA.

The Legion of Decency, also founded in 1934, was an interest group under the control of the Roman Catholic bishops. To give advice to Catholics, the largest religious denomination in the nation, it developed a four-part classification system that included a "condemned" rating. Because most Catholics took an oath to support Legion ratings, many Catholic moviegoers avoided the movies in the condemned category (Black 1994, 1998; Walsh 1996).

Bargaining among the four sets of participants occurred within the boundaries of a shared substantive rationality. Following Enlightenment liberal political philosophy, the censorship boards' standards, the Production Code, and the Legion of Decency regarded sexual displays and dialogue in movies to be dangerous expressions of "passion" (Black 1994, 1998; Gardner 1987; Vizzard 1970; Walsh 1996; Wirt 1956). *Passion* was the pleasant but irrational or impulsive expression of selfishness, desire, license, and emotion to the detriment of other persons or the self (Hirschman 1977; Holmes 1995, 42–68). Unlike economic wealth, sexual passion was irrational and not a legitimate preference for individuals. Furthermore, as evidenced by their standards, the Code, and the categories, the participants believed that public laws and private rules should police the depiction and discussion of passions.

Between 1934 and 1968, the state and local censors, the Legion of Decency, the studios, and the PCA negotiated the sexual content of motion pictures to control audience exposure to sexual passion. Bargaining especially depended on the substantive rules of the Production Code. The PCA interpreted the Code to try to reduce the risk of a costly condemned rating from the Legion or a censorship board's order to make changes in a completed movie. The PCA also served as the central negotiating site for the participants in movie regulation and developed into a powerful independent participant in censorship bargaining (Black 1994, 170–76; Leff and Simmons 1990, 33–54; Moley 1945, 79, 90–91; Vizzard 1970, 28–56; Walsh 1996, 98–111).

The process of bargaining featured several exchanges. Once PCA staff completed its multistage review of a studio's cut of a film, it recommended that the PCA give the movie the MPPDA seal signifying that MPPDA member exhibitors could show it. After a movie received the seal, it underwent review by state and local censors and the Legion of Decency. From the earliest days of the industry, movie producers designed productions to avoid action by the censorship boards.

The PCA and studios kept records of the boards' activity to avoid granting a seal to movies with content that had been excised in the past. On occasion, PCA or studio representatives communicated with boards to discuss and negotiate standards. The result of negotiated standards and information sharing was that censors' reviews normally produced very few cuts in approximately 90 percent of MPPDA members' films. The majority of the deletions involved a few dozen feet of film with nudity; erotic content such as touching, caressing, body movements, and related erotic and suggestive dialogue; interracial kissing; scenes of childbirth; and profanity and "indelicate" words (Carmen 1966, 166, 173–74, 178, 182, 195–96, 202, 211, 219–23, 268, 276–78, 308–9; Randall 1968, 92–107; Wirt 1956, 240–41).

The PCA also cooperated with the Legion's activities. In the early years of the censorship game, bargaining often involved PCA administrator Joseph Breen, Legion Executive Secretary Father John McClafferty, Archbishop John T. McNicholas of Cincinnati (chair of the Episcopal Committee that governed the Legion), Martin Quigley (publisher, paid consultant for studios, and broker between the studios and the Legion), and Father John Devlin (the official Catholic film adviser chosen by the bishop of Los Angeles). The negotiations involving Devlin, Legion staff, and the studios affected the sexual content of many pictures, including the classics *Gone with the Wind* (1939) and *Rebecca* (1940).

Each participant learned that bargaining about issues regulated by the Production Code could work to their advantage. As predicted by a folk theorem, an equilibrium in the game was reached when participants achieved an outcome that satisfied their independent utilities. The outcome, a bargained agreement on the content of a film, was unenforceable because a studio could abandon it by releasing the movie without a seal, or the state censors or the Legion of Decency could impose different standards. However, the equilibrium in bargaining held because, first, it facilitated "cheap talk," or communication of past and probable future preferences between its staff and studio executives with no direct payoff implications (Farrell and Rabin 1996). Second, because the Code was phrased in generalities, the PCA could negotiate adjustments in its interpretations to secure net benefits to all participants. Finally, bargaining with reference to the Code encouraged the development of trust and norms of reciprocity among these participants. Because of the risk of making a costly, unmarketable movie, the state and local censors and the Legion learned that the PCA would anticipate their criticisms and avoid involving them in costly and protracted bargaining about a movie's content. The substantive rationality supporting censorship thus remained unchallenged. The dangerous passion of sexual displays and dialogue disappeared from the screen, to be replaced by visual allusion and verbal innuendo.

Substantive Rationality, Policy Entrepreneurship, and the End of Censorship

In 1968, the censorship bargaining game failed. Several factors contributed to the failure (Bates, de Figueiredo, and Weingast 1998). First, exogenous to the bargaining game, avant-garde intellectuals introduced new preferences about sexual passion and police powers. Then policy entrepreneurs recognized that these new preferences might help them achieve their policy goals or enhance their power. These entrepreneurs, especially the justices of the Supreme Court, undertook a series of tactical moves to rationalize avant-garde preferences and reduce loyalty to the censorship bargaining game. Policy loyalists, such as the Legion of Decency, PCA staff, and state censors, responded to the entrepreneurs' efforts and conflict ensued, only to be resolved by a creative leader who recognized the need to exit the censorship game and establish a new bargaining game about sex in the movies.

Avant-Garde Policy Preferences

In the early twentieth century, an intellectual avant-garde of U.S. progressive and pragmatic thinkers proposed that lived experience should guide the rational construction of the sociopolitical order (Purcell 1973). They believed that empirical information about experience, gathered through scientific study, should direct the rational development of ethical standards, personal liberty, and the enhancement of individual lives. From scientifically grounded assumptions about the substantive rationality of preferences, especially as fostered by intellectuals in the fields of psychology and law, the avant-garde predicted that a scientific critique of the danger of sexual passion and policing of expression would arise.

Sexual liberation. A critical intellectual redefinition of preferences resulted from the "liberation" of sexual preferences emerging from the theory of unconscious sexual drives proposed by the new science of psychology. Sigmund Freud's repressive theory was the most significant product of early twentieth-century scientific investigations of the unconscious aspects of sexuality. In Freudian theory, repression meant that the superego causes the ego to push even reasonable sexual desire and energy into the unconscious (Freud [1923] 1960, 15–29). Freud concluded that repression, including the policing of sexual drives by the state and family, was coercive and harmful. Religion and political regulations especially operated as a "communal superego" in an attempt to dominate the pleasure principle that is an expression of the sexual passions seething in the id (Freud [1933] 1961; Freud [1938] 1946, 45–57). Each individual thus gives up sexual pleasure to join civilization: "a rule of law to which all—except those who are not capable of entering a community—have contributed by a sacrifice of their instincts

. . . and which leaves no one—again with the same exception—at the mercy of brute force" (Freud [1933] 1961, 42).

Freud never promised the elimination of sexual repression, but some of his most influential interpreters and popularizers spoke of his work as constituting the basis for a nonrepressive social and political regime (Hale 1971, 332–60, 1996; d'Emilio and Freedman 1988, 223–29). Certain neo-Freudians, especially Norman O. Brown (1959, 1966), Herbert Marcuse (1955), and Wilhelm Reich (1971, 1983), argued that sexual liberation was an essential component of an overall liberation of the self from the decadence of social and political manifestations of the repressive superego. Influenced by these neo-Freudians, popular conception of legitimate sexual preferences underwent a reassessment. For example, public opinion data from many surveys in the 1960s suggest greater approval of premarital sex, pornography, sex education, and birth control (Smith 1990, 415–35). Consequently, policy entrepreneurs interested in the expansion of personal liberties and economic entrepreneurs interested in the sale of movie tickets could now claim that sexual passion was not a preference outside the boundary of rational policy choice.

Jurisprudence and the conception of rights. Another change in substantive rationality originated with the redefinition of personal rights first proposed by the early twentieth-century jurisprudential-political movement called *sociological jurisprudence*. Among their concerns, sociological jurisprudents such as Zechariah Chafee of Harvard sought to restrict the use of police powers to impose moral values that restricted free expression. Chafee formulated a new legal standard to define the boundary between rights and the police power: the clear and present danger test. As applied by Justice Oliver Wendell Holmes (*Schenk* v. *U.S.* 249 U.S. 47 [1919]; *Abrams* v. *U.S.* 250 U.S. 616 [1919]), the test imposed an obligation to protect expressive rights and to prefer individual liberties against the state's police powers. Chafee and Holmes supported this standard with a crude empirical calculus. As captured by the metaphor "a marketplace of ideas," their logic was that, in a free market, good ideas would be "bought" by the public and bad ideas would not be "sold" (Graber 1991, 18–41).

Legal realism, an academic movement of the 1920s and 1930s, developed the sociological jurisprudents' theory of rights further and attempted to provide empirical information about the harm caused by inefficient applications of state police powers. Legal realists thought that social science evidence of the consequences of law would support the creation of new laws that could protect expressions of individual autonomy (Kalman 1986, 3–44). Leading free speech advocates of the New Deal and post–New Deal era drew on legal realism to develop a general theory of free speech that would encourage individual autonomy and democratic politics. Some of these advocates, such as Thomas Emerson, also regarded obscenity law as a danger to liberty caused by political pressure on courts. He proposed that the legal regulation of sexual displays be limited to incidents of physical or empirically defined harms, especially harms affecting children. He argued that when such evidence was absent, a market in these products should exist (Emerson 1963, 1–15, 89, 1970, 495–503; Graber 1991, 165–80).

Policy Entrepreneurs and Their Policy Objectives

During the 1950s and 1960s, several sets of policy entrepreneurs employed avant-garde preferences about sex and law to pursue various policy and economic goals in the field of movie censorship. They included the American Civil Liberties Union (ACLU), the U.S. Supreme Court justices, studio executives and directors, and Jesuit intellectuals within the Roman Catholic Church. In contrast to the depictions of change in morality policy discussed in other chapters of this book (Chapters 4, 7, 9, 10, and 12), what is striking is that these entrepreneurs destabilized the censorship bargaining game without organizing a social movement, without reference to mass political demand for more sex in movies, without support from the members of mass interest groups, without opposition from a countervailing social movement, and without extensive lobbying of federal and state legislators. They did not have to mobilize persons to shift the demand curve for sex in movies (Meier, Chapter 2, this volume). Instead, they seized opportunities and advanced new preferences with surprisingly limited opposition and without the need to justify their position of standing up for sin shown to a broader public.

The ACLU and the "obscenity bar." The ACLU, the leading opponent of obscenity regulation, was interested in expanding the constitutional protection of personal rights (Kobylka 1987, 1064; 1991, 27–34). It supported the belief that First Amendment rights by political dissidents should trump any exercise of police power, a conception of political rights promoted by the legal realist defenders of freedom of expression. Limited membership and financial resources and hostility to its message restricted the ACLU from organizing a mass movement and lobbying in the legislative process. Rather, its leadership turned to the courts to defend free expression. However, the ACLU never had a formal national litigation strategy on obscenity (Kobylka 1991, 33). Instead, local ACLU chapters supported suits brought by their members or others against police and censorship board actions.

Because of these considerations, the ACLU entered its first significant movie censorship case, *Burstyn, Inc.* v. *Wilson* (343 U.S. 495 [1952]), by filing an amicus curiae brief to challenge the New York censor's decision that a movie, *The*

Miracle (1948, U.S. release 1950), was sacrilegious (Walker 1990, 231–32). Thereafter, national ACLU leaders encouraged local chapters to initiate litigation or to support suits by film distributers. Although local chapters or distributors often lost these cases initially, their appeals and the inclusion of ACLU amicus briefs allowed the U.S. Supreme Court to review state movie censorship (Kobylka 1987, 1068; Walker 1990, 231–36). As an entrepreneur of a legal realist version of First Amendment rights, the ACLU helped create opportunities for the justices to write opinions that challenged governmental censorship of the movies.

Twenty-four other interest groups also brought obscenity litigation to the Supreme Court in the decade prior to 1968 (McGuire and Caldiera 1993, 718). These groups operated independently of one another, and most were not directly concerned with motion picture censorship. However, the lawyers for these groups and the ACLU became a sophisticated set of litigators—an "obscenity bar"—who were employed in the litigation of the cases brought by a variety of groups with some success (McGuire and Caldiera 1993). Especially during the 1950s and 1960s, these lawyers wrote briefs for the ACLU and other interest groups and helped set the agenda for policy entrepreneurship by justices interested in developing legal realist theories of expressive liberty. Thus, a small interest group and a professional elite represented a "support structure" that conveyed avant-garde preferences to the Court and provided the justices with the opportunity for more comprehensive policy entrepreneurship on movie censorship (Epp 1998, 17–22).

Supreme Court justices. As a consequence of these groups' briefs and the appointment of justices who had taught or learned about legal realism, by the 1950s legal realist preferences about rights had entered into the policy discussions of the U.S. Supreme Court. Gradually, shifting majorities of the justices increased the costs of maintaining the movie censorship game. By applying a legal realist interpretation to antitrust statutes and precedents, the justices increased the studios' cost of making movies under the Production Code. By applying a legal realist approach to the review of state and local regulations of obscenity, they increased the cost of conducting censorship.

During the New Deal, the federal government's policy was that a healthy movie industry was more important than antitrust action to end price fixing, vertical integration, or collusion among the studios (an example being the Production Code). In 1946, however, the Justice Department undertook an antitrust suit against the studios, citing various anticompetitive practices. In *United States v. Paramount Pictures, Inc.* (334 U.S. 131 [1948]), the Supreme Court held that the studios' ownership of theater chains violated antitrust law (Moley 1945, 198–212; Izod 1988, 84–123). Writing for the Court, Justice William O. Douglas embraced an interpretation of the Sherman Antitrust Act associated with legal realism, assuming that economic efficiency, democracy, and fairness in markets were promoted by protecting small business from larger corporations. His conclusion about the effects of collusive price fixing was that "size carries with it the opportunity for abuse." He concluded that various collusive and exclusive practices had to end and that the studios had to divest themselves of theater ownership (*U.S. v. Paramount Pictures* 1948, 174–75).

Paramount Pictures significantly altered the movie business. The studios' divestiture of theaters meant that the PCA could no longer stop the exhibition of movies that violated the Production Code. The experience of the 1953 film *The Moon Is Blue* demonstrated the significance of this change. The PCA denied a seal to that movie, which took a light-hearted approach to sexual relationships and contained sexual banter. However, anticipating (correctly) a profit, many exhibitors ran the film. The divestiture of theaters also made the booking process—and profits—more precarious and eliminated studio profits from theater chains (Ayer, Bates, and Herman 1970, 803–5; Cassady 1958, 150–80; Conant 1960, 107–53). The *Paramount Pictures* decision created economic uncertainty for studios just when they also faced decreased profits because of the relocation of the audience to suburbs far from theaters and the appearance of a competitive technology—television (Gomery 1991). Gradually forced toward bankruptcy, in the 1960s many studios began to sell off their Hollywood facilities. Eventually, they were bought by media conglomerates and turned into movie and television distribution businesses. Independent production companies began to make most general release movies for conglomerate distributors (Izod 1988, 124–43; Leff and Simmons 1990, 269–70; Miller and Shamsie 1996).

These changes in the organization of movie production affected the sexual content of films. First, independent production meant that the PCA could no longer control movie content by bargaining with a handful of studio executives. Second, with profits falling, bolder sexual displays were thought to be needed to draw audiences to theaters. The success of several movies with sexual themes, such as *Baby Doll* (1956) and *Lolita* (1962), stimulated profit-seeking independent producers to press for more sexual themes, dialogue, and imagery in movies. Third, because of *Paramount Pictures,* PCA control of the movies exhibited in theaters vanished.

Four changes in the Supreme Court justices' interpretation of First Amendment rights also affected the movie censorship game. First, in the *Burstyn* case (1952), the justices overruled the *Mutual Film* decisions and treated movie content as a form of expression subject to possible protection by the First Amendment. The reaffirmation of *Burstyn* in *Kingsley International Pictures Corp. v. Regents* (360 U.S. 684 [1959]) made it plain that any government censorship of movies had to survive First Amendment analysis. Second, in *Roth v. United States* and *Alberts v. California* (354 U.S. 476 [1957]), the justices severely restricted the prior restraint that government censors might impose on book and magazine content. Although these decisions placed obscene materials outside the protection of the First Amendment, much shifting of obscenity standards ensued in subsequent cases because of tactical choices made by Justice William Brennan. A policy entrepreneur, Brennan attempted to build a majority coalition that would use a legal realist definition of expressive freedom to define when states might restrict the distribution of obscene publications (Heck 1982, 417–25). Even though not fully successful, his efforts led the Court to an obscenity policy that, by 1966, was radically more lenient than the pre-1957 policy.

Third, combining the extension of the First Amendment to movies with their obscenity standards, the Supreme Court justices redefined the authority of state and local movie censors. The *Burstyn* decision left the standards used by state and local movie censors in a dubious constitutional status. In a series of decisions, the justices rejected censors' efforts to ban movies with certain racial and sexual displays or dialogue they judged not to be obscene (*Gelling* v. *Texas* 343 U.S. 960 [1952]; *Superior Films, Inc.* v. *Dept. of Education of State of Ohio* 346 U.S. 587 [1954]; *Holmby Productions* v. *Vaughan* 350 U.S. 870 [1955]; *Times Film Corp.* v. *Chicago* 355 U.S. 35 [1957]; Carmen 1966, 47–66; Jowett 1996; Randall 1968, 25–32). In *Freedman* v. *Maryland* (380 U.S. 51 [1965]), the court clarified the constitutionality of censorship processes. Justice Brennan's decision, citing legal realist Thomas Emerson, began with the proposition that censorship presented a danger to constitutionally protected speech. He then suggested a series of procedures that the state could adopt to prevent endangering rights. The *Freedman* decision's requirements prevented state and local censors from banning films for nonsexual content and from cutting segments because of sexual references or displays that did not violate the Court's definition of obscenity.

Finally, the justices carved out special doctrine affecting the access of children to sexual materials and their inclusion in sexual displays. The justices determined that obscenity affected minors and adults differently, and they permitted states to establish a different definition of obscenity for movies exhibited to or featuring children (*Ginsberg* v. *N.Y.* 390 U.S. 629 [1968], 638; *Redrup* v. *N.Y.* 386 U.S. 767 [1967]). Extending this position, they required state and local censors to develop specific criteria for restricting the admission of juveniles to some movies with sexual content that were not obscene for adults (*Interstate Circuit, Inc.* v. *Dallas* 390 U.S. 676 [1968], 685–88).

The justices therefore created a new institutional context with new costs for state censorship. State and local movie censors lost power over the content of all but obscene movies. Movie censorship by the state now required a costly, difficult process—the passage of a new statute with precise definitions of obscenity and the sexual displays that children might see, public prosecution, trial, and appeal. The filmmakers no longer faced the threat of preemptive governmental editing of alluring costumes, sexual innuendo, or sexual themes. The exposure of juveniles to the obscene was now the primary concern of censorship bargaining.

Studio executives. Confronted with economic and legal changes, studio executives redefined bargaining about sexuality in movies. Studio executives framed the issue in economic terms. In the changing market of the 1950s, they tried to attract audiences to movies by the inclusion of more sexual content (Ayer, Bates, and Herman 1970, 797–800; Sklar 1994, 269–304). This included producing more controversial "social message" pictures with subliminal sexual implications, westerns with hints of sexual immorality, and musicals with subliminal sexual messages. The blockbuster based on biblical or ancient themes and with direct references to "pagan" sexual practices was another effort to entice an audience to theaters. Despite significant profit from movies without such themes, such as *The Sound of Music* (1965), the executives assumed that sex sells tickets.

Consequently, Hollywood studio executives of the 1950s and 1960s produced a series of films that created problems in the eyes of the PCA, state censors, and the Legion of Decency. The most significant event was the PCA's refusal to grant a seal to *The Moon Is Blue*. Defying the PCA, United Artists released it, and the movie returned a profit. Pictures condemned by the Legion of Decency for their sexual innuendo, such as *Baby Doll* and *Lolita*, also produced profits. By 1967, studio executives had learned that the lack of an MPAA seal or a condemned rating from the Legion did not obstruct their ability to make money (Izod 1988, 143–70; Leff and Simmons 1990, 189–203, 270).

However, more sexuality in their films did not save the studios from financial crisis. As losses mounted, media conglomerates bought the studios. Executives of the conglomerates regarded the PCA regulatory process as costly overhead and a deterrent to profits (Monaco 1984, 29–42). In this context, the appeals of PCA decisions to the MPAA board resulted in incremental policy changes. For example, the MPAA changed the Production Code to allow the release of films with some Production Code violations if they carried the advertisement "suggested for mature audiences" (Leff and Simmons 1990, 241–64).

Motion picture directors. After 1945, the arrival of Italian neorealist and French New Wave films caused many directors to reexamine their work. Formerly manufacturers of an entertainment product for a big business, more directors came to regard their work as making an artistic statement about the human condition. In the 1950s, directors such as Elia Kazan made the artistic movie a more popular and profitable medium. For Kazan, the aim was to express his conscience on topics of oppression and alienation (Pauly 1983, 113–247). Directors' artistic statements about alienation also caused them to explore neo-Freudian ideas about the danger of sexual repression. Throughout the 1950s and 1960s, popularized Freudian themes about the harm of sexual repression appeared in the more "artistic" U.S. movies. Again, conflict with the PCA occurred, and tensions intensified between directors and the PCA.

Jesuit intellectuals and the Legion of Decency. In 1957, alarmed by less than wholehearted Catholic opposition to sexuality in movies, Martin Quigley and Francis Cardinal Spellman of New York, a politically powerful moral conservative, sought to coopt the Legion's liberal critics (Cooney 1984, 108–10, 196–203; Walsh 1996, 115, 172, 250–59). As a token symbol of liberalization, they secured the appointment of the more liberal Father Patrick J. Sullivan, S.J., as assistant to the Legion's executive secretary. Sullivan, a Jesuit theology professor, shared the concerns of the critics of the Legion and church censorship policies. Critics within the church, almost all of whom were Jesuit proponents of religious pluralism, argued that church policy should allow intelligent Catholics to make their own decisions on moral matters, such as the decision to avoid obscenity (Murray 1956, 445–46; Gardiner 1958, 15, 103, 152). These critics contended that the church's canon law and related dogma did not compel Catholics to obey the classifications made by the Legion of Decency (Black 1998, 143–47).

Once named to his post in the Legion, Sullivan would not be coopted to a more conservative position by Spellman and Quigley. Instead, he engaged in a series of tactics that reflected his commitment to the pragmatic moral ideas of his Jesuit colleagues. Under Sullivan's leadership, the Legion revised its rating scheme and began to use a separate, unlettered classification for movies that were morally legitimate but with elements "beyond the capacity of some adults" (Black 1998, 176–229; Walsh 1996, 282–323; Walker 1968, 257–69). Sullivan found support for these changes in the implicit anticensorship messages in the policies of the Office Catholique International du Cinéma and the papal encyclical *Miranda Prorsus* (Black 1998, 176–80). During the 1960s, many U.S. bishops no longer required Catholics to support the Legion's decisions. In 1965, after the bishops changed the name of the Legion to the National Catholic Office on Motion Pictures (NCOMP), Sullivan's primary objective became the adoption of an age-based rating system to guide moviegoers. Sullivan's tactics thus produced important incremental changes in Legion of Decency/NCOMP policies. Jesuit reformers had begun to signal a different role for Catholic interests in the movie censorship game.

The consequences of entrepreneurship. The opposition to censorship by studio executives, movie directors, the ACLU, and the Jesuit reformers of the Legion of Decency was sporadic, uncoordinated, and often failed to take advantage of the institutional opportunities for adjusting the censorship game. These entrepreneurs invested little organized effort in opposing censorship, letting a majority of the Supreme Court's justices lead the fight against movie censorship.

Because of its special institutional power—judicial review—the Court succeeded in imposing costs on those participants loyal to the policy of movie censorship.

The Loyalists: Supporters of Movie Censorship

To prevent the failure of a bargaining game under assault by entrepreneurs, participants loyal to the game can try to impose costs on these entrepreneurs. The capacity of loyalists to offset the actions of entrepreneurs and enforce existing policy depends on a mix of information and tactics that can impose costs on the entrepreneurs (North 1990, 68–69). First, loyalists can communicate their objectives, frame political discourse, and shape the political agenda. Such tactics can raise the costs of entrepreneurship (Lichbach 1995, 78–79, 95–96; Hirschman 1970, 92–98). Second, loyalists can provide opportunities for allegiant behavior and disincentives for behavior that threatens the equilibrium established by a bargaining game (Knight 1992, 130–31). Third, loyalists can mobilize allies in support of their goals. Finally, loyalists can support incremental change that reinforces the existing bargaining game. However, loyalists to the censorship bargaining game failed to use any of these tactics in ways that imposed severe costs on the entrepreneurs who sought to alter the game.

The collapse of the movie censorship game was greatly abetted by inefficient communications by the loyalists who supported it, including the leadership of the MPAA, the PCA, and the Legion of Decency. The PCA especially failed to frame political discourse and shape the political agenda in ways that offset the communications of the entrepreneurs. As early as 1953, the trade publication *Variety* featured a story about the PCA's loss of power. Its alleged loss of power, attributed to the success of *The Moon Is Blue*, really stemmed in part from the PCA's inability to justify the costs of its censorship practices in a social environment that increasingly regarded the repression of sexuality as old-fashioned or harmful. In the 1950s, the PCA remained very sensitive to Catholic censorship of the movies. Even the more liberal Geoffrey Shurlock, the PCA director after 1956, assumed that a negative Legion of Decency rating could spell box office danger for a film. By attending to the Legion's desires, the PCA continued to frame the issue of movie sexuality from a perspective of moral danger. Yet the PCA did not offer any scientific or psychological knowledge to buttress its position, nor did it organize a publicity campaign to help manage information critical of censorship or to argue the benefits of censorship. The result was that the PCA appeared to support the religious and extremist attack on sexuality in the movies. To entrepreneurs favoring changes in censorship policy, the Bulwerism of the PCA appeared to be irrational and offered no basis for incremental adjustment of policy bargaining.

The MPAA and PCA were also ineffective in devising tactics to resist the entrepreneurs and encourage loyalty to the censorship bargaining game. For example, because PCA director Shurlock took a more liberal attitude toward the meaning of the Production Code (Schumach 1964, 41–48; Miller 1994, 166–80), he often did not defend it strongly against the criticisms of the entrepreneurs. In 1956, he supported changes in the Production Code that permitted movies about drug addition, prostitution, and childbirth within the "grounds of good taste," and he encouraged the PCA staff to allow slight exceptions to Production Code requirements. Thus, through incremental adjustments, his administration of the PCA gradually compromised the rigid sexual morality of the Production Code (Vizzard 1970, 299–317). Far from satisfying their economic and artistic concerns, however, Shurlock's leniency only gave the producers and directors the incentive to press for more leeway in sexual depictions by defecting from Production Code standards (Leff and Simmons 1990, 250–53; Miller 1994, 196–99; Walker 1968, 185–209).

As challenges to censorship arose, the MPAA and the PCA found few allies for their cause. After the arrival of Father Sullivan in 1957, the Legion of Decency was locked in internal debate and could not generate strong and unified Catholic support for its own classification system, the Production Code, or state censorship of movies. State legislators acquiesced with the Supreme Court's limitation of the power of censors, and they often undertook the elimination of censorship. State censors themselves had little independent power and few resources that they could use to defend their positions. Other moral traditionalists lacked the organization, power, and resources to develop a national response to the entrepreneurs' attack on censorship.

Finally, the loyalists failed to devise incremental changes in censorship that satisfied the entrepreneurs. For example, in response to conflicts among PCA, the Legion, and producers over the revisions in *Who's Afraid of Virginia Woolf?* (1966), Production Code language was revised to permit more discretion by the PCA and to allow the PCA to award seals to pictures with the advertisement "suggested for mature audiences" (Walker 1968, 255–57). The PCA then immediately faced the task of defining suitable "mature" content. Depictions of nudity in *Blow-Up*, implicit fellatio in *Hurry Sundown*, and voyeurism in *Charlie Bubbles*, all movies "suggested for mature audiences" in this period, only created uneasiness and conflict between the PCA, producers, and studios (Walsh 1996, 329–48; Valenti 1996).

The mature audience label, an incremental change, did not resolve the conflict about sexual content in movies. By 1968, uncertainty affected all participants in the censorship bargaining game. Changes in sexual preferences and the legal status of censorship, exploited by studio executives and directors in their search for economic and artistic benefits, had destabilized the censorship game. Loyalists' efforts failed to buttress it. Support for the Production Code by the Legion of Decency became less robust when Father Sullivan became its director. The PCA itself weakened its opposition to changes in the Production Code. The entrepreneurs' actions and the loyalists' inaction had allowed avant-garde preferences to become substantively rational. An asymmetry developed between the bargaining power of the loyal participants and the entrepreneurs who opposed the game (Knight 1992, 145–51; North 1990, 86). The censorship bargaining game was on the verge of collapse; a nonmarket failure was at hand.

The Exit Point

An "exit point" opportunity exists to replace a bargaining game when the costs of satisfying preferences through incremental adjustment of the existing game are outweighed by the anticipated benefits possible by a reconstitution of the game (Hirschman 1970, 4, 21–29; Bates, de Figueiredo, and Weingast 1998, 239–44). Failure of a bargaining game therefore occurs first when participants calculate a low expected utility for their preferences by incremental changes in an existing game. However, to choose to exit from the game, a participant must also possess information about the opportunity to establish a new equilibrium through the establishment of a new game (North 1990, 24, 27–35). Therefore, the exit point is characterized by both a perception of high costs under existing bargaining practices and some sense of the benefits a new game might offer (Bates, de Figueiredo, and Weingast 1998, 243; Wolf 1993, 35–55, 68–79).

By the early 1960s, Supreme Court justices, the ACLU, studio executives, directors, and the Jesuit leadership of the Legion of Decency felt the need to modify movie censorship. This modification, these entrepreneurs claimed, would benefit personal rights, liberate human behavior in a healthy manner, and improve the financial condition of the industry. However, Catholic traditionalists, the PCA, and state and local censorship boards remained loyal to a substantive rationality that defined sex as a dangerous passion. Therefore, discourse about a right to view sex, artistic freedom in the expression of sexuality, and any exploitation of sex for profit was incomprehensible to them. By 1968, entrepreneurs' and loyalists' preferences had so diverged that neither side could perceive incremental adjustments in the bargaining that would reduce the conflict about the censorship of sex in movies. The Supreme Court's 1968 decisions about obscenity and the differentiation between adult and general-audience movies promised legislative battles and contests within the MPAA about revisions in censorship codes, more litigation, and associated transaction costs. Thus, in 1968, the exit point was at hand; however, the participants had to recognize it.

Leadership: Jack Valenti Confronts a Nonmarket Failure

With the studios in economic trouble and challenges to the Production Code bedeviling the PCA and MPAA, in June 1966 the MPAA selected Jack Valenti, former special assistant to President Lyndon Johnson, to become MPAA president (Motion Picture Association of America, n.d.). Initially, Valenti attempted to routinize the incremental evolution of PCA policies, cement cooperation with the Legion, satisfy the economic concerns of studios and producers, and meet the artistic concerns of directors by a selection of tactics from preexisting repertoires. By 1968, however, he recognized that the mismatch between entrepreneurs' and loyalists' preferences about sexual displays and dialogue in movies was preventing them from adjusting the movie censorship game. This recognition was a necessary, but not a sufficient, condition for the appearance of a nonmarket failure and an exit point. At the exit point, a leader must define the costs of the failure in the existing bargaining game for the participants, suggest exit from the game, and define the benefits of a new game that relies on a different substantive rationality.

In 1968, Valenti abandoned his support for revisions in the Production Code. Determined to make a comprehensive change in the control of movie content, he proposed the abolishment of the Production Code and its replacement with a system of ratings. Changes in the immediate political context, especially the Supreme Court decision in *Interstate Circuit, Inc.* v. *Dallas* (1968), which provided different definitions of obscenity for adults and children, encouraged Valenti to engage in such bold action. He wanted to avoid the costs to the industry of an inefficient patchwork of new legal restraints that he called "variable obscenity," a situation in which several states adopted different definitions of movies that were appropriate for adults but not children (U.S. House 1977, 3). During summer and fall 1968, negotiations involving Valenti, MPAA attorney Louis Nizer, the trade association of theater owners, studio executives, unions, critics, the Legion, and other interest groups produced a decision to rate movies and ban children from some films. Valenti later refined the rating system to include additional categories designating whether children of various ages should see a film (U.S. House 1977, 3–4; Ayer, Bates, and Herman 1970, 821–28; Valenti 1996).

Under this new system, the viewer (or parent of the viewer) would become the primary censor. New MPAA Objectives, produced by negotiations among the parties, stated that "we believe self-restraint, self-regulation to be in the American tradition" (Farber 1972, 114). In light of the Supreme Court's decisions, the MPAA Objectives were to identify sexual film content suitable for children but held that "parents have the primary responsibility to guide their children in the kind of . . . movies and other entertainment to which they are exposed" (Farber 1972, 112). The rating system therefore permitted sexual dialogue and displays in films that adults might choose to view. Because of the Supreme Court's distinction between the First Amendment rights of adults and those of children, the ratings system could require exhibitors to ban children from films with overt sexual displays—rated X—and encourage parents to police access to films with very brief sexual displays or innuendo, profanity, or violence—rated R and M (M later was replaced by PG and PG-13) (Farber 1972, 14–15).

What Valenti had accomplished was, first, to convince the loyalists that the Production Code was so costly that it had to go. He also convinced the MPAA executives about the benefits of ratings and outlined how the contours of bargaining about ratings might improve the profitability of the industry by allowing the exhibition of movies with more adult appeal. He then negotiated a scheme of movie rating that would protect producer, exhibitor, director, and ACLU preferences about sex in the movies in the new political context created by the Supreme Court. Ratings allowed studio executives to offset the potentially costly threat of new forms of censorship legislation or Court battles. He could not prevent the states or religious groups from evaluating movies, but the ratings scheme permitted them to reduce their costs and let the industry and popular tastes govern the content of movies.

Valenti therefore searched beyond the substantive rationality that bounded censorship bargaining and proposed a bargaining game that accepted as rational the preferences identified with liberated sexuality and expressive rights. His actions illustrate how leadership is important for initiating cooperation when preferences and opportunities induce nonmarket failure. He was able to propose a new game because of his information about the range of possible changes in movie regulation, his strategy of consultation, and the incentives that he offered the MPAA and studios, the directors, the Legion, the ACLU, and state censors (Bianco and Bates 1990, 133–47; Calvert 1992, 17–19). Valenti's effort to initiate a new bargaining game ran into surprisingly little opposition from the religious bodies and interest groups that had long supported censorship. Although he possessed few resources and no official authority to punish participants, most participants had already calculated that the costs of adjusting the movie censorship game outweighed the benefits of exit. Sporadic harassment prosecutions by local governments and protests against the theaters that showed X-rated pictures occurred (Randall 1976, 450–52), but no national campaign against the new MPAA rating plan developed.

The Ratings Bargaining Game: Sex in the Movies after 1968

The demise of PCA censorship of the movies resulted in a comprehensive replacement of the censorship bargaining game with a ratings bargaining game. In the new game, a substantive rationality that had assumed the danger of sexual passions and the value of government regulation of passions gave way to the assumption that market-based practices would permit persons to cope with sexual passion. Within the revised substantive rationality, sex was no longer dangerous. People assumed that sex in movies was a commodity that should be immune from public censorship. In the new ratings game, all of the old regulatory practices vanished. A reduced set of participants engaged in a three-party bargaining game including a Code and Rating Administration (CARA, an MPAA agency), independent producers, and media conglomerates. Despite the lesson of *Paramount Pictures*, the conglomerates effectively integrated distribution, exhibition, and aspects of production in the industry (Fox 1992; Wasko 1994). By 1981, the three participants established an equilibrium in which no participant had an incentive to shift unilaterally to another strategy. The change in bargaining game had three important consequences: the diminishment of public control of movie content, the disappearance of Catholic participation in movie censorship, and the enhancement of corporate power to specify the sexual content of movies.

State and local film censorship boards lost much of their enforcement power because they could regulate only narrowly defined "obscene" movies. Even these decisions could be subject to costly litigation, so by 1981, state governments chose simply to phase out censorship.[2] The courts even restricted governments from participating in or using the results of ratings bargaining. For example, in 1990, a New York state court concluded that CARA standards were "unprofessional" and that the rating was "a marketing standard, a tool to aid in promoting films" (*Miramax Films Corp.* v. *MPAA* 560 N.Y.S. 2d 730 [1990], 8; see also *Maljack Productions* v. *MPAA* 22 U.S.P.Q. 2d [BNA] 1867 [1992]). By treating CARA ratings as marketing tools, judges avoided judicial oversight of whether a CARA rating harmed expressive liberties. Federal district courts in Pennsylvania and Wisconsin concluded that a CARA rating could not even be used by a city to determine whether a film could be viewed by minors (*MPAA* v. *Specter* 315 F. Supp. 824 [E.D. Pa. 1970]; *Engdahl* v. *City of Kenosha* 317 F. Supp. 133 [E.D. Wisc 1970]).

Initially, CARA remained sensitive to procensorship interest group criticism of the ratings process. Both Valenti and CARA administrator Aaron Stern consulted regularly with Father Sullivan of NCOMP. However, strained relations developed between Valenti and Sullivan over CARA standards and the MPAA's failure to secure the enforcement of ratings by theaters. NCOMP withdrew its support for the rating system in June 1971. Thereafter, CARA simply abandoned any effort to negotiate with NCOMP (Black 1998, 234–36; Farber 1972, 97–98; U.S. House 1977, 16). Decisions by the Catholic bishops about personal responsibility for moral choices and the costs of its operations resulted in the closure of NCOMP in 1981 (Black 1998, 236–38). Since 1981, Catholic protest of sexuality in movies has become quite rare. Other interest groups' protests about movies have occurred sporadically, but they usually challenge the political rather than the sexual content of movies (Lyons 1997, 53–80, 107–45). Interest groups thus have no role in the ratings game.

CARA became a cataloging agency in the rating game, bargaining only about the fit of a sexual display or dialogue with a rating letter to account for producers' or conglomerates' decisions about the market for the sexual content (and violence and profanity) in a movie. CARA does not judge whether the sexual content serves artistic or commercial purposes. It thus has legitimated conglomerates' and producers' discretion over movie content. Since media conglomerates and producers wanted movies with enough sexuality to interest an audience but not forms of sexual content that could discourage exhibitions, producers began to keep accounts of consumer reactions to sexual dialogue and displays. The consequence has been the infusion of sexuality into movies solely to secure ticket sales to a select group of consumers identified through market research. By claiming that CARA's rating system forewarns consumers about the extent of sexuality in a movie, producers and conglomerates also have prevented overt criticism of sexuality in movies by passing the blame for morally distasteful presentations to their ill-informed consumers. Therefore, the outcome of the ratings game is a situation in which a customer, caveat emptor, can purchase a commodity, a ticket to gaze at what conglomerates think is marketable movie sex.

Conclusion

The collapse of movie censorship and the emergence of ratings represent a marked change in the freedom of expression about sexual morality. It occurred quite suddenly when the distribution of the "resource" of sexuality in movies failed to match a change in the substantive rationality of sexual preferences held by movie studio executives, directors, and the Catholic interests represented in the censorship game. When the Supreme Court's entrepreneurship to secure a new, legal realist rationality for rights and economic competition radically diminished the bargaining power of state and local censors and when studio executives and directors created costly problems for the PCA, the collapse of the game became imminent. At that point a leader, Jack Valenti, convinced the participants of the benefits of exit. He designed a new bargaining game to regulate the sexual content of movies that eliminated government and religion from participation in the definition of morality in the movies. Within a few years, corporate interests controlled the message of sexual morality presented in general release movies.

Although the collapse of movie censorship illustrates only one situation of synoptic morality policy change, it suggests that changes in the substantive rationality of preferences initiated by an avant-garde exogenous to a policy bargaining game can have major consequences for the stability of policy-bargaining games that support a morality policy. New preferences developed by an avant-garde are a resource that policy entrepreneurs can employ to displace the substantive rationality in which a policy-bargaining game takes place. This chapter also suggests that had the loyalist participants' knowledge of alternative preferences or their assessment of the costs of alternatives been different, the nonmarket failure of the censorship game might not have transpired. Furthermore, had leadership been absent, the new bargaining game might not have emerged and a quite different resolution to the issue of the control of sexuality in the movies could have occurred. Consequently, because of the mix of preferences, opportunities, and leadership in each situation, policy change will differ as changing variables affect different morality policy bargaining games.

These findings pose challenges for future research on policy change. Beyond the need for more studies that permit comparative analysis of policy change, such studies can provide an explanation of how an avant-garde idea percolates into the preferences of policy entrepreneurs. As this chapter has shown, entrepreneurs may employ such avant-garde preferences in specific contexts, particularly when interests are poorly organized and adopt faulty tactics, to destabilize morality policy bargaining and create synoptic policy change. More also needs to be known about how exogenous institutional rules, such as judicial review, affect how entrepreneurs choose their tactics, how a leader spots an exit point, how a leader devises a new bargaining game, and how unanticipated consequences for public morality emerge as participants play the new bargaining game. These are complex problems, but continued study will permit deeper insights on how the perception of rational political and economic preferences affects the formation of state and local morality policy.

Case References

Abrams v. *United States*, 250 U.S. 616 (1919)

Burstyn, Inc. v. *Wilson*, 343 U.S. 495 (1952)

Engdahl v. *City of Kenosha*, 317 F. Supp. 133 (E.D. Wisc. 1970)

Erznoznik v. *City of Jacksonville*, 422 U.S. 205 (1975)

Freedman v. *Maryland*, 380 U.S. 51 (1965)

Gelling v. *Texas*, 343 U.S. 960 (1952)

Ginsberg v. *New York*, 390 U.S. 629 (1968)

Holmby Productions v. *Vaughan*, 350 U.S. 870 (1955)

Interstate Circuit, Inc. v. *Dallas*, 390 U.S. 676 (1968)

Jacobellis v. *Ohio*, 378 U.S. 478 (1964)

Kingsley International Pictures Corp. v. *Regents*, 360 U.S. 684 (1959)

Maljack Productions v. *Motion Picture Association of America*, 22 U.S.P.Q. 2d (BNA) 1867 (1992)

Memoirs v. *Massachusetts*, 383 U.S. 413 (1966)

Miller v. *California*, 413 U.S. 15 (1973)

Miramax Films Corp. v. *Motion Picture Association of America*, 560 N.Y.S. 2d 730 (1990)

Motion Picture Association of America v. *Specter*, 315 F. Supp. 824 (E.D. Pa. 1970)

Mutual Film Corporation v. *Industrial Commission of Ohio*, 236 U.S. 230 (1915)

Mutual Film Corp. of Missouri v. *Hodges*, 236 U.S. 248 (1915)

New York v. *Ferber*, 458 U.S. 747 (1982)

Osborne v. *Ohio*, 495 U.S. 103 (1990)

Paris Adult Theatre I v. *Slaton*, 413 U.S. 49 (1973)

Rabe v. *Washington*, 405 U.S. 313 (1972)

Redrup v. *New York*, 386 U.S. 767 (1967)

Renton v. *Playtime Theatres, Inc.*, 475 U.S. 41 (1986)

Roth v. *United States, Alberts v. California*, 354 U.S. 476 (1957)

Schenk v. *United States*, 249 U.S. 47 (1919)

Superior Films, Inc. v. *Department of Education of State of Ohio,* 346 U.S. 587 (1954)

Times Film Corporation v. *Chicago,* 355 U.S. 35 (1957)

Times Film Corporation v. *Chicago,* 365 U.S. 43 (1961)

United States v. *Paramount Pictures, Inc.,* 334 U.S. 131 (1948)

Young v. *American Mini Theatres,* 427 U.S. 50 (1976)

Notes

1. By examining only one bargaining game, this chapter is a situational analysis or a causal explanation of a singular occurrence (Farr 1985). As with the situationally focused approach developed by Bates, de Figueiredo, and Weingast (1998), this chapter evaluates how changes in the rationality of preferences of participants and specific institutional opportunities can create the failure of a policy-bargaining game. It is offered as a step in the evolution of models of the failure and replacement of morality policy bargaining games.
2. The Supreme Court did permit governments to zone or limit public exposure to "adult" enterprises (*Rabe* v. *Washington* 405 U.S. 313 [1972]; *Erznoznik* v. *City of Jacksonville* 422 U.S. 205 [1975]; *Young* v. *American Mini Theatres* 427 U.S. 50 [1976]; *Renton* v. *Playtime Theatres* 475 U.S. 41 [1986]) and to ban child pornography (*New York* v. *Ferber* 458 U.S. 747 [1982]; *Osborne* v. *Ohio* 495 U.S. 103 [1990]).

PART FOUR

Individual Morality Policymaking Behavior

CHAPTER SEVEN

Morality in Congress? Legislative Voting on Gay Issues

Donald P. Haider-Markel

HOW DOES INDIVIDUAL-LEVEL political behavior change when basic issues of morality are under consideration within political institutions? Morality policy issues, such as abortion, school prayer, the death penalty, and homosexuality, have been argued to exhibit an identifiable pattern of politics (Meier 1994). Researchers, however, have tested the theory of morality politics only in aggregate political behavior, including ballot initiatives (Haider-Markel and Meier 1996, n.d.; Morgan and Meier 1980) and comparative state policy (Haider-Markel and Meier 1996; Meier 1994; Meier and McFarlane 1993; Mooney and Lee 1995; Smith, Chapter 12, this volume). Other researchers have examined individual behavior on these types of issues but not explicitly within the framework of morality politics (Adams 1997; Chressanthis, Gilbert, and Grimes 1991; Tatalovich and Schier 1993; Gohmann and Ohsfeldt 1994; Luker 1984; Maynard-Moody 1995; Wattier and Tatalovich 1995). This chapter brings these lines of research together by modeling individual legislative voting behavior on lesbian and gay issues based on the morality politics framework.

My analysis of voting on lesbian and gay issues in the U.S. House of Representatives strongly suggests that the morality politics framework is a useful tool for explaining legislative behavior on issues for which at least one coalition argues its point in terms of morality. As predicted by the framework, legislator partisanship, ideology, religious affiliation, and constituency preferences strongly shape voting behavior. However, my findings also indicate that interest groups may play a more significant role on these issues than the morality politics framework would suggest.

Morality Politics Theory and Legislative Voting Behavior

Public policy is shaped by a variety of factors in the social and political environment, including the activities of interest groups, the salience of the issue, citizen forces, competition between political parties, and the values of political elites (Gormley 1986; Meier 1994). The relative influence of each of these factors, however, may be determined by the perceived intent of the policy under consideration (Lowi 1969; Ripley and Franklin 1991).

When one or more sides attempts to define an issue in terms of morality, the intent of those proposing a policy is often to redistribute values in society through government approval (Gusfield 1963). Morality politics issues are likely to be highly salient to attentive publics and, thus, require little information for those willing to participate. The media builds issue salience on morality issues, even though reporters tend to provide little new information or explore the complexities of the issue. Journalists, focused on conflict and sex, jump to cover these issues, enhancing issue salience, but rarely informing the debate (Cook 1998). High issue salience combined with low information requirements allows for greater participation by citizens and politicians, both of whom are likely to mobilize around religious beliefs (Gormley 1986; Morgan and Meier 1980; Lowi 1969). Compromise between competing views is unlikely since the political battle is waged over core beliefs. Similar to redistributive politics, then, morality politics are likely to appear in competitive political systems, be highly partisan, attract entrepreneurial politicians, seek nonincremental policy change, and revolve around core religious beliefs (Meier 1994).

Bureaucracies and interest groups are unlikely to have much influence on policy adoption in morality politics because their prime resource, information, is not essential. The often high levels of salience associated with morality politics decreases necessity for expert information, thereby increasing participation by nonexperts—everyone is an "expert" on morality (Meier 1994). Furthermore, while politicians and journalists frequently express concern over the apparent excessive influence of interest groups more generally in U.S. politics, empirical evidence demonstrating such influence has been mixed (Smith 1995). Researchers suggest that interest group influence is likely to be highest when decisions take place out of the public eye, when the issue is nonpartisan and nonideological, when the interest group's position is unopposed by other interest groups, when issues are technical or complex, and when the level of issue salience is low (Smith 1995, 94–95)—precisely opposite the conditions we expect in morality politics.

Interest groups may, however, selectively activate sympathetic actors in the policy process by framing the issue in terms that appeal to their core beliefs (Haider-Markel and Meier 1996, 337). Interest groups, then, are likely to try to limit broader involvement in the formulation of policy by keeping issue salience low and focusing their resources on sympathetic political elites or, in Schattschneider's (1960) terms, limiting the scope of the conflict. Furthermore, interest groups can provide politicians with resources other than technical information. These resources include campaign contributions, campaign volunteers, electoral support, and political information on the viability of policy proposals and the views of constituents (Smith 1995). Providing these types of resources may give interest groups more influence in the policymaking process generally and in morality politics.

On gay issues specifically, Haider-Markel and Meier (1996) suggest that legislative adoption of antidiscrimination policies for lesbians and gays is best explained by an interest group politics model rather than a morality politics model. In the interest group politics model, policy adoption is determined by interest group resources, the preferences of political elites, and the normal incremental process of politics. Haider-Markel and Meier's analysis of gay issues, however, is limited in at least two ways.

First, their analysis is limited to only one issue affecting lesbians and gays, antidiscrimination policies, and may not be generalizable to all gay-related issues. For example, research suggests that political dynamics may differ on some gay issues, such as hate crime policy (Haider-Markel 1997). Examining gay issues within an institutional context in which a multitude of gay issues are considered should allow for a better understanding of the political dynamics at work.

Second, the Haider-Markel and Meier (1996) analysis is conducted at the aggregate level and does not attempt to model the behavior of individual legislators on gay issues. As such, their analysis may underestimate the influence of factors specified by the morality politics model in the policymaking process. In fact, because the Haider-Markel and Meier (1996) interest group politics model explicitly includes a variable measuring the preferences of political elites on lesbian and gay issues, the authors fail to recognize that the influence of morality politics factors may work *through* political elites. The preferences of political elites may be shaped by morality politics factors, including member religious affiliation, partisanship, and ideology, as well as citizen forces, including public opinion.

It is interesting to note that interest group influence on individual behavior in morality politics issues may also be visible for some of the same reasons that morality politics variables are likely to be visible. The level of analysis—individual legislators versus aggregate-level policy outcomes—allows for greater variation in the variables and should decrease measurement error. First, variation is increased due to a larger number of cases. Second, measurement error should decrease because the selective appeals made by interest groups are more likely to be reflected in individual legislator voting behavior than in legislative outcomes (Smith 1995).

Within the context of a legislative arena, therefore, what should we expect the dynamics of morality politics to look like? First, we should expect the debate to be highly partisan and ideological (Haider-Markel and Meier 1996; Mooney and Lee 1995). For example, in his study of the abortion issue in Congress, Adams (1997) found that the issue has become increasingly partisan and ideological over time. Mooney and Lee's (1995) study of abortion policy in the states found that ideology had the single greatest influence on policy.

Second, because morality politics is often organized around religious beliefs (Meier 1994; Mooney and Lee 1995), the religious affiliation of legislators should play a role in legislative decision making on issues perceived to involve morality. Legislators affiliated with more conservative religions should prefer legislation that supports the morals of their denomination. In fact, some traditional studies of legislative voting behavior have included measures of religious affiliation to capture the preferences of individual legislators (Benson and Williams 1982; Day 1994; Gohmann and Ohsfeldt 1990, 1994; Green and Guth 1991).

Third, many researchers have assumed that constituencies influence legislative voting behavior (Buchanan and Ohsfeldt 1993; Clausen 1973; Erikson 1978; Fleisher 1993; Jackson and Kingdon 1992; Kingdon 1989). In morality politics, citizens are more likely to participate in the policymaking process because information costs are low, the issue is salient, and the issue evokes strong emotions (Meier 1994). Higher levels of citizen participation should make legislators more responsive to citizen preferences. Indeed, studies of morality politics have found that citizen preferences, usually measured by religious affiliations, do influence morality policy (Mooney and Lee 1995; Morgan and Meier 1980). However, the influence of citizen preferences may be conditioned by the level of issue salience, with higher influence under conditions of high salience (Haider-Markel and Meier 1996).

Fourth, interest groups may be able to influence legislator behavior at the margins by mobilizing selective publics to put their own "spin" on the issues (Haider-Markel and Meier n.d.). Even if interest groups are unable to control the legislative outcome of a policy, they should be able to use their resources to sway potentially sympathetic legislators. Interest group influence, like citizen preferences, will be conditioned by the level of issue salience, with interest group influence more likely under conditions of low salience (Haider-Markel and Meier 1996).

A morality politics model of legislative voting behavior, therefore, should account for legislator party affiliation, ideology, religious affiliation, constituency preferences, and interest group resources. The influence of these factors, moreover, is likely to be conditioned by the salience of the issue. In the following sections, I operationalize these variables for a morality politics model of legislative voting behavior on lesbian and gay issues.

Variables: Operationalization and Measurement

Dependent Variables

Determining what issues are of concern to lesbians and gays is no easy task. Gay groups sometimes adopt public positions on issues that are only remotely related to homosexuality, and gay-related legislation does not always use terms such as *homosexuality* or *sexual orientation*. I determined relevant votes on lesbian and gay issues in four steps. First, I created a list of House votes by using the index of the *Congressional Quarterly Almanac* to find all bills, amendments, and motions mentioning AIDS, gays, hate crimes, homosexuality and homosexuals, lesbians, and sexual orientation. Second, I supplemented my list with congressional actions discussed in Adam (1995) and Thompson (1994). Third, I contacted the two largest national gay and lesbian interest groups to determine which votes they found important and/or actively lobbied on.[1] The two national groups are the National Gay and Lesbian Task Force (NGLTF) and the Human Rights Campaign (HRC). NGLTF and HRC track congressional member voting records on gay issues. The information provided by both groups helped to expand my list but also included votes on issues not directly related to lesbians and gays.[2]

Finally, I confirmed that votes in each session constituted gay issues by factor analyzing the votes in each session. My minimum requirements in including votes from each session entailed that one factor account for more than 50 percent of the variation in session votes and that each session vote loaded in a single factor at 0.36 or above.[3] My final list includes votes for the House from the 101st Congress through the 104th Congress. Each session averaged about ten votes on gay-related issues.[4] My measure of support for gay and lesbian issues is simply the overall percentage of time a legislator voted in a pro-gay position on gay and lesbian issues during a congressional session.[5] For example, if a legislator cast one pro-gay vote of a total of four votes during a session, the legislator would receive a score of 25 percent.

Independent Variables

Party affiliation. Morality politics often inflames partisan conflict. As morality issues, gay issues frequently divide Republicans and Democrats, with Republicans tending to view homosexuality as a threat to traditional moral values (Haider-Markel 1997). Democrats, meanwhile, are more likely to define homosexuality in less negative terms and be more supportive of gay and lesbian civil rights (Seltzer 1993). I measure party affiliation as a dichotomous variable, coded 1, for Democratic legislators.[6] I expect that Democratic partisanship will be positively related to pro-gay voting support.

Member ideology. Morality politics often invokes strong ideological divisions, with conservatives defending traditional values and norms, while liberals argue for tolerance and an acceptance of nontraditional lifestyles (Buchanan and Ohsfeldt 1993). I measure the ideology of U.S. House members with the American Conservative Union (ACU) rating for each legislator in the relevant Congress.[7] I expect that higher ACU ratings will be associated with lower levels of pro-gay support.[8]

Religious affiliation. The crux of the morality politics framework is that at least one coalition in the debate must define the issue in moral or "sin" terms (Meier 1994). In the case of homosexuality, many religious denominations have historically framed homosexuality as immoral and as a threat to religious values (Diamond 1995). Protestant fundamentalists, evangelical Christians, and fundamentalist Christians are the least likely to have positive attitudes toward homosexuals (Woodward 1993, 81). Therefore, it seems likely that legislators who are affiliated with conservative religious denominations are less likely to be supportive of a pro-gay position on roll call votes. To test this, I include a variable coded 1 if the legislator is affiliated with a conservative religious denomination.[9]

Constituency interests. Another key component of the morality politics model is the vocal participation of citizens in the policymaking process. The potential for greater citizen participation should ensure that legislators pay heed to constituency preferences on morality politics issues and others such as race (Miller and Stokes 1963). Given the increased salience of lesbian and gay issues in the 1990s, we should expect legislators to be especially responsive to constituency concerns on gay issues. However, measuring constituency opinion on gay and lesbian issues is difficult; no existing surveys have reasonably large district samples. This limitation forces me to simulate constituency opinion on gay issues rather than calculate mean district opinion based on existing samples (Erikson 1978; Gamble 1994; Page et al. 1984).

I simulate constituency opinion on gay issues for each U.S. House district using a two-stage estimation technique on data from Miller et al. (1993a) for the first stage and Miller et al. (1993b) for the second stage (Gamble 1994).

In the first stage of simulating opinion on gay and lesbian issues, I use an additive index based on three survey responses as the dependent variable: (1) opinions on laws protecting homosexuals, (2) opinions on allowing homosexuals to serve in the military, and (3) opinions on permitting homosexuals to adopt children. These questions offer substantial face validity as a measure of opinions on gay issues, and using three indicators rather than one should reduce measurement error (Gamble 1994).

To predict opinion on gay issues, I used the following independent variables: education, age, race, gender, martial status, party identification, mainline Protestant, conservative Protestant, and Catholic (Gamble 1994; Seltzer 1993). The results in Table 7.1 are similar to those found by other researchers predicting attitudes on gay issues; most of the variables are statistically significant, and the model explains a reasonable amount of variation (Gamble 1994; Seltzer 1993).

The second stage in the simulation process is to combine the first-stage results with the actual values of the independent variables from a similar survey that contains large samples and all congressional districts. I do this by creating a regression equation in which the slopes from Table 7.1 are multiplied by the actual values for each respondent in the pooled National Election Studies survey (also see Erikson 1978; Page et al. 1984). The resultant sums for all respondents are averaged within each district. The mean for each district, therefore, is the simulated district opposition to gay issues. Simulated district opposition is expected to be negatively related to pro-gay legislative voting.

Interest group activity. Morality politics theory suggests that interest groups are unlikely to have much influence in policymaking simply because they are denied their prime resource: information. I examine the possible influence of interest groups in three ways. First, I include a measure of gay interest group campaign contributions. The largest gay and lesbian political action committee (PAC) is the HRC, which has contributed to House and Senate candidates since the

TABLE 7.1 DETERMINANTS OF PUBLIC OPPOSITION TO GAY CIVIL RIGHTS

INDEPENDENT VARIABLES	UNSTANDARDIZED BETA (SLOPE)	STANDARD ERROR
Party identification	0.49**	.04
Mainline Protestant	0.76**	.22
Conservative Protestant	2.15**	.22
Catholic	0.49**	.24
Education	−1.28**	.19
Age	0.29**	.01
Race (white)	0.56**	.18
Gender (female)	−1.49**	.19
Marital status (married)	0.67**	.17
Intercept	4.12**	
R^2		.19
Adjusted R^2		.18
SEE		3.55
F		51.29**

Notes: Coefficients are unstandardized regression coefficients.

** = significant at > .05, one-tailed test.

1981–82 election cycle and in the 1995–96 cycle contributed more than $1 million to national campaigns. For each congressional session, I measure HRC campaign contributions as the dollar amount contributed to each legislator during the previous election cycle.

My second measure of interest group activity captures the potential for the grassroots mobilization of gay interest group members. Successful lobbying efforts often hinge on the ability of an interest group to mobilize its members to contact their legislators (Smith 1995, 103–5). I measure the potential for grassroots mobilization by including a dichotomous variable coded as 1 if HRC has established a district coordinator in that district.[10]

Third, because morality politics often involves competing advocacy coalitions, I included a variable to capture the influence of groups likely to be opposed to gay interests. However, two problems thwarted my efforts. First, national groups that are likely to be opposed to gay groups, such as the Eagle Forum or the Christian Coalition, do not release membership data on a congressional district basis. Second, of the conservative PACs that are likely to oppose gay groups, none is specifically organized for this purpose. Most conservative political action committees are concerned with a variety of issues, including the size of government, obscenity, abortion, and school prayer, most of which are only remotely related to the concerns of gay groups.

However, we might expect that PAC contributions from groups that are often opposed to pro-gay legislation would capture the *potential* influence of these groups on legislative voting behavior. Therefore, I include a measure of campaign contributions from the Eagle Forum PAC, which is headed by Phyllis Schlafly and has been staunchly opposed to feminism, abortion, and gay rights since 1972. The Eagle Forum PAC has contributed to congressional candidates since 1977, and during the 1995–96 election cycle, it contributed $309,000 to candidates for federal office. For each House session, I measure Eagle Forum PAC contributions as the dollar amount contributed to each legislator during the *previous* election cycle.[11] I expect Eagle Forum PAC contributions to be negatively related to pro-gay legislative support.

Finally, because my measures of PAC contributions could be influenced by the previous voting behavior of legislators, past voting by individual members should be controlled for. While gay groups may be more likely to contribute money and mobilize constituents in districts in which the legislator has been supportive of gay interests in the past, the Eagle Forum may be more likely to support legislators who have been opposed to gay interests in the past (Grenzke 1989). To control for this influence, I include a measure of each legislator's pro-gay support from the previous congressional session in each model, estimating pro-gay support in the current session.[12] If interest groups simply reward a member for past voting behavior, the inclusion of this control variable should negate the impact of groups in the current session.

Strategy of Analysis and Results

Preliminary analysis of the data indicated high levels of multicollinearity between most of the independent variables and my measure of legislator ideology. Following Wattier and Tatalovich (1995, 174), I reduced the collinearity problems by regressing all of the significant independent variables (except the measure of previous pro-gay support because of its value as a control variable) on the measure of ideology and by using the residuals from this equation in place of the actual values for legislator ideology. This process purges the model of collinearity and allows for

TABLE 7.2   LEGISLATOR PRO-GAY SUPPORT ON ROLL-CALL VOTES, U.S. HOUSE OF REPRESENTATIVES

INDEPENDENT VARIABLES	101ST U.S. HOUSE	102D U.S. HOUSE	103D U.S. HOUSE	104TH U.S. HOUSE
Member ideology	−0.76***	−0.76***	−0.81***	−0.70***
	(.03)	(.05)	(.03)	(.04)
Democrat	31.46***	35.91***	41.28***	32.39***
	(1.70)	(2.17)	(1.47)	(1.70)
Religious conservative	−7.81***	−7.62***	−3.59**	−4.80***
	(1.25)	(1.85)	(1.61)	(1.47)
Simulated constituency opposition to gay rights	−4.61***	−5.68***	−7.72***	−5.98***
	(.54)	(.84)	(.78)	(.75)
Gay contributions	0.0032***	0.0040***	0.0050***	0.0035***
	(.00033)	(.00035)	(.00033)	(.00034)
Gay mobilization	0.65	−2.33	7.91***	7.25***
	(1.13)	(1.71)	(1.40)	(1.36)
Eagle Forum PAC contributions	−0.0092***	−0.0092**	−0.0045***	−0.0049***
	(.0027)	(.0041)	(.0011)	(.0009)
Member's previous pro-gay support	0.19***	0.31***	0.06***	0.23***
	(.03)	(.05)	(.02)	(.03)
Intercept	79.96***	66.35***	84.74***	71.36***
	(13.68)	(7.27)	(7.94)	(7.62)
R^2	.91	.87	.89	.89
Adjusted R^2	.91	.86	.88	.89
SEE	78.40	181.38	148.19	136.05
F	524.30***	336.41***	401.38***	414.73***
n	425	426	408	408

Notes: Coefficients are OLS regression coefficients.
Standard errors are in parentheses.
One-tailed significance test = *** sig. < .01; ** sig. < .05

a more confident interpretation of the regression coefficients; however, it also limits our ability to interpret the distinct influence of legislator ideology.[13]

After conducting F tests as outlined in Hanushek and Jackson (1977, 126–29), I determined that each House session was significantly different from the others, suggesting that pooling the data would be inappropriate.[14] Table 7.2 (p. 123) displays the regression results for each session. Each model predicts pro-gay support quite well, with all models predicting at least 87 percent of the variation in the dependent variables. A comparison of these models demonstrates two facts. First, the performances of the independent variables are consistent across congressional sessions. Second, this is true even though the sessions are dramatically different from one another.

The differences between the sessions can be explained several ways. First, the issues considered by each session are different. For example, the 103d House was the only session to consider the question of gays in the military, while the 104th House was the only one to consider the same-sex marriage issue. Second, the values for the independent variables change over time. Campaign contributions, for example, have generally increased. Third, starting with the 103d Congress, the House has become increasingly Republican—leading to less pro-gay support by individual members. Finally, redistricting after the 102d Congress may have influenced the values of the variables.

As predicted by the morality politics framework, member partisan affiliation and ideology are the most consistent predictors of pro-gay support. In each session, members that were affiliated with conservative religious denominations were consistently less likely to score high on the index of pro-gay votes. The influence of this variable, however, appears to have decreased slightly over time. While this finding may indicate that moral interpretations of gay issues are on the decline in Congress, it nonetheless confirms the importance of religious values in morality politics.

My simulated measure of constituency opposition to policies favoring gays and lesbians performs well across all the models, suggesting that on morality politics issues, legislators are likely to take constituency preferences into account. The fact that legislators pay particular attention to public opinion on gay issues confirms a key component of the morality politics model: that morality politics invokes legislative responsiveness to citizen preferences. It may also indicate that factors specified in the morality politics framework do indeed influence policy but indirectly by influencing legislator voting behavior.

My measures of gay interest group activity—PAC contributions and potential membership mobilization—have a significant positive influence on pro-gay support in most of the models. The variable measuring potential gay interest group mobilization is significant in only two sessions, suggesting that the measure is either too crude or that grassroots mobilization simply did not have any influence during the 101st or 102d Congress. My measure of potential resources of groups likely to be opposed to gay groups—campaign contributions from the Eagle Forum PAC—shows a consistent negative influence on legislator pro-gay voting. The size of the coefficients further suggests that, dollar for dollar, conservative PAC contributions are likely to get more "bang for their buck." Given the surrogate nature of my conservative PAC measure, however, these results should be interpreted with caution. Overall, the performance of the interest group variables suggests that even in morality politics, interest groups have the potential to influence legislative voting behavior.

Are All Issues Created Equal? Issue Salience in Morality Politics

While my analysis has confirmed the pattern of politics predicted by the morality politics framework, one important aspect of the theory has not been examined. As suggested by Haider-Markel and Meier (1996, n.d.), a key aspect of morality politics is issue salience. If a morality politics issue becomes salient, interest group resources are likely to be less important than morality politics factors. I explicitly assumed earlier that gay issues are generally salient in Congress. However, some gay issues may be more salient than others. For example, while the *New York Times* extensively covered legislation concerning gays in the military during the 103d Congress, other gay-related issues, such as legislation concerning the discussion of homosexuality in public school curriculum, were barely mentioned.

To demonstrate the different impact of morality politics forces and interest group forces under different degrees of issue salience, I modeled three specific legislative votes in the 103d House: (1) the final vote on gays in the military, an amendment to HR 2041, (2) a vote on an amendment to HR 2492 that would prohibit the District of Columbia from spending money to implement its domestic partners ordinance, and (3) a vote on an amendment that would remove language from HR 6 that would prohibit local education agencies receiving money under the bill from carrying out programs that encourage or support "homosexuality as a positive lifestyle alternative." The dependent variable for each vote is simply 1 if the member voted for the pro-gay position and 0 if the member voted against the pro-gay position.

Based on coverage in the *Congressional Quarterly Weekly Report*, I ordered these votes in relative rank order, with the first, gays in the military, being highly salient and the last, homosexuality in the curriculum, being relatively nonsalient. I expect that while the estimated coefficients for partisanship, ideology, public opposition, and religious affiliation will tend to decrease with issue salience, the coefficients for interest group variables will tend to increase.

TABLE 7.3   **PROBABILITY OF LEGISLATOR PRO-GAY SUPPORT ON SALIENT AND NONSALIENT LEGISLATION IN THE 103D U.S. HOUSE OF REPRESENTATIVES**

INDEPENDENT VARIABLES	GAYS IN THE MILITARY	DISTRICT OF COLUMBIA DOMESTIC PARTNERS	HOMOSEXUALITY IN CURRICULUM	DIFFERENCE
Relative issue salience	High	Medium	Low	High–Medium Medium–Low
Member ideology	−0.09***	−0.09***	−0.082***	0.000
	(.01)	(.01)	(.013)	−.008**
Democrat	0.90**	2.38***	3.40***	1.48***
	(.45)	(.43)	(.48)	1.02***
Religious conservative	−1.28**	−0.07	−0.16	−1.21***
	(.62)	(.54)	(.46)	.09
Simulated constituency opposition to gay rights	−1.21*** (.28)	−0.63** (.26)	−1.18*** (.26)	−.54** .55**
Gay contributions	0.00068***	0.00085***	0.0022**	.00017**
	(.00011)	(.00018)	(.00099)	.00135**
Gay mobilization	1.60***	0.80*	0.64	−.80*
	(.41)	(.43)	(.44)	−.16
Eagle Forum PAC contributions	−0.015 (.041)	−0.00065 (.00060)	−0.0017* (.00088)	−.01435 .00105
Member's previous pro-gay support	0.0093 (.0064)	0.011* (.0064)	0.006 (.006)	.0017 −.005
Intercept	8.32***	2.88	9.48***	−5.44***
	(2.75)	(2.63)	(2.58)	6.60***
Pseudo R^2	.43	.46	.46	
Model χ^2	303.35*** (df = 8)	328.16*** (df = 8)	317.63*** (df = 8)	
Percentage classified correctly	89.68	89.92	86.92	
Percentage cases in modal category	29.48	38.54	52.31	
n	407	397	390	

Notes: Coefficients are logit coefficients.
Standard errors are in parentheses.
"Difference" is the difference between coefficients left to right.
One-tailed significance test = *** sig. < .01; ** sig. < .05; * sig. < .10

Table 7.3 displays the results of logistic regression for the three votes. The results suggest a general pattern: As salience decreases, so too do the coefficients for the morality politics variables. The coefficients for gay interest group variables, meanwhile, tend to increase. Furthermore, *t* tests suggest that these differences are statistically significant.[15] There are, however, exceptions and findings that deserve more discussion. First, member partisanship and ideology are consistently significant across each vote, and the importance of partisanship actually seems to increase as salience decreases. Contrary to expectations, these results suggest that morality politics may be the *most* partisan when issue salience is low.

Second, constituency opinion performs inconsistently, with a fairly high effect under conditions of both high and low issue salience. This finding may suggest that legislators are consistently responsive to constituency opinion on morality politics issues, regardless of the level of issue salience. Lastly, while the coefficient for PAC contributions increases as salience decreases, the coefficient for gay mobilization at the grass roots is largest under conditions of high issue salience. This result partly confirms the interest group hypothesis but suggests that grassroots supporters may be mobilized and, therefore, have influence only under conditions of high issue salience.

Conclusion

This chapter used the morality politics framework to examine congressional voting behavior on morality issues. My empirical analysis of the U.S. House strongly suggests that the morality politics framework is a useful tool for explaining the behavior of legislators on issues when at least one coalition argues its point in terms of morality. As predicted by the framework, legislator partisanship, ideology, religious affiliation, and constituency preferences strongly shape voting behavior. My findings also indicate that interest groups are able to influence legislative voting behavior through campaign contributions and the mobilization of grassroots supporters. Furthermore, as suggested by Haider-Markel and Meier (1996), morality politics factors seem to have more influence on legislative voting behavior when the salience of the issue is high, but interest groups appear to have more influence when issue salience is low.

Two general conclusions can be drawn from the evidence presented in this chapter. First, the potential role of interest groups in morality politics should not be underestimated, even though it is not yet well understood. In the case of lesbian and gay issues, interest groups are able to influence legislators despite the existence of factors that should lessen their influence: relatively high issue salience, a highly mobilized opposition, and polarized public attitudes toward homosexuals.

As Meier (Chapter 2, this volume) has begun to outline, it may in fact be that we can distinguish between two types of morality politics, one for which the influence of interest group resources is difficult to capture empirically and another for which influence may be more visible. We might define the first type as "sin" politics for which one advocacy coalition has successfully defined the issue solely in terms of sin, thereby making it politically impossible to be caught on the wrong side. In this case, the successful advocacy coalition effectively "wins" in the policy process simply because it was able to monopolize issue definition. The second type of morality politics could be defined as "opposing coalition" politics for which two or more advocacy coalitions successfully define an issue in at least two acceptable ways. In this case, neither coalition is likely to be successful all of the time, thereby giving morality politics the "feel" of redistributive politics. Indeed, interest groups in this case are likely to expend most of their resources attempting to control the scope of conflict, using issue frames to appeal to broad or narrow constituencies. Furthermore, issues are not forever regulated to be one "type" of morality politics or the other. Instead, the pattern of politics may change over time (Meier, Chapter 2, this volume) and, as shown here, is dependent on the specific manifestation of an issue.

The second general conclusion of this chapter is that the morality politics framework can be used to inform studies of individual-level political behavior. While a growing body of literature has established the distinctive pattern of politics associated with morality policy at the aggregate level, morality politics researchers have neglected to examine the role of partisanship, ideology, citizen preferences, and religious orientation in studies of individual-level political behavior. This chapter demonstrates that individual behavior in morality politics is influenced by individual characteristics, but it also highlights the fact that the influence of these forces is conditioned by factors in the political environment, such as issue salience, that are often difficult to control.

Notes

Portions of this manuscript were presented at the 1996 meeting of the American Political Science Association. The data and documentation necessary to replicate this analysis are available upon request from the author.

1. Consulting with an interest group to determine relevant votes is not new; for example, McArthur and Marks (1988) and Fleisher (1993) use those votes thought to be important by the Americans for Democratic Action (ADA), while Combs, Hibbing, and Welch (1984) use scores for representatives compiled by the American Conservative Union (ACU).
2. The HRC scored members according to some votes on abortion issues. These votes were not included in my analysis.
3. I chose 50 percent to ensure at least half of the variation was accounted for and chose a 0.36 factor loading because a loading of 0.35 and above ensures a significant amount of correlation.
4. A complete list of the votes is available from the author or Haider-Markel (1997).
5. I determined the "pro-gay" position on a vote by examining the positions held by NGLTF and HRC on votes in the 100th to 104th Congress. For most votes, the pro-gay position was relatively easy to determine. On some votes, especially

some concerning AIDS, the pro-gay position was impossible to determine, so these votes were not included in the analysis. When a member was absent from a vote, the vote was counted as missing data. A complete list of votes and all possible votes is available from the author.

6. Data are from *Congressional Quarterly Almanac* (various years).

7. Data are from *Congressional Quarterly Almanac* (various years), Duncan (various years), and the ACU.

8. The ACU rating did share some votes in common with my dependent variable. In no case, however, did common votes represent more than 2 percent of the ACU rating.

9. My measure of conservative religious affiliation includes Protestant fundamentalists, Baptists, and those members simply stating Christian. Like Haider-Markel and Meier (1996, 338), I classify Protestant fundamentalists as those legislators with affiliations to the Church of God, Latter Day Saints, Church of Christ, Church of the Nazarene, Mennonites, Conservative Baptist Association, Missouri Synod Lutherans, Pentecostal Free Will Baptists, Pentecostal Holiness, Salvation Army, and Seventh-Day Adventists (data for the U.S. House are from Duncan [various years]).

10. Data on HRC contributions, membership, and district coordinators were provided to the author by HRC.

11. Data on campaign contributions are from the Federal Election Commission.

12. The construction of the pro-gay support variable is explained in the section discussing the construction of the dependent variable. Readers should note that using votes from a prior session is essentially the same as lagging the dependent variable in time-series analysis. As such, the OLS estimator may be biased but can be consistent; the procedure may also overestimate relationships (Kennedy 1994, 140–41). This problem is commonly ignored, but another option, as suggested by Grenzke (1989), would be to estimate the models using instrumental variable (IV) estimation techniques. The validity of IV is highly dependent on the selection of discrete instrumental variables, which creates an inherent weakness in such models (Greene 1997, 710). Simply controlling for votes at $t - 1$, however, provides the easiest and strongest test.

13. I also conducted regression diagnostic tests for heteroscedasticity and influence points. None of these diagnostic tests suggested any problems.

14. Although pooling is inappropriate in this case, I did pool the four sessions to see whether the results were significantly different. The results show that the independent variables perform in a consistent manner across congresses. Because including a control variable for each member's voting behavior in the previous session may underestimate the long-term impact of each independent variable by decreasing the size of each variable's slope coefficient, I also estimated the models with the control. The results indicate that the control variable does decrease the size of the coefficients for the other variables, but the results are only slightly different.

15. The t tests were conducted using a pooled analysis as described in Hanushek and Jackson (1977, 124–29).

CHAPTER EIGHT

Congressional Use of Policy Information on Fact and Value Issues

Malcolm L. Goggin and Christopher Z. Mooney

THE CONTENT, FLOW, and control of policy-relevant information is the driving force behind the legislative process (Krehbiel 1991; Porter 1974; Bauer, Pool, and Dexter 1963, 466–72; March and Simon 1958, 161–69; Mooney 1993). From the design of policy options to the final vote on legislation, what legislators know about a policy, in terms of both facts and opinions, determines the content of law.

Is there a systematic difference between the content and use of information by legislators developing morality policy versus nonmorality policy? Since morality policy is often nontechnical and symbolic, it is likely that the information used by lawmakers in their deliberations on it is less technical than that needed for more instrumental policy for which the goal is to achieve an agreed-upon policy outcome. The morality policy literature suggests that information on the values held by citizens and elites will be more important than technical information and policy analysis (Mooney and Lee, n.d.; Norrander and Wilcox, Chapter 9, this volume; Haider-Markel and Meier 1996). If true, this lack of use of formal policy analysis could have serious implications for the implementation of morality policy (Meier, Chapter 2, this volume).

In this chapter, we address this question by examining how members of the U.S. House of Representatives used information to design one morality policy (on family planning) and one nonmorality policy (on clean air) during the 100th Congress (1987–88). Through interviews of twenty-four people identified as district-based information sources by members of the relevant congressional subcommittee and their staff, we find that information use does vary systematically between morality and nonmorality policy, even in the early phases of policymaking. When designing morality policy, members of Congress and their staff use more information about constituents' personal experiences and other emotive information than technical policy analysis, they seek out less information, and they use the information they receive more selectively than when they are designing nonmorality policy.

Legislative Information Use in Morality and Nonmorality Policy Design

Much of the research on legislative policymaking focuses on roll call voting, explaining the passage of law in terms of various actors giving voting cues and information to members of Congress (e.g., Matthews and Stimson 1975; Kingdon 1989; Wilcox and Clausen 1991; Cox and McCubbins 1993). Given congressional specialization in committees and subcommittees, however, the choices made by subgroups of legislators in the policy design phase clearly define and limit the impact of the broader body at later phases of the process (Deering and Smith 1997; Hall 1998). While rank-and-file members listen primarily to their colleagues and staff when voting on bills developed by committees on which they do not sit, they will expand their informational horizons further when designing a bill in a committee (Mooney 1991; Kovenock 1973). Thus, legislative information flows in a two-step process in which committee members and other specialists gather information from outside Congress on a given bill and then filter it through to their less-involved colleagues (Porter 1974; Sabatier and Whiteman 1985; Zweir 1979). This process makes the use of information by committee members crucial to both the development and passage of legislation.

How might congressional committee members and their staff use information differently when developing morality policy versus nonmorality policy? A crucial characteristic of morality policy here is its less technical nature. Morality policy is about governmental validation of contentious first principles rather than about developing a policy instrument that will achieve an agreed-upon substantive policy outcome (Mooney, Chapter 1, this volume). It is not about what will "work" but about what values will be affirmed. Therefore, much of the formal policy analysis that might be useful in developing more instrumental policy is irrelevant for morality policy development. Rather than technical policy analysis, the morality policy literature suggests that information regarding the values of their constituents is more useful for legislators grappling with such issues (Haider-Markel and Meier 1996; Haider-Markel, Chapter 7, this volume; Fairbanks 1977; Mooney and Lee, n.d.). On these simple, salient issues, risk-averse legislators with a democratic mandate will be especially careful to reflect the values of voters.

Two other dimensions of information use that may vary between morality and nonmorality policy development are the extent to which legislators seek out information and the extent to which they use it selectively. From one perspective, legislators may believe that they are closely in touch with their constituents and therefore need less external information about their values and will use only what information they do hear selectively, based on their own understanding of constituent values (Fenno 1978). Additional information about a subject on which a person feels well informed is superfluous and may in fact be explicitly shunned, especially if it conflicts with preconceived notions (Calvert 1985; Kovenock 1973; Tyszka 1989). There is probably less at stake psychologically for a legislator to admit that he or she does not know about some technical aspect of policy than to admit that he or she is out of touch with the basic values of his or her constituents. On the other hand, salient and simple morality policy may generate more electoral worry for legislators than nonmorality policy, with its narrower implications, therefore giving them a greater incentive to seek out policy-relevant information (Mooney 1993). The relative strength of these two processes—cognitive heuristics versus electoral fear—may determine the extent to which legislators seek out and use information on morality policy.

The District Information Connection: Influence from the Ground Up

To assess our hypotheses of differential information use between morality and nonmorality policy design and development, we examine the use by congressional subcommittee members and their staff of information from interest groups and executive branch bureaucrats from their home districts on two policies that are exemplars of morality and nonmorality policy. First, the two types of nonlegislative actors who supply the most information to legislators in the United States are interest group representatives and bureaucrats (Milbrath 1970; Wright 1996, Chap. 3; Mooney 1991). These people have the advantage of both being interested in the particulars of policy and possessing the detailed information that legislators designing policy often need. Few, if any, other actors in the process are in this uniquely advantaged position. Interest group representatives and bureaucrats are at the core of a network of actors who possess the expertise that a congressperson needs to estimate the short- and long-term consequences of policy alternatives (Kingdon 1984, 35–37; Rourke 1984; Lupia and McCubbins 1994; Browne 1995; Whiteman 1995).

Second, while Goggin's (1995) earlier research focused on how members of Congress and their staff use information from cue givers inside the Beltway, we look at sources of information from their home districts. There is ample evidence that when confronted with having to make a decision about if, when, and how to redesign an existing policy, Washington lawmakers seek the advice of state bureaucrats and members of the attentive public in their home states and districts (Rourke 1984; Fenno 1978; Kingdon 1989; Gray and Lowery 1996; Wright 1996). While Goggin's (1995) earlier research suggests that this district "feedback loop" might not work very well for value-laden morality policy, if legislators want information on the values of their constituents, they could arguably be best able to get it from sources in their districts.[1]

Third, as exemplars of morality and nonmorality policy design, we look at work on family planning and clean air policy in the 100th Congress. During this Congress, family planning was treated by the Reagan administration and the legislature as being directly connected to abortion regulation (Goggin et al. 1990, 163–69; "Family planning legislation" 1987). Social conservatives in the executive branch were convinced that workers in family planning clinics were providing "directive counseling," that is, directing pregnant women to abortion clinics. This concern led the administration to propose a gag rule, preventing anyone working in a family planning clinic receiving federal funds from giving advice about the availability of abortion services. In this manner, a "wall of separation" was to be built between abortion and family planning services. Abortion, the quintessential morality policy issue (Studlar, Chapter 3, this volume), therefore became the focal point of the debate. Congressional deliberations centered on the reauthorization of the family planning provisions of Title X of the Public Health Service Act.

Our exemplar of nonmorality policy development is Congress's 1988 attempted redesign of the Clean Air Act. The issues involved in this debate were technical and focused on the impact of various proposals on the environment and economy of different sections of the country ("Clean Air Bill Fails to Move" 1988). These were bread-and-butter issues for the legislators involved, not issues of abstract first principles. The debate pitted legislators from northeastern states concerned about acid rain against those from coal-mining states where jobs were threatened. Legislators from smog-filled southern California fought those from automobile-manufacturing states in the Midwest. The technical points of debate included the annual tonnage of sulfur dioxide and other chemicals that could be emitted safely into the air, the efficacy of new technologies for burning coal more cleanly, and electricity price impacts. These points were debatable in terms of facts supported by science and analysis. The development of this clean air policy in the 100th Congress was a classic nonmorality policy.

Aside from being clear exemplars of morality and nonmorality policy design, these cases were selected on the basis of similarities that helped to control for extraneous influences on information use (George 1979; Goggin 1986; Lijphart 1975). The clean air and family planning bills were being considered for redesign (1) at the same time (2) by the same members of Congress (3) sitting on the same House subcommittee, namely, the Health and Environment Subcommittee of the

House Energy and Commerce Committee, chaired in the 100th Congress by Henry Waxman (D-Calif.).[2] Studying these cases helps rule out alternative explanations for differences in legislative behavior across these two issues based on time, the members involved, district, and subcommittee.

Research Design

Between January and September 1988, the first author conducted face-to-face interviews in Washington, D.C., with twenty-five people from fifteen congressional offices in which the member served on the House Energy and Commerce Committee's Subcommittee on Health and Environment (Goggin 1995). Nine of the interviewees were members of Congress, and sixteen were legislative aides who specialized in either environment or health issues for their members.[3] Each interviewee was asked to identify individuals or organizations in her or his home district with whom she or he had communicated about these issues, either by actively soliciting or by receiving unsolicited advice or information. Based on responses to these questions, a list of twenty-four district-based information sources was compiled. Seventeen of these sources were state government bureaucrats, and seven were members and officers of interest groups. These sources came from eight states and the District of Columbia.[4]

These twenty-four people identified as information sources by congresspersons and their aides were interviewed by telephone about their perceptions of the congressional use of their information. The focus of each interview was the nature and extent of information use on clean air or family planning policy during this subcommittee's deliberations in the 100th Congress. Respondents were asked a number of open-ended and fixed-response questions. The following questions solicited the responses reported in Table 8.1:

Offered unsolicited information? "In the past two years, have you personally contacted anyone in Washington about (the Title X family planning provisions or the Clean Air Act) that Congress has been trying to revise?"

Was solicited for information. "Has anyone from Washington, D.C., ever asked you for your advice about (Title X family planning or the Clean Air Act)?"

Type of information provided? "How, if at all, did you use the results of research in these contacts?" "How, if at all, did you use your own or others' experiences with the state's (family planning or clean air) policies in these contacts?"

Perceived use of information. "In your opinion, to what extent are the U.S. Senators and Congresspersons that you contacted listening to or learning from the results of research or to the experiences of people like you?"

TABLE 8.1   **DISTRICT-BASED BUREAUCRATS' AND INTEREST GROUP OFFICIALS' PERCEPTIONS OF INFORMATION USE BY CONGRESSIONAL POLICYMAKERS ON MORALITY AND NONMORALITY POLICY**

	NONMORALITY POLICY (CLEAN AIR)	MORALITY POLICY (FAMILY PLANNING)
Offered unsolicited information?[a]		
Yes	10 (90.9%)[b]	13 (100%)
No	1 (9.1%)	0 (0%)
Was solicited for information?		
Yes	10 (90.9%)[c]	6 (46.2%)
No	1 (9.1%)	7 (53.8%)
Type of information provided[d]		
Experiential knowledge	4 (26.7%)[c]	9 (69.2%)
Formal policy analysis	11 (73.3%)	4 (30.8%)
Perceived use of information		
Policymakers *listened* to all	9 (81.8%)[c]	2 (15.4%)
Policymakers *listened* selectively	2 (18.2%)	10 (76.9%)
Policymakers did not *listen*	0 (0%)	1 (7.7%)
Policymakers *learned* from all	3 (27.3%)[e]	0 (0%)
Policymakers *learned* selectively	2 (18.2%)	9 (69.2%)
Policymakers did not *learn*	0 (0%)	1 (7.7%)
Don't know	6 (54.5%)	3 (23.1%)

Note: Data are from telephone interviews with persons named by members of the House Energy and Commerce Committee's Subcommittee on Health and Environment and their staff as sources of information and advice during the design of clean air and family planning policies in the 100th Congress.

   a. See the text for the wording of questions.

   b. The number of respondents giving this answer with the percentage in parentheses.

   c. Using Fisher's exact test, we determined that the percentages of these responses were statistically distinct between the types of policy at the .05 level (Blalock 1979, 292).

   d. Respondents were allowed to report that they used both experiential and analytical information if this was the case. For this reason, the number of total responses is larger for this question.

   e. Because too many cells were empty and more than two categories of response were used, no statistical inference could be validly conducted on these results.

Findings

Table 8.1 compares the responses of district-based information sources in the clean air policy area with those in family planning. While the sample is small, due to the highly specialized nature of these respondents, the results suggest systematic differences in legislative information use in morality and nonmorality policy design.

Offering Information and Advice

Table 8.1 indicates that virtually all of those interviewed reported that at some point during the process of designing each of these policies, they had tried to place unsolicited information into the hands of policymakers in Congress. On this behavior, there was no substantial difference across policy type. This indicates that these information sources were actively seeking to inform (and perhaps influence) congressional policy design on these issues, confirming their role as active information sources. It also shows that activists on both morality and nonmorality policy try to influence legislative deliberations through the provision of information at an early stage in the process. However, the remainder of our results indicates that legislators and their aides behave quite differently in their use of this information in morality versus nonmorality policy design.

Soliciting Information

Members of congressional offices were much more likely to solicit information from sources in their districts if the issue under consideration was a technical, nonmorality policy (clean air) rather than a less technical, morality policy (family planning).[5] As Table 8.1 indicates, 90.9 percent of those information sources active in clean air reported that they were contacted by a member of a congressional office, while less than 50 percent of those activists on family planning were contacted for information. Beyond these raw figures, more than half of the eleven persons interviewed who were involved in the clean air issue said that they were solicited for information frequently.[6]

The Type of Information Provided

Policy expertise is usually based on either experiential knowledge gleaned from day-to-day familiarity with the policy in question or formal policy analysis, perhaps in the form of the results of evaluation research. It is important to note that considerable amounts of both types of information were available to members of congressional offices from our respondents on both of the issues under study. Our respondents were asked two open-ended questions about how they used their experiences and the results of research in their contacts with congressional offices.

As is clear from Table 8.1, the results of formal policy analysis and evaluation research were used far more often in designing the nonmorality policy than the morality policy. When state family planning–policy experts did pass information along, it was based on the results of formal research only 30.8 percent of the time. Qualitative evidence from the interviews with family planning informants points to a reliance on emotional appeals and the superiority of personal testimony over facts. On the other hand, clean air information sources stressed the importance of facts, with 73.3 percent of the respondents indicating that formal policy analysis was the main information that they provided to congressional offices. This information was usually couched in terms of how the state or district would be affected by changes in the Clean Air Act.

Perceived Use of Information by Policymakers

While putting information into the hands of policymakers is a necessary condition for action and influence, it is not sufficient. Perhaps the most important measure of the success of a policy activist is the extent to which a policymaker actually listens to and learns from the information she or he presents. Our respondents were asked whether or not they believed, based on their perceptions of the policy design processes under study, that members of Congress and their staff listened to and learned from all points of view, selectively, or not at all. While the perception of being listened to and learned from is not equivalent to the fact of being listened to and learned from, our respondents were experienced policy activists whose perceptions are likely to be reliable. The actual use of information is notoriously difficult to assess empirically (Whiteman 1995), and these perceptions are a useful surrogate for this.

Again, the results of the interviews suggest a clear difference between how policymakers use information on morality and nonmorality policy. Based on their experiences with members of this congressional subcommittee and their aides, 81.8 percent of the information sources on clean air believed that policymakers in Washington listened to all points of view. In contrast, only 15.4 percent of information sources on family planning believed that congresspersons listened to all points of view. Most of our respondents in the family planning attentive public—76.9 percent—were convinced that those in congressional offices from their states listened only selectively to policy information.

On the question of whether policymakers actually learned from various sources of information, there is a different distinction between morality and nonmorality policy information sources' perceptions. More than half (54.5 percent) of the clean air sources admitted that they did not know if policymakers learned from the information they and others provided. Of the family planning informants, however, most (69.2 percent) believed that policymakers learned selectively from the information supplied to them, and none of the respondents believed that they learned from all sides on the issue.

This contrast between the breadth of congressional information use on these different issues was also apparent from the qualitative judgments of our respondents. For example, while several of the clean air informants expressed satisfaction with the open-mindedness of their states' congressional delegations, none of the family planning informants had similar impressions. More typical of the family planning informants was the perception that policymakers listened and learned only selectively and that their own information often "fell on deaf ears."

Conclusion

This study of the redesign of the Clean Air Act and the Title X family planning program shows that members of Congress use policy-relevant information differently, depending on the type of policy under consideration. When developing policy on the fact-based, instrumental issue of clean air, members of Congress and their aides tended to solicit much outside information, rely heavily on formal policy analyses, and listen to policy experts with a wide range of views. In contrast, when designing policy on the morality policy issue of family planning, with its implications for abortion regulation, members of Congress and their aides tended not to solicit information as often, to rely more on information based on the personal experiences of their informants and others, and to listen and to learn from this information only selectively. In short, members of Congress and their aides appear to solicit, gather, and use policy-relevant information differently, depending on whether the content of the issue at stake is defined as morality or nonmorality policy.

Legislative policymakers, like citizens, appear to assess morality policy more with preconceived notions, perhaps based on their own values and/or those they perceive their constituents to hold, rather than being open for more in-depth, multisided, and formal policy analysis. The cognitive heuristic of ignoring information that conflicts with these preconceived notions apparently trumps the electoral fear that legislators feel at potentially misrepresenting the values of their constituents. Legislators may be (perhaps realistically) confident that they know their constituents well enough that they do not have to bother assessing more information on morality policy, especially when the positions are as clearly staked out as on abortion-related issues.

While these strategies of ignoring formal policy analysis and selectively using other information on morality policy may be good cognitive economy for individual members of Congress, they have at least two broader implications. First, since less objective, technical policy information is used in the development of morality policy, there is a good chance that its implementation will have unforeseen impacts and complications (Meier 1994; Chapter 2, this volume). Without thorough and formal consideration of the actual consequences of a policy, based on the best technical assessments, there is often no telling what a new law may do to people, government workers, and businesses when it is implemented.

The second important implication of these findings is that since legislative policymakers, even those working in the policy development phase, are less likely to seek out and use objective information, especially that which may contradict what they already believe, morality policy may be very difficult to resolve to the satisfaction of even most sides (Mooney, Chapter 1, this volume). If information from a variety of sources and at an in-depth level is going to be used anywhere in the legislative process, it is in the policy design phase (Mooney 1991; Porter 1974; Zwier 1979). This type of information is needed for the deep understanding, serious deliberation, and resolution of public problems. The fact that our findings indicate that this type of information is not used much in the design of morality policy does not bode well for the resolution of morality policy in the U.S. legislative process.

Notes

This is a revised version of a paper presented at the 1996 meeting of the American Political Science Association in San Francisco. We wish to thank Michael Pagano, Peter Kobrak, and three anonymous reviewers for their helpful comments on this project.

1. Ideally, the types of comparisons we make in this chapter would be made using the full range of information sources, both in- and outside the Beltway. But these data were not collected to make such comparisons possible during the 100th Congress. We argue, however, that our data still allow us to make valid judgments about differences between information use on morality and nonmorality issues, albeit with somewhat less generalizability. Because the primary factor that differentiates these two policy developments is their morality versus nonmorality policy status (e.g., the same Congress, the same subcommittee, the same members and staff, the same location of the information sources), any differences in the use of information between them may reasonably be attributed to this difference.

2. During the 100th Congress, the first author was a guest scholar at the Brookings Institution and had direct access to members of Congress on this subcommittee and their aides for an extended period of time.

3. Most of the members of Congress were interviewed twice. One interview focused on the members' use of information during the redesign of the clean air bill, and a second interview focused on the members' behavior when the Title X family planning provision was being considered in subcommittee for reauthorization. Rarely did a single legislative aide specialize in both health and environmental issues.

4. These information sources were from Texas, California, Michigan, Pennsylvania, Illinois, Iowa, New York, Virginia, and Washington, D.C.

5. Fisher's exact test was used to assess whether the differences in the percentages in the response categories were statistically distinct between these policy types (Blalock 1979, 292).

6. More details on the results of these interviews are available from the first author.

PART FIVE

Aggregate Patterns of Morality Policy Adoption

Public Opinion and Policymaking in the States: The Case of Post-*Roe* Abortion Policy

Barbara Norrander and Clyde Wilcox

IN 1989, THE U.S. SUPREME COURT in *Webster* v. *Reproductive Health Services* (492 U.S. 490) gave states an ambiguous authority to regulate access to legal abortions. This ruling seemed to invite states to experiment with restrictions on abortion, and several states and territories quickly accepted that invitation (Halva-Neubauer 1993). What role did the opinions of states' citizens play in the passage of these new abortion laws? One could argue that public opinion would have a strong effect on morality policies, including the regulation of abortion. On morality issues, citizens are likely to have strong, stable opinions. Such intense preferences should lead citizens to become active in interest groups, and these interest groups should reflect the public's positions in their lobbying of state legislators. The starkly polarized positions of abortion interest groups (Woliver 1998) also may move the political parties to adopt distinctively different sets of policy options in contrast to the more moderate positions hypothesized by the model by Downs (1957). The two parties' national platforms indeed have offered contrasting pro-choice and pro-life positions since 1980 (Daynes and Tatalovich 1992). With a strong message coming from the public, interest groups, and political parties, state legislators could more easily perceive and incorporate public preferences into abortion policy.

On the other hand, state legislators could receive mixed messages from these groups of actors. Although the public has strong positions on abortion, these are not necessarily polarized positions. A plurality of Americans favor abortion in some, but not all, circumstances (Cook, Jelen, and Wilcox 1992). Interest groups and parties, however, may cater to the more extreme positions on this issue. State legislators themselves also may have strong preferences on abortion, and, adopting a trustee role, legislators may incorporate their own preferences into public law. Thus, the influence of state public opinion on abortion policies needs further investigation. In attempting to clarify the role of public opinion and organized interests on state abortion policy, we employ new measures of state public opinion, interest group activity, and abortion policy to assess the consequences of public opinion on abortion laws.

Abortion Policy and the Politics of Morality

Early research on public policy in the U.S. states focused almost exclusively on economic issues, such as state welfare expenditures or highway construction, and sought to test the relative importance of economic and political factors in explaining variations in public policy (Asher and Van Meter 1973). More recently, however, attention has turned to diversity in morality policy, such as the regulation of drugs, alcohol, and sexual conduct. Morality policy has several distinctive characteristics: The issues are not technically complex, they are highly salient to the public, and the policy debates evoke a wide variety of citizen participation (Gormley 1986). Moreover, compromise is more difficult to achieve in morality than economic policy (Lowi 1988; Mooney and Lee 1995). Although contending sides in a tax dispute may easily negotiate differences on the wording of a loophole or even on the proposed rate of taxation, greater difficulty arises for the antagonists in debates over abortion, sex education in schools, and drug laws.

Previous studies of morality policy suggest that patterns of policy adoption differ substantially from those of other types of state policies (Mooney and Lee 1995). In *The Politics of Sin*, Meier (1994) draws several conclusions about state morality policies: Political actors have their own preferences on morality issues that influence their decisions, citizens influence public policy, and morality policies tend to be debated as redistributive policies. In a sense, morality policies are redistributing values. Thus, these issues bring on heated partisan debates and frequent battles between opposing advocacy coalitions.

Public opinion has been demonstrated to match public policy in the United States (Stimson, MacKuen, and Erikson 1995; Wlezien 1995; Page and Shapiro 1992). The effect of public opinion is thought to be especially strong on morality policy. Morality policies are generally not complex, allowing a wide range of citizens to participate (Gormley 1986; Mooney and Lee 1995). Moreover, religious institutions frequently mobilize their members in an effort to influence morality policy (Morgan and Meier 1980; Fairbanks 1977). These circumstances make it more likely that even relatively amateur state legislators will respond to public sentiments.

Of course, the impact of public opinion on morality policymaking in the states is likely to vary across issue areas. In general, we expect that public opinion will have the greatest impact on morality policies for which individual and aggregate opinion is relatively stable, opinion is represented by organized interests, an issue is sufficiently salient to influence voters' decisions, and the political parties take reasonably distinctive positions. The accurate perception of public preferences is a difficult task for legislators. Only when a consistent message is received from multiple sources should we expect a high level of representation of public preferences in state policies.

These conditions may exist for the abortion issue. Abortion is a nontechnical issue that has been debated continually and loudly in the United States since *Roe v. Wade* (410 U.S. 113 [1973]). Most citizens hold a position on abortion. Indeed, the percentage of respondents who do not express an opinion on abortion questions in national surveys is very small. In the 1996 American National Election Study (ANES) survey, only five respondents, 0.3 percent of the sample, indicated that they had no opinion on the abortion question. Individuals' positions on abortion are also quite stable. In the 1992–94 ANES panel, the correlation between abortion attitudes across time is .76**, comparable to the stability in party identification where $r = .79$** (** means statistically significant at the .01 level). Moreover, for many Americans, abortion is a highly salient issue—one that mobilizes them to activism (Verba, Schlozman, and Brady 1995). The political parties have gradually diverged on abortion, providing voters with elite cues that make issue voting easier (Adams 1997). There is strong evidence that once voters realized that state officeholders could affect abortion policy after *Webster*, abortion became an issue affecting vote choice in ensuing elections (Cook, Jelen, and Wilcox 1994; Cook, Hartwig, and Wilcox 1993). All of this suggests that state abortion policies should reflect public opinion on the abortion issue.

Public opinion could play a lesser role on morality politics, however, when policymakers themselves hold highly salient personal positions influenced by religion, when interest groups distort aggregate public opinion significantly, and when parties position themselves to attract the energies of interest group activists rather than the median voter. Under these circumstances, state legislators receive distorted cues and may even be unaware of the public's true opinions. All of these factors also apply to the abortion case. Interest groups have organized around the strictly pro-life and pro-choice positions (Tribe 1990), but a majority of Americans take a more nuanced view that supports abortion under some but not all circumstances (Cook, Jelen, and Wilcox 1992). Thus, interest groups distort opinion, and legislators are likely to interact with interest group activists.

Finally, the political parties have moved away from the median voter on abortion in an effort to attract the energies and financial support of interest group activists, frequently confronting moderate voters with strictly pro-choice and pro-life candidates. Right-to-life groups hold Republican candidates to strict pro-life pledges (Rozell and Wilcox 1996), and pro-choice groups hold Democratic candidates to strict pro-choice pledges.

The personal and partisan preferences of legislators may interfere with the linkage between public opinion and abortion policy. Because several religious groups (most notably evangelical Protestants and Catholics) condemn abortion, many legislators have strong personal views on the issue that may conflict with those of their constituents. Indeed, political elites are far more divided on abortion than are the mass public and take more extreme positions (Jackson and Clayton 1996). Although party elites are generally more ideologically extreme than their electorates (Erikson, Wright, and McIver 1993), the gap is truly large on abortion policy. This might indicate that party control of state government will be a far better predictor of abortion policy than state opinion. States with Republican majorities in the legislature may enact generally strict sets of abortion requirements, and states with Democratic majorities may protect abortion rights, regardless of general public opinion.

Moreover, because aggregate and individual opinion on abortion is relatively static, there is less opportunity for state legislatures to respond to shifting opinion. Although there is some evidence that abortion opinion has shifted in the aggregate at the national level (Franklin and Kosaki 1989; Cook, Jelen, and Wilcox 1992), these changes have been quite modest. Yet it may be that the *Webster* decision changed the dynamics of opinion representation in state legislatures without making a major impact on opinion. After *Webster*, pro-choice activists became much more active, providing greater equality in the interest group environment. The impact of public opinion on state abortion policy is therefore a somewhat controversial issue theoretically, one ripe for exploration.

Gauging State Opinion

Researchers attempting to measure state abortion opinion have relied on proxy measures such as state National Abortion Rights Action League (NARAL) membership or the percentage of residents who are Catholic or evangelical Christians (Berkman and O'Connor 1993). These are reasonable operational definitions in the absence of actual measures of opinion (Haider-Markel and Meier 1996), but more direct measures of opinion are clearly preferable.[1] Moreover, NARAL and church membership may tap the importance of organized interests rather than state opinion per se. Others have relied on measures of state ideology and abortion opinions pooled from national samples (Hansen 1993). Ideological orientation, however, does not necessarily match abortion opinion, and pooled national samples do not guarantee accurate state measures.

Other studies use data from the 1990 Voter Research and Surveys Exit Polls, which asked voters in forty-two states their opinion on abortion (Cohen and Barrilleaux 1993; Cook, Jelen, and Wilcox 1993; Goggin and Kim 1992; Goggin and Wlezien 1993). These extensive state samples provide more accurate measures of state opinion than do the proxy measures, but they include only voters. Turnout rates in off-year elections vary systematically according to political culture and the presence of statewide gubernatorial or senate elections, so in some states these surveys represent a higher portion of the population than in others. Moreover, it is possible that in relatively low-turnout elections, people with more extreme views on abortion are more likely to vote. Finally, the states in the 1990 exit polls do not include Utah and Louisiana, the two states that have passed the most restrictive legislation.

To develop a more broad-based and direct measure of abortion attitudes, we use the 1988, 1990, and 1992 Senate National Election Study (SNES) surveys. Unlike most National Election Study surveys and most academic and commercial polls, the SNES contains representative samples from each state rather than the nation as a whole. By using the pooled 1988, 1990, and 1992 Senate surveys, we were able to aggregate sufficient cases to obtain a reliable measure of state public opinion on abortion. Moreover, the SNES has questions on more than one abortion policy area, making it ideal to study opinion policy congruence in detail.

The Senate election series contains three questions on abortion. The general abortion question asks, "Do you think abortion should be legal under all circumstances, only legal under certain circumstances, or never legal under any circumstance?" The funding question inquires, "Would you favor or oppose a law in your state that would allow the use of government funds to help pay for the costs of abortion for women who cannot afford them?" A follow-up question ascertains whether these opinions were strongly or not so strongly felt. Finally, the parental consent question asks, "Would you favor or oppose a state law that would require parental consent before a teenager under 18 could have an abortion?" This question also is followed up by a strength question. The funding and parental consent questions were not asked in the 1988 survey, but the abortion question was asked in all three years.

Because the small number of cases per state raises some concerns about reliability, O'Brien's (1990) generalizability coefficient was calculated for each of the abortion questions.[2] O'Brien's coefficient indicates the reliability of estimating a characteristic of a group, in this case state public opinion, based on the responses of a sample of group members, in this case the survey respondents. The generalizability coefficient when using mean responses from state respondents to represent general abortion positions is .87, demonstrating very high reliability. The coefficients for the other two abortion questions are .62 for parental consent and .76 for government funding. Both values indicate good reliability.[3] Table 9.1 shows considerable variation in the percentage of residents in each state holding liberal abortion opinions: supporting abortions under all circumstances, strongly favoring government funding of abortions for the poor, and strongly opposing parental consent for abortions for minors.

These three abortion attitudes are interrelated but not identical. Opinions are the most liberal on the general abortion question and most conservative on parental consent. Mean state positions for these abortion opinions find the strongest correlation between the general abortion attitude and government funding of abortion ($r = .83**$). Opinions on parental consent are least similar to the other two, with the correlations with general opinion at $-.50**$ and with funding at $-.57**$ (parental consent is coded in the opposite direction as the other two questions). With these separate indicators of different elements of the abortion controversy, we can test whether policies on specific aspects of abortion match opinion in these same areas or whether legislation reflects the public's more general abortion attitudes.

TABLE 9.1   STATE-LEVEL PUBLIC OPINION ON ABORTION

STATE	ALL CASES	GOVERNMENT FUNDING	PARENTAL CONSENT	n^a
Kentucky	14.5	16.5	26.8	127–193
Missisisppi	15.6	26.0	23.5	100–179
West Virginia	15.6	21.6	19.3	148–205
Arkansas	16.9	26.0	10.5	104–166
North Dakota	18.5	16.8	14.0	95–168
Louisiana	19.5	18.8	15.9	126–169
Tennessee	22.4	19.7	13.7	137–201
Kansas	23.4	15.8	14.0	120–192
Utah	24.1	17.5	9.3	97–162
Missouri	24.2	17.5	12.5	96–161
Wisconsin	24.4	18.4	10.1	98–160
Alabama	24.6	16.9	23.3	129–191
Wyoming	25.0	18.1	12.3	127–196
Pennsylvania	25.2	21.5	11.7	93–155
South Carolina	25.8	20.2	15.6	118–182
Georgia	26.3	20.6	15.6	96–167
South Dakota	26.7	12.2	13.4	119–195
North Carolina	27.2	19.4	17.4	132–202
Nebraska	27.8	18.3	17.3	109–180
Idaho	28.0	19.0	8.0	137–207
Texas	28.2	20.7	15.0	120–170

TABLE 9.1 (CONTINUED)

STATE	ALL CASES	GOVERNMENT FUNDING	PARENTAL CONSENT	n^a
Ohio	28.8	19.8	14.6	86–163
Oklahoma	29.3	18.9	15.7	140–208
Michigan	30.4	30.4	18.9	132–194
Iowa	30.9	20.6	21.3	141–188
Indiana	31.6	25.0	13.2	112–187
Minnesota	32.8	21.0	23.1	119–195
Florida	33.5	25.8	18.6	97–155
Virginia	33.6	21.7	19.5	82–146
New Mexico	34.1	24.6	19.2	118–176
Illinois	35.9	29.2	17.7	120–170
Maryland	36.3	39.8	22.9	105–157
Montana	36.8	24.2	13.7	124–182
Hawaii	37.4	34.8	19.1	115–147
Delaware	38.3	21.6	20.0	120–188
Massachusetts	39.8	25.6	22.7	128–171
Rhode Island	40.2	33.3	20.9	115–164
Maine	40.4	25.6	25.2	121–208
Connecticut	41.3	37.6	23.8	101–160
Alaska	41.8	32.4	23.6	108–184
Washington	42.2	41.1	25.8	93–154
Nevada	42.6	32.2	12.9	115–169
Oregon	43.2	27.9	30.5	111–183
New York	43.7	38.1	23.5	97–142
California	43.9	34.1	14.9	134–180
Colorado	44.9	28.7	23.5	136–196
New Jersey	45.6	33.1	22.5	118–160
New Hampshire	47.3	34.4	23.3	120–169
Vermont	47.4	34.0	26.0	97–152
Arizona	47.8	31.5	15.4	104–161
Low	14.5	12.2	8.0	82–142
High	47.8	41.1	30.5	150–208
Mean	32.1	25.0	18.3	116–176
Standard deviation	9.4	7.2	5.2	

Source: Miller et al. 1993.

Note: Data are percentages of respondents favoring abortions in all cases, strongly favoring government funding of abortions for the poor, and strongly opposing parental consent requirements for minors seeking abortions, 1988 to 1992.

a. Range of numbers of respondents per state. The government funding and parental consent questions were asked only in 1990 and 1992.

State Abortion Policies

Previous studies relating state public opinion to state policies use a variety of indicators of abortion policy. Some focus on calls by states for a constitutional convention to ban abortions (Cohen and Barrilleaux 1993), although most of this action took place soon after *Roe*. Others investigate state funding of abortions for poor women (Berkman and O'Connor 1993; Hansen 1993; Meier and McFarlane 1993) or parental consent and notification laws (Berkman and O'Connor 1993). Still other scholars construct indices that span a range of abortion policies (Halva-Neubauer 1993; Hansen 1993; Goggin and Wlezien 1993).

In this chapter, we use both single and combined indicators of state abortion policy. Table 9.2 lists a variety of abortion laws that were on the books in the U.S. states in 1992. A plurality of states (1) has some regulations of abortions for minors, (2) allows the use of government funds for abortions only to

TABLE 9.2   STATE POLICIES ON ABORTION

	NUMBER OF STATES	
	Total	Enforced
Regulation of abortion for minors		
Written consent of parent(s)	8	1
Written consent or judicial bypass	12	9
Parental notification	4	3
Parental notification or bypass	9	4
Counseling of minor	3	0
No law	14	
Government funding of abortions		
Only to save woman's life	30	
For some other exceptions	8	
For most abortions	12	
Spousal notification or consent		
Spousal consent	3	
Spousal notification	7	
No law	40	
Required waiting periods and counseling		
Waiting periods of 24–48 hours	11	
Counseling	14	
No law	25	
Ban on most or all postviability abortions		
Bans	35	
No law	15	
Current or future bans on abortion		
Current (unconstitutional) bans	2	
Law promising bans when legal	3	
Law promising fullest regulation	6	
No law	39	
Pro-choice legislation banning clinic harassment or promising to keep abortions legal		
Pro-choice legislation	7	
No law	43	

Source: NARAL 1992.

save the woman's life, (3) has no laws on spousal notification, (4) bans most postviability abortions, (5) has no laws promising future bans on abortion, and (6) has no laws guaranteeing access to abortions. States are evenly divided on requiring waiting periods or counseling (NARAL 1992).[4]

To investigate the impact of public opinion on public policy, we examine three types of relationships. We analyze the relationship between general abortion attitudes and each of these policies. We also examine the relationship between specific opinions and regulation of abortions for minors and government funding of abortions for poor women. Finally, we study the relationship between general abortion attitudes and a combined abortion policy scale.

A general abortion policy index was created by combining the seven types of abortion laws listed in Table 9.2. Standardized scales were calculated for each of the seven policy variables, and scores on these scales were summed and divided by 7 to develop the final policy scale. Cronbach's alpha for this scale is .62. Low scores on this abortion policy index indicate conservative (pro-life) policies, and high scores indicate liberal (pro-choice) policies. Our measure is highly correlated with Halva-Neubauer's (1993) index of abortion regulations (.72**) and moderately correlated with state actions calling for a constitutional convention to pass a human life amendment (.46*).

The Abortion Policy Environment

The simplest model of opinion representation in public policy has state legislators, using the directed delegate role, accurately perceiving constituency opinion and enacting laws reflecting these public values, perhaps because they fear electoral defeat. The linkage between public opinion and policy outputs by a state legislature may be mediated by two types of variables. First, interest group activity may influence legislators' votes. Opinions expressed through organized interest group activities, including those of various religious bodies, may shape lawmakers' judgments on the preferences of their constituencies. Moreover, interest groups represent the attentive public, which may be more important in electoral politics than the more moderate middle. Second, the types of individuals who serve in a legislature may influence policy outputs. Representation may come through shared values between legislators and constituents along party lines (Miller and Stokes 1963). The growing party divide on abortion suggests that legislatures dominated by a single party may produce policy that is not entirely consistent with public preferences. Moreover, research has found that the number of women representatives in a legislature plays a key role in influencing abortion policy (Berkman and O'Connor 1993).

Although some attempts have been made to measure interest group activity at the state level (Lowery and Gray 1993), no available state-level data exist on lobbying or lobbyists on the abortion issue. Yet lobbyists are probably not as important on the abortion issue as sheer grassroots pressure from mail, phone calls, and other forms of direct contact with policymakers. As a proxy for pro-choice grassroots pressure, several scholars have used statewide membership in NARAL (Berkman and O'Connor 1993; Hansen 1993; Meier and MacFarlane 1993). The National Right-to-Life Committee has been less forthcoming in disclosing its statewide membership totals, so scholars have substituted the number of Catholics and evangelical Protestants within the state.

In this chapter, we introduce a new measure of state interest group activity. We identified the number of individuals in each state who contributed at least $200 to national or state pro-life or pro-choice political action committees and the amount of money these individuals contributed.[5] Individuals who contribute to abortion PACs are presumably the most likely to write letters to policymakers and to otherwise apply grassroots pressure.[6] We use the number of individual contributors from each state as our measure of interest group activity, adjusted for state population.[7] A single interest group measure for each state was made by subtracting the pro-life interest group measure from the pro-choice interest indicator to create a new scale measuring the net advantage (or disadvantage) of liberal (pro-choice) groups over conservative (pro-life) groups.

A large Catholic presence in a state may represent an organized interest group effort or may influence legislators' perceptions of their constituents' opinions. State percentages of Catholic adherents are taken from *Churches and Church Membership in the United States, 1980* (Quinn et al. 1982). Partisan control of state offices is measured as (1) the average percentage of state legislative seats held by Democrats from 1980 to 1992[8] and (2) the number of years that Democrats controlled the governorship in that same time period. Gender representation in state legislatures is the percentage of upper and lower house seats held by women in 1991.

In addition to these variables that may influence the relationship between opinion and policymaking, we control for a variety of other factors that might influence abortion policy. Such controls are necessary to limit the possibility of finding spurious correlations. General political liberalism for state residents or in state policy overall also may determine state abortion policy. Although national legislators devote considerable effort to determining their constituents' views on specific policy matters such as abortion, state legislators may lack the resources, and in some states even the incentive, to devote to such effort. Yet state legislators may well have a general idea of the ideological orientations of their constituents and respond to the general ideology of their state rather than to citizen views on abortion. Data on public ideology is taken from the 1988–92 SNES surveys in the same manner as the abortion attitudes. A high score indicates that a state has a more conservative public. States differ in their policy culture, with some states consistently adopting conservative or liberal policies. To control for this policy culture we include Klingman and Lammers's (1984) measure of liberal public policies.[9]

We also controlled for demographic characteristics that influence abortion opinion at the individual level: per capita income, urbanization, education (percent of college graduates), party identification (from the SNES), normal vote, interparty competition, political culture (Sharkansky 1969), and southern residence. In addition, we controlled for the percentage of state populations who are members of a variety of religious denominations (evangelical, Pentecostal, fundamentalist Baptist, Mormon, and Jewish) and various combinations of these religious denominations (e.g., conservative Protestants). None of these controls added significantly to the R^2s of the regression models or affected the basic results presented later, so we do not include them in the final models. In part, several of these alternative independent variables, such as fundamentalist religions and political culture, coincide with a north-south division of the states. This regional aspect is already incorporated in our model through the variables measuring public and state policy ideology.

The Determinants of State Abortion Policies

The effect of abortion opinions and these policy environment variables are explored in Table 9.3 (p. 154), which reports the results of separate OLS regressions for the composite abortion index and for parental consent and public funding.[10] The first column under each policy shows a model with all variables included. In these full models, the effects of abortion opinion and interest group support are not statistically significant. This is so because the interest group measure is highly correlated with each of the opinion measures ($r = -.64^{**}$ for general abortion opinion, $-.74^{**}$ for government funding, and $.53^{**}$ for parental consent). In the abortion policy arena, legislators are receiving similar messages from interest groups and the public. To judge whether either avenue is more effective at communicating public sentiments, we estimated separate models using abortion opinion first and then interest group measures. For the two specific abortion policies, we also added a third equation testing the significance of specific attitudes on this policy versus a more generalized abortion opinion. In these models, we include only variables that are statistically significant. These results appear in the subsequent columns under each of the policy categories.

The two models for the composite abortion index show that state legislators are influenced by opinion and interest group support. A similar result holds for public funding of abortions: specific opinion on this issue coincides with

TABLE 9.3 COMPETING MODELS EXPLAINING LIBERAL STATE POLICIES ON ABORTION

	COMPOSITE ABORTION POLICY INDEX			NO PARENTAL CONSENT LAW				GOVERNMENT FUNDING OF ABORTIONS			
	Full	General Opinion	Interest Group	Full	Specific Opinion	General Opinion	Interest Group	Full	Specific Opinion	General Opinion	Interest Group
General opinion	-0.64 (0.39)	-0.81* (0.32)				-2.94* (1.36)		-0.32 (0.52)		-0.76[a] (0.43)	
Specific opinion				1.43 (1.40)	0.62 (1.18)				-0.74* (0.34)		
Interest group	0.11 (0.07)		0.14* (0.06)	0.60* (0.26)			0.56* (0.23)	0.11 (0.12)			0.18* (0.08)
Catholic	-0.02** (0.01)	-0.02** (0.01)	-0.02** (0.01)	-0.02 (0.03)				-0.02* (0.01)	-0.02* (0.01)	-0.02* (0.01)	-0.02* (0.01)
Democratic legislature	0.01** (0.00)	0.02** (0.00)	0.01** (0.00)	0.03 (0.02)				0.02* (0.01)	0.01* (0.01)	0.02* (0.01)	0.01* (0.01)
Democratic governor	-0.01 (0.02)			-0.09 (0.08)				-0.02 (0.03)			
Women legislators	0.03* (0.01)	0.02* (0.01)	0.03** (0.01)	0.12** (0.04)	0.09* (0.04)	0.06 (0.04)	0.09* (0.03)	0.02 (0.02)			
Liberal state policies	0.33** (0.10)	0.35** (0.09)	0.31** (0.10)	0.80[a] (0.42)	0.60[a] (0.35)	0.55 (0.33)	0.51 (0.33)	0.63** (0.16)	0.65** (0.15)	0.68** (0.15)	0.63** (0.15)
Conservative public	0.57 (0.44)			4.68** (1.73)	3.83* (1.53)	5.18** (1.59)	5.09** (1.53)	0.13 (0.71)			
R^2	0.54**	0.51**	0.50**	0.32**	0.18[a]	0.25**	0.27**	0.48**	0.45**	0.43**	0.45**
Adjusted R^2	.46**	0.45**	0.44**	0.18**	0.11[a]	0.19**	0.21**	0.38**	0.40**	0.38**	0.40**

Notes: Entries are unstandardized regression coefficients from OLS regression and, inside parentheses, standard errors.

** = significant at 0.01.

* = significant at 0.05.

a. = significant at 0.10.

$N = 50$.

Opinion for general abortion (high = conservative); for parental consent (high = liberal); for abortion funding (high = conservative).

general abortion opinions, and both match interest group support and influence public policies. For policies covering parental consent for abortions performed on minors, however, specific opinion has no influence on public policy in this area. In contrast, interest group strength and general abortion opinion do influence state policy. Precisely why specific opinion on parental consent should not influence state policy in this area is not clear. It may be that state legislators find it difficult to determine attitudes on specific abortion policies and respond to more general abortion opinion. Although majorities or pluralities in most states generally favor allowing adult women to receive abortions, majorities also support parental notification and consent, and, thus, on this issue, general opinion and specific opinion clash.

Beyond the influence of public opinion, the composite index model shows that abortion policies in the fifty U.S. states are influenced by the dominant policy culture. States that have historically enacted liberal policies also pass liberal abortion policies, as demonstrated by the significant coefficient for the past policy variable. In addition, Democratic legislatures are significantly more likely than Republican-dominated legislatures to pass liberal abortion policies once the conservative orientations of southern legislatures are accounted for in other areas of public policy. Thus, general political factors such as party control of political institutions and policy culture are important predictors of state abortion policies. Dynamics specific to the abortion question, nevertheless, also contribute to the development of state abortion statutes. The presence of a large Catholic population results in more conservative abortion policies, and a large number of women legislators results in more liberal abortion policies. While we are able to explain half of the variation in general abortion policies, some states are outliers in the composite index model. We are least able to explain policies in Colorado, Montana, and Maine, which have more conservative abortion policies than expected, and in New Jersey and Connecticut, which have more liberal policies than the model predicts. (These five states have standardized residuals greater than 1.5.)

The explanation of state policies on public funding of abortions closely matches that of the composite index model. A liberal tradition of policies in other areas and a Democratic legislature produce liberal policies on abortion funding. The presence in a state of a large number of Catholics once again leads to more conservative policies. Indeed, the models are quite similar, except that larger numbers of women legislators do not increase the probability that a state will adopt public funding. Once again, Colorado is a state with significantly more conservative policies than expected, as is Michigan. North Carolina, West Virginia, Vermont, and Alaska have policies more liberal than the model would predict.

The models explaining parental consent requirements for minors seeking abortions are the least satisfying. The amount of variance explained is only 50 percent of that found for the other two policy areas, and the 20 percent of variance explained is quite low for a U.S. state policy model. Moreover, an important predictor variable—public ideology—has an unexpected sign, with states with generally more liberal public opinion having more conservative parental consent laws. We are not certain why the models have such a poor fit to the data, but parental consent is a policy that is generally popular with voters, so even traditionally liberal states may enact such a law. More conservative states have a range of policies to enact when attempting to regulate abortion, and some may satisfy conservative voters with waiting periods instead of parental consent. Alternatively, the influence of public opinion on parental consent laws may have been on the timing of the enactment of this fairly widely adopted law. It is important to note that even the parental consent model suggests that state legislators are responding directly to more generalized opinions on abortion, or indirectly through the support of interest groups. Finally, women legislators lend a liberal influence on parental consent measures. This time our model finds California and Alaska joining Colorado in having more conservative than expected laws, while Ohio, North Carolina, and New Jersey have more liberal parental consent laws than the model would predict. These outlier states might be the locus of future research to identify the political sources of state abortion laws.

Conclusion

Whether and how public opinion would influence abortion policies in the fifty U.S. states was an unanswered question, with arguments supporting and refuting claims that public opinion is likely to shape morality policies. Representation of public sentiment in public policy is a difficult task. If the public, interest groups, and the political parties send similar messages, representation is more likely. Yet mixed messages could also arise from these three sources. Our results suggest that public opinion and interest groups do influence abortion policy in the states. Although the number of cases prevents us from sorting out the independent effects of each, they are highly correlated, and both are strongly associated with state policy after controls for a variety of other variables.

On more specific aspects of abortion policy, the role of public opinion is less clear. In the area of public funding, abortion policy is strongly associated with both general abortion opinion and opinion on public funding. Yet on parental consent, only general abortion opinion matters. This may mean that state legislators do not perceive the subtle distinctions among various abortion policy preferences but merely reflect the general policy views of their constituents on the abortion issue. Public sentiment on abortion in general does match more closely preferences on government funding than on parental consent. The greater politicization of parental consent since 1992 may have increased state legislative awareness of this issue so that today opinion and policy on it may be more consistent. Since 1992, a number of states have passed parental notification and parental consent laws, and GOP candidates and Christian conservatives have begun to frame abortion debates around this popular policy. Additionally, it should be noted that efforts to pass parental notification and consent laws are attempts to redistribute values, and in other studies of this type of morality policymaking, mass opinion has not been shown to have a significant impact on policy (Mooney and Lee 1997). Not to be overlooked, however, is that we did find general abortion opinions to influence the two more specific abortion policies.

Although public opinion and interest group strength do influence state abortion policy, other factors also affect it. States with large Catholic populations are more likely to produce conservative abortion policies and are less likely to fund abortions. This is true even after controlling for the effects of Catholic opinion and Catholic support for pro-life groups. Interestingly, membership in other conservative denominations—including fundamentalist and Pentecostal churches—does not predict more conservative policy. It may be that the hierarchical Roman Catholic Church is better able to muster its political resources than in the more fragmented community of orthodox Protestants. It may also be that Catholics are simply more numerous in states with liberal abortion opinion overall, while fundamentalist Protestants are more numerous in the more conservative South. Thus, Catholicism is not as highly correlated with state opinion and is therefore statistically distinguishable from mass sentiment. Holding constant opinion and interest group activity, Democratic legislatures produce more liberal policy on general abortion restrictions and on government funding. Legislatures with more women members produce more liberal abortion policy and are more likely to resist passing parental consent laws. This suggests that elite opinion as well as public opinion is an important predictor of abortion policy adoption.

In the opening sections of this chapter, several conditions that could enhance or decrease the influence of public opinion on morality policies were discussed. The abortion case is clearly one for which public opinion plays an important role. The stability and clarity of public preferences and the reflection of these preferences in grassroots interest group activity provide two avenues for state legislators to perform a representative role in abortion politics. Representation also can be sought through party politics, since the parties have staked out clear alternatives and partisan control of state legislatures is linked with abortion policies. Although public opinion, interest group activity, and partisan control account for abortion policies, several states are significant outliers. Future research might focus on those states in which policy does *not* match opinion as well, both on abortion and in other policy areas. It may be that careful consideration of these deviant cases will help us further develop our theories of morality policymaking.

Notes

1. NARAL membership is a measure of mobilization, not of state opinion. Norrander and Wilcox (1993) showed that interest group mobilization stimulates countermobilization, so NARAL membership may be higher in some conservative states than in other more moderate ones. Cook, Jelen, and Wilcox (1993) report that Catholics are more opposed to abortion in majority Protestant states than in majority Catholic states.

2. The O'Brien (1990) generalizability coefficient is affected by the sample size in each unit (here states) and the variation within each unit versus the variation across units (Jones and Norrander 1996). The O'Brien measure is similar to the approach used by Erikson, Wright, and McIver (1993). The highest reliability would be obtained with large state sample sizes, small variances within states, and considerable variation in means across states. Changes in public attitudes across the three pooled cross sections would decrease the reliability of an aggregated public opinion measure by increasing the variation within states. The reliability for the general abortion attitude measure is somewhat depressed by a national trend of slightly increasing liberal responses to this question (mean response in 1988 = 2.7, 1990 = 2.6, 1992 = 2.5, F = 11.63, significance $\le$ .01). Attitudes did not differ between the two cross sections containing questions on parental consent (F = 0.99, significance = .32) and public funding of abortions (F = 1.86, significance = .17).

3. With only 82 to 208 cases per state, sampling error may be a concern, but state values have predictive criterion validity. For the forty-two states that overlap between the 1990 Voter Research and Survey exit polls and the SNES, the correlations on the general abortion questions is .82**. Similarly, the correlation between state means from the SNES and census data on percentages of residents with college diplomas is .92**.

4. Of course, states vary within these categories as well. Informed consent laws vary in the amount and type of information that must be conveyed, from written informed consent to a waiting period after lectures about fetal development replete with photographs. Similarly, although most scholars who have examined Medicaid funding of abortions have coded states into a few categories, in fact states vary in the circumstances in which they fund abortions.

5. These data come from the Federal Election Commission (FEC) and cover the period from January 1989 through March 1992. A $200 contribution is the minimum level that the FEC will report for individual contributions.

6. Brown, Powell, and Wilcox (1995) show that individuals who are solicited by direct mail are very likely to write to policymakers, and nearly all abortion PACs solicit their funds through direct mail.

7. A measure based on total PAC money correlates with state abortion policy at the same level as the measure based on number of contributors.

8. The national mean of 60.38 percent Democratic legislators was assigned to Nebraska's nonpartisan legislature.
9. The Klingman and Lammers (1984) measure of state policy liberalism is quite similar to the Erikson, Wright, and McIver (1993) measure. Both measures contain some of the same policies, and the two measures correlate at .91**. We use the Klingman and Lammers measure because it is available for all fifty states, while the Erikson, Wright, and McIver measure excludes Alaska and Hawaii.
10. We choose to model abortion policy as dependent on public opinion rather than to estimate a reciprocal model for several reasons. First, although research has shown that aggregate opinion is somewhat responsive to abortion policy (Franklin and Kosaki 1989), abortion opinion is incredibly stable at both the aggregate and individual levels. Second, research has shown that policy is generally far more responsive to opinion than opinion is to policy (Stimson, Mac-Kuen, and Erikson 1995).

CHAPTER TEN

Variations in the Diffusion of State Lottery Adoptions: How Revenue Dedication Changes Morality Politics

Patrick A. Pierce and Donald E. Miller

RESEARCH ON MORALITY POLICY has generally focused on the politics of its adoption (see Meier 1994 for an exception in looking at implementation) and has used theory drawn from the diffusion of innovations to explain the pattern of policy adoption (Rogers 1983). Katz, Levin, and Hamilton (1963) note that a central theoretical issue in the study of diffusion of innovations is the nature of the "item" that is diffusing across space and time. "It is the problem of how to classify items so that the results obtained are generalizable to other items. . . . Unless some scheme of classification exists . . . each study simply becomes a discrete case which cannot be generalized" (p. 243; see also Walker 1973 on the same point). The converse of this difficulty is equally damaging. An overly broad scheme of classification will result in generalizing to cases to which the results *do not apply*. Morality policy has too often been considered a coherent and distinctive set of policies that would diffuse across the states according to one particular model. This study takes issue with that assumption and demonstrates that important differences exist in policy diffusion even for seemingly similar morality policies—different types of state lotteries—that can be explained by using the issue typology of symbolic politics. Furthermore, we argue that the symbolic politics literature can help better define the nature of morality policy, enabling researchers to develop studies that can be generalized validly to other cases.

The Politics of State Lotteries

Researchers have explored fairly comprehensive models to explain the adoption of state lotteries (Berry and Berry 1990, 1992; Winn and Whicker 1989–90; Filer, Moak, and Uze 1988). Briefly, the process has been modeled as the diffusion of an innovation (Canon and Baum 1981; Clark 1985; Crain 1966; Menzel and Feller 1977; Feller and Menzel 1978; Foster 1978; Glick and Hays 1991; Sigelman, Roeder, and Sigelman 1981) affected by (1) the motivation to innovate and (2) the availability of resources for overcoming obstacles (Berry and Berry 1990, 399; Frant, Berry, and Berry 1991; cf. Mohr 1969). For example, poor fiscal health provides motivation to opt for a lottery to raise revenue, and neighboring states running a state lottery provide a resource of information that may overcome the resistance to a lottery created by the existence of sizable numbers of religious fundamentalists.

Existing studies, however, fail to consider the possibility that the politics of lottery adoption varies with the *purposes* for which the lottery's revenue will be used. The two most prevalent uses of lottery funds are for the state's general fund and for education. As of 1990, twelve states had dedicated all or part of their lottery revenue to fund education, and twelve states had funneled their lottery revenue into their general funds (NASPL n.d.) (see Table 10.1, p. 162). If different types of innovations or policies face different obstacles and experience different levels of participation and conflict, lotteries dedicated to different purposes may generate different politics (Lowi 1972; Hayes 1978; Wilson 1973; Greenberg et al. 1977). This perspective is drawn from Lowi's thesis (1972) that policy affects politics; that is, characteristics of the policy will affect who participates and how they participate in the process. Lowi's perspective would lead us to hypothesize that lotteries for education and lotteries for the general fund might generate different types of politics: factors that make lottery adoption more likely should be expected to differ for these two types of lotteries.

In the case of lottery adoption, the cause of these differences may well lie in the *process* of agenda setting and policy legitimation and the role of issue or policy entrepreneurs (Mintrom 1997; Baumgartner and Jones 1993; King 1988; Kingdon 1984; Schneider and Teske with Mintrom 1995; Kelman 1987). Mintrom (1997, 739) characterizes policy entrepreneurs as strategic political actors who engage in "identifying problems, networking in policy circles, shaping the terms of policy debates, and building coalitions." These activities are central to the politics of the policy process. For the purposes of morality policy, the first and third activities—problem identification and issue definition—are particularly important. Policy networking and coalition building are more characteristic of interest group politics than of morality politics (Haider-Markel and Meier 1996).

TABLE 10.1 EDUCATION AND GENERAL-FUND LOTTERY ADOPTIONS

STATE	YEAR OF ADOPTION	PURPOSE	METHOD OF ADOPTION
Arizona	1981	General fund	Initiative
California	1984	Education	Initiative
Connecticut	1972	General fund	Legislation
Delaware	1975	General fund	Legislation
Florida	1986	Education	Referendum
Idaho	1986	Education	Referendum
Illinois	1974	Education	Legislation
Iowa	1985	General fund	Referendum
Maine	1974	General fund	Referendum
Maryland	1973	General fund	Referendum
Michigan	1972	Education	Referendum
Minnesota	1990	General fund	Referendum
Missouri	1984	Education	Referendum
Montana	1986	Education	Referendum
New Hampshire	1964	Education	Legislation
New Jersey	1971	Education	Referendum
New York	1967	Education	Referendum
Ohio	1974	Education	Legislation
Rhode Island	1974	General fund	Referendum
South Dakota	1986	General fund	Referendum
Vermont	1978	General fund	Referendum
Virginia	1987	General fund	Referendum
Washington	1982	General fund	Legislation
West Virginia	1984	Education	Referendum

Policy entrepreneurs will use problem definition and issue definition as related tactics in their strategic plan to advocate a particular policy (Mintrom 1997). Policy entrepreneurs seeking to place the lottery on the state agenda have uniformly identified the problem as insufficient revenue. General-fund lotteries are proposed as a response to a *general* need for revenue, whereas education lotteries are defined as a response to a need for *specified* revenue to fund education. As policy entrepreneurs attempt to use "need" or, similarly, "crisis" as a justification for placing an issue on the agenda, they seek to define the issue in ways that expand and contract the scope of conflict to their advantage once the issue is on the agenda (Cobb and Elder 1983a, 1983b; Mintrom 1997; Kingdon 1984; Schattschneider 1960). Issue definition of morality policy typically centers around the use of symbols to expand the scope of conflict. Symbols are words, pictures, sounds, and other stimuli that evoke an emotional response (Edelman 1967; Cobb and Elder 1983a, 1983b). Unlike more detailed presentations of issues, symbols require little or no political sophistication to generate a response. Given the abundant evidence of minimal political sophistication among the mass public (Converse 1964, 1975; Zaller 1992; Kinder and Sears 1985; Luskin 1987;

Bennett 1989; Delli Carpini and Keeter 1996), strategic policy entrepreneurs will use symbols to expand public involvement in the scope of conflict (see the similar discussion of easy issues in Carmines and Stimson 1980, 1989).

Different issues will, however, present opportunities to use different problem definitions and symbols. In the case of state lotteries, different purposes of the lottery will structure the availability of symbols to policy entrepreneurs. If the purpose of the revenue is left unspecified and indeterminate (the general fund), there is less opportunity for advocates of the lottery to generate a powerful symbolic response to the symbol of "sinful" gambling that opponents might raise. Thus, we expect general-fund lottery adoptions to be sensitive to the symbolic politics connected with pietistic or fundamentalist antigambling sentiment (Mooney and Lee 1996).

On the other hand, education lottery proponents could employ a symbol of their own ("the education of our children") to *counter* the moralistic symbol of sinful gambling. Edelman (1967) notes that the use of such symbols is particularly effective when the symbol itself is threatened. In this case, using education as a symbol would be most effective if the public widely believed that children's education were in danger. In that case, appeals to education would be plausible and powerful. Therefore, educational need would affect *both* problem identification *and* the use of symbolic politics. In the case of general-fund lotteries, no specific positive competing values can plausibly be brought to bear. Although spending for education can be related to potent symbols—"our children's future"—more government spending and even tax cuts are far more amorphous and therefore do not allow for the use of similarly powerful symbols.

We therefore hypothesize that the factors affecting lottery adoption will differ significantly for the two types of lotteries. General-fund lottery adoptions will be related to the existence of more sizable fundamentalist populations, but fundamentalists will not exercise a similar influence on education lottery adoptions. General-fund lotteries will diffuse among the states in ways that are structured by a single symbol (the sinfulness of gambling). However, education lotteries diffuse throughout the states according to the availability of the competing symbol of educational need for revenue. Inadequate education spending makes the symbol of children's education available to issue entrepreneurs. These entrepreneurs can then use the symbol to promote the lottery, making its adoption more likely, thus defeating the fundamentalist opposition (Cobb and Elder 1983a; Mintrom 1997).

Data

This study follows Berry and Berry (1990) in employing an event history analysis model (Allison 1984). We are thus attempting to explain the adoption of a state lottery by any state in the risk set (i.e., those states that have not yet adopted a lottery).[1] We basically employ the same independent variables to explain lottery adoption as those used by Berry and Berry (1990) plus some used by Winn and Whicker (1989–90). These variables indicate the fiscal health of the state (state revenue, expenditures, and debt) and its citizens (personal income and taxes),[2] the nature of party control of the state (Democratic Party strength of control and extent of control regardless of party), the timing of the electoral cycle, and the adoption of a lottery by neighboring states. We refer the reader to these studies for the theoretical justification of each of these variables. As with other studies, spatial diffusion of the policy is indicated by the relationship between the number of neighboring states with a lottery and the state's adoption of a lottery (see Mooney and Lee 1995 for a discussion of this approach). However, we will also test for the possibility suggested by Mooney (1997) that the hazard rate for adoption is not constant across time. To that end, annual dummies will be employed.

Our central hypothesis concerns the differential effect of citizens' religious fundamentalism. We hypothesize that fundamentalism will be a significant factor affecting general-fund lottery adoption when there is no compelling competing symbol but will be insignificant in affecting education lottery adoption as a result of the availability of the competing symbol "children's education."

Results

The purpose of this chapter is to reveal differences in the politics of different types of lotteries. Hence, we apply the same model to explain the adoption of a lottery for education and adoption of a lottery to add revenue to the state's general fund. The results are displayed in Table 10.2.[3] See appendix (p. 168) for definition of the variables and how they were measured.

First, we may note the general failure of any of the variables in our model to have a significant impact on the adoption of education lotteries. Although general-fund lotteries diffuse spatially (note coefficient for Neighbor) and are more likely to be adopted in states with higher levels of personal income, neither of these variables has a statistically significant impact on education lottery adoption.

Our central hypothesis, however, concerns the differential impact of fundamentalists on general-fund and education lottery adoption. The results in Table 10.2 support that hypothesis. Religious fundamentalism poses a significant hurdle to adopting a general fund lottery (t ratio = -2.051, $p < .03$, one-tailed test) but has an insignificant impact on education lottery adoption (t ratio = -1.545, $p < .10$, one-tailed test).

We may also note that the model fits general-fund lotteries much better than it does education lotteries. As a result of the highly skewed distribution of the dependent variable, a chi-square statistic is the best measure for goodness of fit (Hagle and Mitchell 1992). Whereas the chi-square for the model for gen-

TABLE 10.2 MODEL PARAMETERS FOR GENERAL-FUND AND EDUCATION LOTTERY ADOPTIONS, 1966–90

Independent Variable	GENERAL-FUND LOTTERIES Coefficient (t ratio)	EDUCATION LOTTERIES Coefficient (t ratio)
Neighbor	0.22246	0.14139
	(2.09)	(1.36)
Electyr	0.18404	0.39091
	(0.62)	(1.44)
Fiscal	−0.01494	0.01872
	(−0.75)	(0.94)
Income	16183.8	12856.0
	(1.93)	(1.53)
Taxes	27581.7	−73523.0
	(0.25)	(−0.65)
Fundment	−0.07241	−0.02980
	(−2.05)	(−1.55)
Party	0.21131	0.00134
	(0.52)	(0.00)
Control	0.02810	−0.16121
	(0.20)	(1.16)
Intercept	−3.97510	−3.40041
	(−3.82)	(−3.30)
Model χ^2	29.97	17.38
	($p<.005$)	($p<.03$)
n	832	832

eral-fund lotteries is significant at $p < .005$, the chi-square for the education lotteries model is significant at $p < .03$.

The poorer fit of our model in explaining the adoption of lotteries to fund education is relevant to our central hypothesis. If we misspecify our model, we can draw inappropriate conclusions concerning the impact of fundamentalists in opposing education and general-fund lotteries. In general-fund lotteries, the revenue *need* being addressed by lottery revenue is a general need, hence Berry and Berry (1990) used a general measure of fiscal health. However, education lotteries purportedly fund education *specifically*; a more appropriate model would substitute education spending for general fiscal health. Table 10.3 (p. 166) presents the revised model for education lottery adoptions, using real education spending per capita rather than general fiscal health.

Although the coefficient for Educspend is not quite significantly related to education lottery adoption ($p < .10$, one-tailed test), its impact is clearly greater than the general measure of fiscal health. States with lower levels of real education spending per capita were somewhat more likely to adopt an education lot-

TABLE 10.3   MODEL PARAMETERS FOR EDUCATION LOTTERY
ADOPTIONS, INCLUDING EDUCATIONAL NEED

VARIABLE NAME	COEFFICIENT (t RATIO)
Neighbor	0.17307
	(1.57)
Electyr	0.38227
	(1.40)
Educspend	−140028
	(−1.43)
Income	17349.8
	(2.08)
Taxes	−21607.7
	(−0.18)
Fundment	−0.01848
	(−1.06)
Party	0.007809
	(0.02)
Control	−0.17892
	(−1.27)
Intercept	−3.33743
	(−3.31)
Model χ^2	18.64
	($p<.025$)
n	832

tery. The overall model had marginally better fit, but the real point is to test a more theoretically reasonable model of education lottery adoption to enhance the validity of our findings concerning religious fundamentalism.

Most important, therefore, the coefficient for Fundment remains insignificant. Indeed, its impact *declines* when placed in the more theoretically appropriate model of Table 10.3. The political importance of fundamentalists diminished when they faced opposition aroused by issue entrepreneurs calling for more revenue for education. Thus, our findings suggest that the prevalence of fundamentalists affected the likelihood of general-fund lottery adoption but not education lottery adoption.

Discussion

In this chapter, we explored the possibility that different types of lotteries would generate different types of politics. Consideration of a general-fund lottery seems to occasion politics somewhat similar to those for lotteries in general; however, education lotteries are quite different. Significant differences in the policy process exist for different types of lotteries. Studying lotteries in general and generalizing the findings to all types of lotteries is misleading. In at least this limited sense, Lowi's (1972) claim that the politics of a policy are affected by characteristics of that policy gains support. Education lotteries generate different politics than do general-fund lotteries. Seemingly minor changes in the substance of a morality policy (the lottery) can significantly change the impact of "moral" political forces (fundamentalists).

Our finding that fundamentalists significantly affected the likelihood of general-fund lottery adoption but not education lottery adoption raises a question for further research. If fundamentalists did not effectively oppose education lotteries, what forces were responsible? We suggest that there are two reasonable avenues to pursue.

First, the possibility of more complex symbolic politics in a lottery providing funds for education may parallel abortion politics for which competing sides can argue that "life" or "the right to choose" should be protected (Meier and McFarlane 1992). Issue entrepreneurs supporting an education lottery could claim that the "education of our children" rather than the "sinfulness of gambling" should frame the issue. However, general-fund lotteries seemingly involved only one symbol, the sinfulness of gambling. Hence, Meier's (1994, 4) association of morality policy with redistributive policy ("one segment of society attempts by government fiat to impose its values on the rest of society") may have applicability to general fund lotteries but not to education lotteries. As a result, education lottery adoptions might be affected by a different set of grassroots "moralistic" forces, responding to a competing symbol.

A second possibility is suggested by Haider-Markel and Meier (1996). Their study of gay and lesbian rights demonstrated that policies that are conventionally considered morality policies can generate *interest group politics* when issue salience is low. In this case, perhaps state education lobbies were mobilized to support education lotteries. Given the strength of education lobbies across the nation (Thomas and Hrebenar 1990), interest group support of education lotteries could plausibly explain fundamentalists' failure to stop education lotteries.

In conclusion, our study demonstrates the importance of understanding the substance of any policy being studied. Even as students of morality policy have emphasized its distinctiveness from "normal" policy, we need to appreciate the variation *within* the general category of morality policy. Morality policy differs from other forms of policy because values can stimulate symbolic politics with the attendant unusual levels of public involvement. However, different morality policies can involve different constellations of values. Identification of those values yields important insights into the nature of the politics of that policy.

Appendix: Measurement of Variables

Dependent Variable

Lottery adoptions (general-fund, and education): 0 = not adopted; 1 = adopted.

Independent Variables

Neighbor: Number of neighboring states with a lottery enacted in that year.

Electyr: 0 = not year of gubernatorial election; 1 = year of gubernatorial election.

Fundment: Percentage of population identified as belonging to a fundamentalist sect
(Source: Johnson et al. 1974; Quinn et al. 1982; Bradley et al. 1992). Fundamentalist percentages varied so minimally over the time period that they were treated as constants for each state. We checked the 1980 and 1990 data to validate this approach taken by Berry and Berry (1990). Data from 1980 were used.

Fiscal: [(Total state revenue − Total state expenditures)/Total state expenditures] * 100.
Revenue and expenditures in millions of dollars, adjusted by the implicit price deflator for personal consumption expenditures (1987 dollars) (Source: Council of State Governments, *Book of the States* [various years]; U.S. Bureau of the Census, *State Government Finances* [various years]; price deflator from *Economic Report of the President, 1994*).

Income: Personal income per capita, in millions of dollars, adjusted by the price deflator
(Source: Council of State Governments, *Book of the States* [various years]; U.S. Bureau of the Census, *State Government Tax Collections*; price deflator from *Economic Report of the President, 1994*).

Taxes: General and sales taxes per capita, in millions of dollars, adjusted by the price deflator
(Source: Council of State Governments, *Book of the States* [various years]; U.S. Bureau of the Census, *State Government Tax Collections*; price deflator from U.S. President, *Economic Report of the President Transmitted to Congress, 1994*).

Party: Office of governor and control of the upper and lower houses of the state legislature coded 0 for Republican control, 1 for Democratic control, and 0.5 for evenly divided. The sum is then divided by 3 to produce a 0 to 1 range.

Control: 2 * (abs[1.5 − (gov + sen + house)]) where gov, sen, and house are coded as in the previous item; range from 0 to 3.

Educspend: Total state spending for education, in millions of dollars per capita, adjusted by the price deflator (Source: Council of State Governments, *Book of the States* [various years]; U.S. Bureau of the Census, *State Government Tax Collections*; price deflator from U.S. President, *Economic Report of the President Transmitted to Congress, 1994*).

Notes

This study was supported by a grant to both authors from the Center for Academic Innovation at Saint Mary's College. The authors wish to acknowledge the assistance of Erin O'Neill and Beth Urban in data collection and data entry, respectively. We also benefited greatly from comments by Joe Stewart, Chris Mooney, and Neil Berch on previous drafts of this chapter.

1. New Hampshire, the first state to adopt a lottery, is excluded from the analysis. Event history analysis treats the initial incidence of the event as the beginning of a contagion. Thus, only states adopting *after* New Hampshire are susceptible to the contagion and amenable to analysis.
2. All fiscal measures are adjusted by the 1987 price deflator to take into account inflation over the period. We also use per capita measures of the income and tax variables. This practice is consistent with that of Berry and Berry (1990).
3. Analysis also indicated that spatial diffusion of each type of lottery was indiscriminate; that is, lotteries diffused from neighboring states regardless of the type of lottery they had passed. Hence, the variable indicating the number of neighbors with a lottery included neighbors with *any* type of lottery. Furthermore, the model for general-fund lottery adoption was tested from 1966 to 1990, similarly to the model for education lotteries. Although the first general-fund lottery (which might theoretically be the start of the "contagion") was passed in 1971, it could be argued that the initial lottery in 1965 began the "contagion." At that point, policymakers could easily consider applying the revenue to a variety of items in the budget, including the general fund. Empirically, the model fit better for the extended time period; analytically, comparisons between the two types of lotteries are easier and more valid if the same time frame is used. These results are available from the authors. Finally, contrary to Mooney (1997), we did not find evidence that the hazard rate varied significantly over time. We would note that we use a slightly different model and probit (Berry and Berry 1990) rather than logit analysis.

CHAPTER ELEVEN

The Temporal Diffusion of Morality Policy: The Case of Death Penalty Legislation in the American States

Christopher Z. Mooney and Mei-Hsien Lee

SHOULD A STATE be allowed to execute some of its criminals? Is the death penalty morally acceptable or, indeed, morally imperative under certain circumstances? These questions, along with questions regarding abortion, gambling, homosexual rights, pornography, and animal rights, are among the most controversial and prominent that have faced U.S. state legislatures in recent years. The common thread among these issues is that each has generated significant conflict over first principles; that is, each involves *morality policy* (Haider-Markel and Meier 1996; Tatalovich, Smith, and Bobic 1994; Smith 1975, 90–126; Mooney and Lee 1995). These are not the types of question with which state legislatures typically work, nor are these bodies well equipped to handle them. An important question for students of state policy is, what happens when state legislatures are faced with this unusual and significant type of issue, as they have been increasingly in the past thirty years?

In this chapter, we examine an important and well-researched manifestation of state policy decision making—the temporal diffusion of policy through the states—to understand the impact of basic moral conflict on that process. Copious empirical and theoretical work in this area provides clear expectations for the general pattern of state policy diffusion, based on a specific conception of how decisions are made in organizations generally (e.g., Walker 1969; Gray 1973; see Rogers 1995 for a review). However, it has been suggested that the characteristics of the policy being diffused may have a significant impact on the decision-making process involved and therefore on the patterns of diffusion that follow from that process (Walker 1973, 1189; Savage 1985; Gray 1973). This suggestion has yet to be considered thoroughly in the literature. We ask, does a policy diffuse in the usual way when it is as unusual as morality policy and what are the implications for our understanding of political decision making if it does not?

We hypothesize that the temporal diffusion of morality policy varies with the context of public opinion and the purity of the morality debate surrounding it. By examining state death penalty laws that vary on these characteristics, we show that the diffusion patterns of popular and unpopular morality policies can be very different from each other and from the usual diffusion pattern of nonmorality policy. We also show that if an unpopular morality issue can be "demoralized," that is, redefined so that it no longer exhibits the characteristics of morality policy, it diffuses like nonmorality policy. These findings indicate that political decision making for morality policy is distinctive from that typically used for nonmorality policy.

The Temporal Diffusion of Public Policy through the States

One of the most intriguing characteristics of U.S. public policy is its variability among the states. The question of why one state pursues one set of policies and another state pursues a different set of policies has long interested scholars and citizens alike, especially for the light it can shed on political decision-making processes and political values (e.g., Dye 1966, 1990; Walker 1969; Erikson, Wright, and McIver 1993; Mintrom 1997). An important facet of this variability is how it develops in the first place, that is, the patterns by which policy is adopted across the states over time.[1] An exploration of this process of temporal diffusion can tell us a great deal about political decision making in the states.

In trying to understand state policy diffusion, political scientists early on turned to the well-developed literature on the general diffusion of innovations in the disciplines of agricultural economics, communications, and sociology (see Rogers 1995 for a review). Drawing on insights from this literature, political scientists explained state policy diffusion as being the result of a social learning process, in which policymakers applied interstate analogies to the public problems they faced (Walker 1969; Gray 1973; Katz, Levin, and Hamilton 1963; Freeman 1985). Instead of synoptically evaluating the pros and cons of every option to solve a problem, state policymakers were said to look for shortcuts to rational decision making, and an important shortcut was the emulation of policies of other states facing similar problems. This explanation fit well with theories of bounded rationality and incrementalism that were prominent when the early state policy diffusion researchers were writing (Simon 1958; Lindblom 1959). The decision-making process they envisioned was one of political decisionmakers struggling to come to grips with technical and instrumental policy uncertainties under conditions of little information or broad public interest and heavy time pressures.

A clear pattern of temporal diffusion follows from this social learning model of decision making (Gray 1973). First, one or two pioneering states adopt a new policy while other states wait to see how it works there before passing judgment on it. As time passes, a few more relatively adventurous states adopt the policy, and, as its benefits become clear, more and more states adopt it with increasing frequency. Nonadopting states begin to feel pressure to adopt, as the policy "gain[s] a stamp of legitimacy" and is viewed as "something all states ought to have" (Walker 1969, 890). Finally, after the bulk of states adopt the policy in a relatively short time, the last few laggards adopt less frequently as the reluctance of these most resistant states gives way slowly.

These three phases—the slow initial set of a few adoptions, the short burst of many adoptions in the middle period, and the final, gradual mopping up of the laggards—yield a cumulative frequency distribution of adoptions across time that has the S shape of a typical social learning curve (Rogers 1995, 257–61). This pattern of temporal diffusion has been seen not only in a variety of state public policies (Gray 1973) but also in the diffusion of a wide range of innovations in various institutions (Rogers 1995, 260).

However, Gray (1973) provides evidence that perhaps not all state policies diffuse in this way. Why would we see variation in temporal diffusion patterns among state policies when the agricultural economics, communications, and sociology literatures are replete with studies of adoptions of innovations that diffuse in just this pattern (Rogers 1995, 260)? The explanation may be that the decision-making process behind state policymaking is at least sometimes different than that behind the innovations studied in these other disciplines. The diffusions examined in those studies were largely of technical innovations that fulfilled a commonly held value, such as improving health or economic production (e.g., Wellin 1955; Hagerstrand 1965). Decision making in such cases could readily be understood as simple learning since a decision maker would need only to be shown the benefits of the innovation to adopt it virtually automatically. Is such a learning process always driving policymaking in the states? In the next section, we explore how morality policy may trigger a different decision-making process and therefore may yield a different pattern of temporal diffusion.

The Temporal Diffusion of Morality Policy

What characteristics of morality policy could affect decision making regarding it and, thereby, its temporal diffusion? Morality policy involves issues on which there is significant disagreement about first principles. These are not questions about which policy might best achieve a commonly held goal, but they are debates over basic policy goals themselves. Meier (1994, 4) argues that morality policy closely resembles redistributive policy, in which "one segment of society attempts by government fiat to impose its values on the rest of society" (see also Gusfield 1963).[2] Ripley and Franklin (1987, 145) hold that redistributive policy "attempts to reallocate items and symbols of value among different groups in society." Since morality policy validates certain basic values and rejects others, it redistributes moral values just as surely as a progressive income tax scheme redistributes economic values.

Two characteristics of redistributive policy that help determine its unique politics are even more prominent in morality policy than in economic redistributive policy: the potential for high saliency and technical simplicity. First, since these policies allocate basic values, they can be highly salient to the general public (Meier 1994, 4; Sharp 1992; Ripley and Franklin 1987, chap. 6; Gormley 1986). When their economic or moral values are threatened, people care. This threat may well excite deeper passion in certain people when the government bans abortion or executes a criminal, for example, than when it enacts a new social welfare program. The link to one's economic values in the latter case may be tenuous, but for many people, the threats to their basic moral values in the former cases are palpable and a stimulus for political action.

Second, redistribution is often technically simpler than other types of policy: one side wins, and the other side loses. This enhances the potential for issue salience and widespread public participation, especially among the losers (Gormley 1986; Carmines and Stimson 1980). In addition, moral value redistribution is likely to be even less confused by technicalities than is economic redistribution (Meier 1994, 4–5). For instance, although the average person might not understand the nuances of a progressive income tax, he or she may well feel knowledgeable about the propriety of banning alcohol sales. This belief in having an informed opinion on a morality issue is often justified since the debate is at root not about whether a policy instrument will have a particular effect but whether or not a given value is validated.

Given that morality policy involves the redistribution of values through simple and potentially salient public policy, what patterns of decision making and temporal diffusion can we expect to see associated with it? An important consideration here is the distribution of the values in question among the citizens. We expect a very different type of diffusion pattern when the status quo policy reflects the values of the minority than when it reflects the values of the majority.[3]

When the majority of citizens disagree with the values represented by the currently enacted morality policy, there is little political risk for policymakers to pursue a new policy; indeed, there is great incentive to do so. This simple and salient reform can easily be communicated to a receptive public with great political advantage accruing to its advocates. This situation will yield high-speed entrepreneurial politics as individual politicians and parties compete for public favor by promoting popular reforms of this sort (Riker 1986; Mintrom 1997; Meier 1994, 210; Mooney and Lee n.d.). The decision-making process is therefore not one of incremental learning, but it is one of competition to validate majority values. Therefore, we posit the following hypothesis:

> *Hypothesis 1: The pattern of temporal diffusion for majority-favored morality policy will be one of swift adoption with little or no introductory learning period.*

What would we expect the temporal diffusion pattern to be for morality policy that reflects values held only by the minority? Of course, one might not even expect such a policy to come onto the political agenda in a democracy, much less to be passed into law. When the minority is significantly large and aligned with one political party (Key 1949), when the intensity with which the minority holds its values is such that ignoring them could be detrimental to the system (Truman 1958), or when there is a movement toward fulfilling these minority values for some other reason, policymakers may consider such policy. Even under these conditions, however, they will indeed be very difficult to pass.

The usual way majority-to-minority economic redistribution policy is enacted in the United States is, ironically, by being redefined as distributive policy (Ripley and Franklin 1987, 148). Instead of being advocated as a policy through which the minority gains at the expense of the majority, this policy is advocated as one through which all (or at least many) parties can benefit. For example, the Model Cities program was changed from targeting only certain economically depressed urban areas to being a general federal subsidy for cities (Ripley and Franklin 1987, 164–66).

This method of passing minority-benefiting policy points out another important difference between moral and economic redistribution. Whereas economic redistribution can be adopted as a compromise with one group "buying off" its opponents by reducing costs or making side payments, with morality policy, the values involved are not so easily divisible. When values of fundamental right and wrong are at stake, compromise is unthinkable (Epstein and Kobylka 1992, 309). Either a state holds that human life is sacred, or it does not; either a state holds homosexuality to be an unacceptable perversion, or it does not. Morality policy cannot, therefore, be redefined as distributive policy in the same way that economic redistributive policy often is.

Advocates of minority-supported morality policy may succeed, however, if they redefine it, again ironically, to lose some of the characteristics that made it a morality policy in the first place (Haider-Markel and Meier 1996; Jacobs 1988). If advocates can successfully characterize the policy as being one of incremental change, low salience, and high complexity, it may pass through the legislative process quietly and unmolested. The political environment needs to be like that surrounding regulatory or government administration policy; that is, the policy needs to be "demoralized" (Pierce and Miller, Chapter 10, this volume). Under these conditions, the redistribution of basic values from the majority to the minority may occur through the routine social learning decision-making process, as with the nonmorality policy it is redefined to be. Therefore, we hypothesize:

> *Hypothesis 2: If it can be successfully "demoralized," a minority-favored morality policy will diffuse temporally in the typical S-curve pattern.*

The Data: The Death Penalty as Morality Policy

To evaluate these hypotheses, we examine the temporal diffusion patterns of three state death penalty policies. However, the first question that must be answered is whether the death penalty is a morality issue. Certainly, some of the arguments used in the death penalty debate are not based on first principles, such as those based on its deterrent effect (Tullock 1974; Baldus and Cole 1975) and the potential for arbitrariness, bias, and mistakes (Black 1974). These are largely side issues, however, that distract advocates from the fundamental moral question. As pro–death penalty scholar Walter Berns argues (1979, 8–9), "The real issue is whether justice permits or even requires the death penalty." That is, given a deterrent effect and unbiased implementation, does the state have the right or duty to put a human being to death under certain circumstances? A state must answer this question affirmatively if it is to adopt the death penalty, and it is at root a question of first principles over which people passionately disagree.

The conflict of first principles is obvious even in the scholarly debate over the death penalty about which advocates on both sides "advance their arguments as self-evident and morally compelling" (Bowers 1984, xxiii). This is perhaps best exemplified in that the same arguments are often used *both* to support and to oppose the death penalty. The death penalty is seen as "an affront to human dignity" (Bedau 1977, 11) and as an acknowledgment of the criminal's humanity (Berns 1979, 154); as more and less humane than life imprisonment (Camus 1961; Bedau 1977, 6); as in and out of step with biblical teaching (Vallenga 1967; Kazis 1967); as good and bad because it provides retribution (Berns 1979, 8–9; Black 1974, 23). Death penalty scholars even resort to using cheap emotional allusions to support their cases. Graphic descriptions of executions and horrifying crimes are common in what can seem to be an embarrassed, frustrated admission that the normal channels of logical and empirical argument are inadequate (e.g., Black 1974, 21; Berns 1979, 118–19, 154–55, 172–73, 180). While one might expect such argumentation tactics from interest groups and politicians, the fact that legal and policy scholars engage in them is strong indication that the debate has been reduced to first principles and that policy arising from such a debate can be characterized as morality policy.

The state policies we investigate involve legislation making the death penalty discretionary for murder (1838–1963), abolishing it (1846–1969), and reestablishing it after the 1972 *Furman* v. *Georgia* (408 U.S. 238) U.S. Supreme Court decision that vacated all state death penalty statutes (1972–94).[4] The abolition of the death penalty is pure morality policy as a simple, nonincremental, and potentially salient state validation of a certain set of first principles. Reestablishment of the death penalty after *Furman* is also a clear morality-based redistribution but in the opposite direction of abolition. Discretionary sentencing legislation is a redefined and demoralized death penalty policy because it is more complex, incremental, and less salient than either abolition or reestablishment. Under this reform, juries and trial judges can impose a sentence of imprisonment in lieu of death for those convicted of murder. Along with instituting humane methods of execution, specifying degrees of first degree murder, and eliminating public executions, the goal of this reform was to mitigate "the rigidity and brutality" of the death penalty, thus addressing many of the public's objections to it (Bedau 1967, 14–15; Mooney and Lee 1999). While addressing some technical side issues, these reforms had the effect of focusing the debate over the death penalty more and more clearly on the basic first principles involved in execution.

Since we have hypothesized that the diffusion of morality policy will be influenced by the distribution of citizens' values, we need evidence regarding U.S. public opinion on the death penalty. Although no systematic polling data exist on this issue for the entire period of interest, irregular national polls dating back to 1936 indicate majority support for having the death penalty available for murderers (Stanley and Niemi 1994, 33).[5] In only one poll (July 1966) of forty from 1936 to 1991 did opposition surpass support for it. Except for the period 1956–72 when respondents' support averaged 49.7 percent and opposition averaged 39.3 percent, the ratio of support to opposition has typically been 65/35. While their citizens' death penalty support varies among the states, evidence from the only two comparative state-level polls on the subject (which were taken in very different periods, 1936 and 1990–92) indicates that in only one instance did a majority of a state's citizens oppose the death penalty, and this was slight opposition[6] (Cantril 1951, 94; Norrander 1997). There is also evidence from state initiatives of high levels of support for the death penalty over an even longer period (Cannon 1995, 2; Allen 1967; Dann 1967; Bedau 1977, 64–65). In sum, it is probably true that majority sentiment in almost every state has been consistently in favor of the availability of the death penalty in the period under study.

Therefore, due in part to the Supreme Court's *Furman* decision, the three policies we examine represent three distinct contexts for morality policy change— two pure morality policies, one with majority and one with minority public support, and a demoralized policy whose underlying position (anti–death penalty) has minority support. Table 11.1 reports the year in which each state adopted each of these reforms.

TABLE 11.1   YEAR OF ADOPTION OF DEATH PENALTY LEGISLATION

STATE/TERRITORY	DISCRETIONARY SENTENCING FOR MURDER	ABOLITION (REESTABLISHMENT)	POST-*FURMAN* REESTABLISHMENT[a]
Alabama	1841		1976
Arkansas	1899	1957	
Arizona	1885	1916 (1918)	1973
Arkansas	1915		1973
California	1874		1973[b]
Colorado	1901[c]	1897 (1901)	1974[b]
Connecticut	1951		1973
Delaware	1917	1958 (1961)	1974
Florida	1872		1972
Georgia	1861		1973
Hawaii	1955	1957	
Idaho	1911		1973
Illinois	1867		1974
Indiana	1881		1973
Iowa	1878[c]	1872 (1878) 1965	
Kansas	1935[c]	1907 (1935)	1994
Kentucky	1873		1974[b]
Louisiana	1846		1973
Maine	—[d]	1876 (1883) 1887	
Maryland	1908		1975
Massachusetts	1951		1979
Michigan	—[d]	1846	
Minnesota	1868	1911	
Mississippi	1872		1974
Missouri	1907	1917 (1919)	1975
Montana	1907		1973[b]
Nebraska	1893		1973
Nevada	1912		1973
New Hampshire	1903		1974
New Jersey	1916		1982
New Mexico	1939	1969	1973
New York	1963	1965	1974

TABLE 11.1   (CONTINUED)

STATE/TERRITORY	DISCRETIONARY SENTENCING FOR MURDER	ABOLITION (REESTABLISHMENT)	POST-*FURMAN* REESTABLISHMENT[a]
North Carolina	1949		1974
North Dakota	1883	1915	
Ohio	1898		1973[b]
Oklahoma	1890		1973
Oregon	1920[c]	1914 (1920) 1964	1978
Pennsylvania	1925		1974
Rhode Island	—[d]	1852	1973
South Carolina	1894		1974
South Dakota	1883	1915 (1939)	1979
Tennessee	1838	1915 (1916)	1974
Texas	1879		1973
Utah	1876		1973
Vermont	1911	1965	
Virginia	1914		1975
Washington	1909	1913 (1919)	1975
West Virginia	1870	1965	
Wisconsin	—[d]	1853	
Wyoming	1915		1973

Source: Bowers 1984, 9, 11, 526–31.

a. The date of the first legislative enactment after *Furman*, regardless of subsequent court or legislative action.

b. Year of passage, but enactment was on 1 January of the following year.

c. First established discretionary sentencing for murder after repealing abolition.

d. Abolished the death penalty before making it discretionary for murder.

The Temporal Diffusion of State Death Penalty Policy

Our first hypothesis is that when a change in morality policy is favored by a majority of citizens, it will diffuse rapidly without the slow introductory phase indicative of social learning. This is the type of opportunity that entrepreneurial politicians, demagogue or democrat, should be able to exploit effectively (Riker 1986; Mintrom 1997; Meier 1994, 210). By raising the public salience of such a simple and popular issue, an entrepreneur should be able to push it through the legislature with ease, and woe to those who raise arguments in opposition, be they morality or utility based. Learning will be unimportant because the issue is simple, and its high salience can generate an irresistible demand.

Such a scenario requires an unfulfilled demand for a popular morality policy, which is probably a very unusual circumstance. The U.S. Supreme Court's decision in *Furman* v. *Georgia* (1972) created such a circumstance, allowing us to

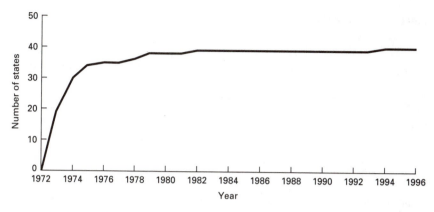

FIGURE 11.1 CUMULATIVE NUMBER OF STATES REESTABLISHING THE DEATH PENALTY AFTER *FURMAN*

Source: Bowers 1984, appendix B.

assess our hypothesis. Figure 11.1 shows the cumulative distribution of post-*Furman* death penalty reestablishment, demonstrating clearly the effect of what Epstein and Kobylka (1992, 131) describe as state legislatures that "could barely wait to reconvene and pass new laws, which given the *Furman* majority and informed commentary on it, were of dubious constitutionality." State legislatures did not pause to learn from the experiences of other states before they reestablished their death penalties, and they did not move cautiously. Legislators were so energized by this threat to the values of the bulk of their constituents, and citizens were so outraged by this clear and simple attack on their values, that the death penalty diffused through the states rapidly, not in the typical S-shaped learning curve pattern, thus substantiating our hypothesis (Zimring and Hawkins 1986, 41–42; Schwed 1983, 144–45).[7] This is clearly not a diffusion process driven by social learning.

Next consider the diffusion of policy that has at its root a value not held by the majority. The only way for advocates to succeed in such a case is to pursue a demoralizing strategy (Haider-Markel and Meier 1996; Jacobs 1988). We hypothesize that if advocates succeed in demoralizing this type of issue into technical, nonsalient, and incremental policy, it will diffuse across time in the S-curve cumulative distribution pattern indicative of a boundedly rational social learning decision-making process.

Figure 11.2 (p. 180) shows that the temporal diffusion of discretionary sentencing reform does indeed display this pattern.[8] Adoptions of these laws came very infrequently in the early period, increased in frequency from 1870 to 1915, and

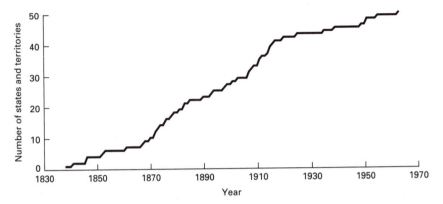

FIGURE 11.2 CUMULATIVE NUMBER OF STATES AND TERRITORIES WITH DISCRETIONARY SENTENCING REFORM

Source: Bowers 1984, 11.

then came more slowly again as the laggard states finally adopted. This anti–death penalty policy was so watered down, so technical and incremental, that is, so demoralized, that it failed to incite the type of highly salient, first principle debate that precludes social learning. Decision making regarding its adoption proceeded quite normally: quietly, technically, and in a boundedly rational way.

Can all minority-favored policies be demoralized so completely? The cumulative distribution of death penalty abolitions in Figure 11.3 shows a pattern that is markedly different from the S-curve seen in Figure 11.2, as well as being different from the steep and permanent diffusion pattern seen in Figure 11.1. In Figure 11.3, we see the starts, stops, and reverses of the various abolition movements over the course of 123 years. This sawtooth pattern reflects the fact that this is the only one of these three policies that was repealed during the periods of study. What decision-making process could have led to such a temporal diffusion pattern?

We suggest that this diffusion pattern is the result of a series of failed attempts to demoralize and adopt abolition through the normal social learning process. Although each of these attempts to demoralize the issue produced at least a few abolitions, at some point in each of these attempts, the issue became salient to the public. Since the moral questions had not been purged completely, quick reestablishments occurred to realign policy with majority opinion, much like the reestablishments that followed *Furman.* Between each of these reform movements was a period of quiescence for salience on the issue to recede. Therefore, the temporal diffusion pattern of death penalty abolition is a series of very truncated normal S-curves and quick reestablishments, separated by periods of inac-

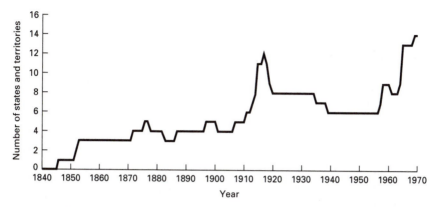

FIGURE 11.3   **CUMULATIVE NUMBER OF STATES AND TERRITORIES ABOLISHING THE DEATH PENALTY**

Source: Bowers 1984, 9.

tivity on the issue, as seen in Figure 11.3. The four waves of death penalty abolition activity are separated by approximately twenty-year periods of quiescence. The first wave of the 1840s and 1850s involved only three states, and these reforms were indeed sustained. In the next two waves, in the 1870s and the Progressive Era of the early twentieth century, however, most of the states that abolished the death penalty readopted it, sometimes very quickly (Table 11.1, pp. 177–78). The fourth wave was artificially truncated by *Furman*, so we cannot judge the final outcome of these abolitions with certainty. Legislatures in three previously abolitionist states (Rhode Island, New Mexico, and New York) voted to reestablish the death penalty within fifteen months of *Furman*, suggesting at least some backsliding would have occurred in the absence of that decision.

While the temporal diffusion pattern displayed in Figure 11.3 is consistent with this scenario, strong historical evidence also supports it from some of the states in which the death penalty was abolished and then reestablished. The 1958 Delaware abolition was an insider affair, for which reformers developed a lengthy technical report and focused their efforts on state legislators (Cobin 1967). Missouri's abolition came quietly on a day (17 April 1917) when legislators were far more concerned about U.S. entry into World War I than about the death penalty, which, after all, reformers argued, was rarely used in Missouri (Guillot 1967). Similar stories of low-key abolition efforts backed with technical arguments come from other states, as well (Bedau 1967, chap. 7). In contrast, the reestablishment of the death penalty usually followed a speedy, public, and emotional campaign, often sparked by a well-publicized crime. For example, Delaware's reestablishment was instigated by the murders of three elderly white people by young African American parolees when race relations in the state were strained because of civil rights activities (Cobin 1967). In Missouri, two police officers were killed in a shootout in 1918, causing public outrage and so quick a reversal in policy that the abolition law was never even published in the Revised Statutes (Guillot 1967).

Conclusion

The temporal diffusion patterns of these three death penalty laws offer important insight into the policymaking process and the effect of first principle conflict on that process. First, when advocates can demoralize a minority-favored morality policy, policymakers may employ the typical boundedly rational social learning process used in the adoption of so many other innovations by governments, other organizations, and individuals. When the conflicts of first principle cannot be suppressed, however, social learning by political decision makers no longer drives the process. Rather, because these issues are technically simple and involve basic moral judgment, citizens have both the interest and the ability to draw their own conclusions and make their views known strongly to policymakers. Therefore, policymakers are not forced to use their own routine decision-making strategies, nor are they given the political leeway to do so. Democracy supercedes learning, and reasoned analysis or even boundedly rational lesson drawing becomes unnecessary and irrelevant.

This interpretation of our results fits well with the findings of other research into morality policy that indicates that the values held by citizens are well reflected in pure morality policy, whether through religious affiliation or political ideology (Norrander and Wilcox, Chapter 9, this volume; Berry and Berry 1990; Mooney and Lee 1995; Fairbanks 1975). Our findings also suggest that the distinction between morality policy and nonmorality policy is certainly not objective but resides in the issue definitions and arguments that surround a given policy debate (Pierce and Miller, Chapter 10, this volume).

Notes

An earlier version of this paper was presented at the 1997 meeting of the Western Political Science Association.

1. Another important aspect of state policy diffusion is the way that policies spread geographically across the country (Walker 1969; Berry and Berry 1990; Mooney and Lee 1995). We do not address geographic diffusion in this paper.

2. It may also be the case that morality policy takes on different characteristics, depending on the context of public opinion surrounding it (Meier, Chapter 2, this volume; Mooney and Lee n.d.). While we begin to explore this idea here, it is still useful at this stage in the theoretical development of morality policy studies to think about at least some morality policies as redistributive.

3. Note that if the minority is too small, the issue fails to involve any significant controversy, and it is of little interest to political scientists. An example of such a nonissue would be legislation outlawing murder.

4. Death penalty implementation is highly variable. Most states have always allowed the death penalty, but few states have executed more than a handful of prisoners in recent times (Zimring and Hawkins 1986, chap. 7). If death penalty legislation is therefore largely symbolic, it is no different in this way than legislation in many other areas (Edelman 1964). Since the debate here is about basic values, symbols matter. There is a fundamental difference in the values of a state that allows executions and those of a state that does not. We investigate the pattern of the development of these differences in this chapter.

5. Bedau (1967, 68) raises the point that it is "difficult to answer . . . *what* the present high levels of public support for the death penalty really support. Is it only the *legal threat* of the death penalty, coupled with the ritual trying, convicting, and occasionally sentencing a murderer to death, rather than *actual executions?*" Since this chapter examines only the adoption of death penalty legislation, public support for this "legal threat" is our concern.

6. In the 1936 poll, citizens of Wisconsin opposed the death penalty, 51 percent to 49 percent (Cantril 1951, 94).

7. Also of interest is why a few states failed to reestablish their death penalties rapidly. We address this issue elsewhere (Mooney and Lee n.d.).

8. If death penalty abolitions are not included in this analysis, the S-shape is even more pronounced.

PART SIX

Implementation of Morality Policy

CHAPTER TWELVE

Clean Thoughts and Dirty Minds: The Politics of Porn

Kevin B. Smith

UNDERLYING MUCH OF the research examining the regulation of pornography is an unresolved question, does the state regulate sexual expression primarily in response to real or perceived threats to social order, or is it simply an effort to legitimate one group's moral norms? (Daynes 1988; Davies 1997; Childress 1992; Kutchinsky 1973). If the answer is the latter, the normative implications are substantial; this answer suggests that the state is willing to suppress individual liberties not because their exercise is a threat to society as a whole but simply because their exercise is an offense to other groups in society. Yet the emerging theory of morality politics suggests that exactly such outcomes are predictable products of competing value agendas within society. While this framework does not preclude social harm as a driving force behind the regulation of sexual expression, it is strongly suggestive that this policy arena will be dominated by efforts to use the coercive power of the state to legitimate one set of moral norms while outlawing others.

This chapter adopts the morality politics framework to assess empirically the framework's ability to predict the regulation of sexually explicit materials. The results indicate that the politics of porn are indeed less about the struggle to balance individual freedom and social harm than about an effort by one group to impose its moral taboos on everyone else.

Pornography and Public Policy

In the United States, sex and politics have always made for a volatile mix. As recreation or entertainment, sex is often viewed as a threat, something with the power to alter norms of behavior, undermine morality, and erode social order (Daynes 1988). On such grounds, the coercive power of the state has long been used to define, regulate, and suppress sexually explicit material. Regulating sexually explicit material, or "pornography," brings into conflict two core values: (1) the individual freedoms considered necessary to liberty and guaranteed by the First Amendment and (2) a set of behavioral norms—often with religious foundations—considered important to a stable society.

This collision of values results in the viewing of pornography as both a civil right and a civic threat. According to the Rev. Jerry Kirk of the National Coalition for the Protection of Children and Families, "Pornography is anti-children, anti-woman, anti-family, anti-church and anti-God" ("Ohio Minister Urges Charlotte to Fight Local Pornography" 1995, 13). According to Nadine Strossen (1995) of the American Civil Liberties Union, pornography covers such a broad area of sexually related speech that it should be protected as a political freedom. The public seems to hold these contradictory viewpoints simultaneously; opinion polls indicate that most people view pornography as a threat to community standards and moral norms, yet there is a broad and consistently high demand for these same sexually explicit materials in virtually every community in the nation (Daynes 1988). As Meier (1997) has noted, few politicians are willing to stand up for "sin," and this raises the possibility that one set of these values is going to be overrepresented in the policymaking process.[1] There is generally only one acceptable political position on pornography: opposition. Officials may label themselves pro–First Amendment, but few are willing to call themselves propornography.

Not surprising, balancing freedom of speech and sexual autonomy with social morals and norms has been an elusive political goal. State and federal governments have passed numerous laws regulating sexually explicit material, and in various challenges, the Supreme Court has consistently ruled that obscenity has no First Amendment protection and may be outlawed. Instead of providing a framework for resolving such conflicts, these decisions have fueled them. The basic problem of these efforts was most famously articulated by Justice Potter Stewart in his concurring opinion of the 1964 case *Jacobellis* v. *Ohio* (378 U.S. 184, 197). Stewart admitted that "perhaps I could never succeed in intelligibly [defining obscenity]. But I know it when I see it."

The 1973 *Miller* decision set three criteria for judging obscenity (*Miller* v. *California* 413 U.S. 49, 24): (1) the "average person, applying contemporary community standards, would find that the work, taken as a whole, appeals to the prurient interest," (2) the work "depicts or describes in a patently offensive way, sexual conduct specifically defined by the applicable state law," and (3) taken as a whole, the work "lacks serious literary, artistic, political, or scientific value." These guidelines were subsequently incorporated into federal and state statutes as the most common approach to identifying obscene materials. They have not resolved the problem of definition articulated by Justice Stewart, however, and there is nothing approaching a consensus on what constitutes obscenity. States legally define offensive sexual conduct in different ways, and the community standards criteria embedded in the *Miller* test have created questions of whether what is legal differs not just between states but also within them. Such terms as *obscenity, pornography, erotica*, and *smut* tend to elicit different responses from different individuals and have proven to be amorphous concepts resistant to specific definition, legal or otherwise.[2]

This vagueness in state attempts to balance moral behavioral norms with sexual expression has long concerned civil libertarians. They fear that laws regulating sexually explicit material will be used as vehicles to impose one group's moral norms on the rest of society. A number of examples of arbitrary and selective enforcement support their case. For instance, during the Reagan and Bush administrations, the National Obscenity Enforcement Unit of the Justice Department was repeatedly charged with being a conservative "morality brigade" that trampled individual freedoms in an attempt to impose behavioral codes favored by religious fundamentalists. Established in the 1980s by Attorney General Edwin Meese, the unit hired lawyers from avowed antipornography groups, pushed the prosecution of the rap group 2 Live Crew and the exhibitors of Robert Mapplethorpe's photographs, and appeared to be highly selective in choosing jurisdictions in which to pursue convictions (Dority 1992; Stone 1994).

These patterns strongly suggest that pornography fits within the theoretical framework of morality politics and that the politics of regulating sexual expression can be explained and predicted by this value-based framework. Formulating and enforcing laws with strong moral content has long been approached by scholars as a subset of redistributive or regulatory policy (Meier 1994; Lowi 1988). In general terms, regulatory policy sets limitations on individual or group action, and redistributive policy manipulates the allocation of wealth within society (Ripley and Franklin 1987, 24–25). Applied specifically to moral issues, social regulatory policy has been defined as "the exercise of legal authority to modify or replace community values, moral practices, and norms of interpersonal conduct with new standards of behavior" (Tatalovich and Daynes 1988, 1). In redistributive terms, morality policy is viewed as an attempt to reallocate values when "one segment of society attempts by government fiat to impose its values on the rest of society" (Meier 1994, 4). These are complementary rather than contradictory approaches; both rest on the same fundamental assumption that morality politics is characterized by a struggle between groups to get government to legitimate one set of values and outlaw another.

This general pattern of morality politics has been documented in such areas as the prohibition or regulation of alcohol (Gusfield 1963), abortion (Luker 1984), sodomy (Nice 1988), the death penalty (Mooney and Lee 1996), guns (Spitzer 1998), and gay rights policies (Haider-Markel and Meier 1996). The common elements of these studies include value-based political conflict, highly salient policy issues, and the limited role of expertise or information in resolving these struggles.

There is a strong prima facie case that pornography regulation should follow these general patterns. To some people, sexually explicit material "is a matter of liberty and privacy, but to others it is an abuse of free expression that is in need of regulation" (Daynes 1988, 41). Calls for tight regulation to defend a set of social norms (often made with religious overtones) are juxtaposed with the high demand within society for sexually explicit materials. Adult video rentals alone constituted a $500 million business in 1995, representing as much as 28 percent of the entire video rental market in some regions of the country (Fishbein 1995). In addition, attempts to regulate porn tend to be high profile but are backed with little analysis or information. As with Justice Stewart, most policymakers have a gut-level, rather than a cerebral, response to the issue of pornography regulation. On this issue, citizens tend to mobilize around sets of preexisting beliefs, allowing politicians and parties to respond to these beliefs with no information costs and to do so in absolutist terms (Haider-Markel and Meier 1996).

Theoretical and empirical consideration thus point to a clear expectation that the regulation of sexually explicit material will be a function of the competing values of groups in society. In turn, this suggests that the adoption and enforcement of such policies will depend on the direction and strength of those values within society. Although this explanation reflects the fears expressed by civil libertarians, it is also likely to be accepted by many favoring the regulation of sexually explicit material. Advocates of regulation, such as the Rev. Kirk, make no secret of the moral basis of their arguments.

However, there are arguments for pornography regulation that do not involve moral judgments. Groups pressing such regulatory demands on government also justify them by arguing that sexually explicit material causes more objective social harm. For example, there is widespread agreement that sexually explicit material is inappropriate for minors. A number of fundamentalist and feminist groups have argued that there is a causal connection between sexually explicit material and sexually related violence, especially rape.[3] These arguments provide grounds for government regulation of sexually explicit materials in the name of protecting individual rights and communal social order rather than moral norms.

These justifications are often particularly associated with a branch of feminism that argues that pornography promotes violence against women, exploits and degrades women, and perpetuates a series of damaging stereotypes that keep women trapped in a second-class political status. As Catharine MacKinnon (1984) puts it, "[P]ornography, with the rape and prostitution in which it participates, institutionalizes the sexuality of male supremacy." The quote is from an article pointedly titled "Not a Moral Issue." Such arguments tie the regulation of sexually explicit material to questions of female political power—specifically that regulation is needed to remove a social barrier that prevents women from attaining full political equality (Jensen 1995; but see also Davies 1997). This suggests that struggles to regulate pornographic materials will depend in part on women's access to political power.

There is a large division within feminist ranks over such arguments. Nadine Strossen (1995) argues that regulating pornography does not empower women but does just the opposite. She argues that the power to regulate sexual expression is a dangerous tool to put into state hands, for it is just as likely to be used to oppress women as to help liberate them. Such arguments also clearly relate the regulation of sexually explicit material to questions of female political power but reverse the cause and effect posited by MacKinnon. Instead of making sexual regulation more likely, increasing female political power will reduce this possibility because the absence of such laws is not the problem—their presence is. Feminists advocating this perspective argue that sexual expression is a category of political speech that should be protected by law, not restricted by it, and that pornography can be a source of female power and pleasure, not an obstacle to the same (e.g., Duggan and Hunter 1995; McElroy 1995).

Regardless of the stance on regulation, some of these arguments can also be viewed in terms of values. The differences between the groups advocating regulation on religion-based morality and on gender-based discrimination could not be more different. One "is characterized by a dislike of traditional political, social and moral structures"; the other is characterized by a strong attachment to them (Kobylka 1991, 61–62). At least in some sense, however, the arguments are mutually reinforcing in that they both can be employed to support calls for regulation. Taken together, these arguments suggest a series of clearly related but conceptually distinct hypotheses to explain why government regulates sexually explicit material:

Hypothesis 1: Regulation is a function of the value-based agenda of groups seeking to force their moral codes on others through government fiat.

Hypothesis 2: Regulation is a function of social harm often associated with sexually explicit material.

Hypothesis 3: Regulation is a function of the political status of women.

The first hypothesis is firmly rooted in existing theoretical and empirical work on morality policy and on the more anecdotal evidence surrounding enforcement of obscenity laws. The second reflects a common justification in calls for regulation, especially when the social harm is sexually related violence against women. The third reflects an underlying agreement in feminist debate on pornography—that regulation is tied to the political status and power of women—although there is a sharp disagreement on whether higher political status for women should or would result in increased or decreased regulation of sexually explicit material. The remainder of this chapter tests these hypotheses empirically.

Data and Methods

Dependent Variable

The biggest challenge facing such an analysis is the conceptualization and operationalization of a dependent variable. Fortunately, I do not have to define what constitutes obscenity or pornography, but I do have to specify and measure what constitutes government regulation of it. It is critical in doing so to provide a reasonable basis of comparison in different jurisdictions with the power to regulate sexual expression. To this end, I used states as the unit of analysis and settled on not one measure but three.

The first measure of pornography regulation is an indicator of the severity of obscenity laws adopted in each state. To construct this measure, I created a baseline offense: an individual convicted of selling or renting fifteen copies of a sexually explicit videotape found to be legally obscene. I then analyzed statutes in all fifty states and recorded the maximum fine that could be levied for such an offense under applicable obscenity laws in 1994. I assumed that the conviction was a first offense and that higher fines reflect harsher laws. The baseline offense was used strictly to create a reasonable basis of comparability; it is not intended to represent a typical obscenity case (if there is such a thing). Although this case provides a reasonable basis of comparison within the technical limits of the law, it admittedly does not measure the undoubted variation in what would be judged obscene in different states.

Having a law and enforcing it are two different things. Tough obscenity laws can be enacted with little or no cost, political or pecuniary, and can serve a purely symbolic function. Enforcing them is much more difficult (Meier, Chapter 2, this volume). It may well be that groups can get their moral codes written into statute. Whether or not they can get them actually enforced on the streets and in the courts is another question. Regardless of the position in the debate, the implementation question may be more important to answer. The obstacle to answering this question is the lack of data.[4] Although any measure of enforcement is likely to be imperfect, reasonable proxies are available, and to help overcome the limitations of any single measure, I use two. The first is a state's 1994 arrest rate for sex offenses as defined and reported by the Federal Bureau of Investigation (1995, 10), including offenses against "chastity, common decency, morals and the like." This is an imperfect measure because it includes enforcement of laws that do not specifically regulate sexually explicit material. I created the second enforcement variable using the Lexis-Nexus electronic database. This database includes searchable access to regional newspapers in all fifty states. For each state, I counted every government enforcement action—arrest, indictment, trial, and conviction—recorded in the database for 1993, 1994, and 1995. I used these data to construct an obscenity enforcement rate per 100,000 population. Again, this is an imperfect measure because not all enforcement actions are going to be reported or recorded in the database, and the variable is to some extent a yardstick of salience (although the three-year period was intended to be long enough to pick up a general pattern rather than just a good news story). However, together these measures should tap into the main concept I am pursuing—the state's attitude toward enforcing regulation of sexually explicit materials—and stable relationships across both variables should provide a solid basis for inference.

Independent Variables

Values supporting regulation. To tap into the strength of the values agenda supporting the regulation of sexually explicit material, I used the percentage of a state's population that was Catholic and the percentage of the population belonging to a Protestant fundamentalist denomination (Bradley et al. 1992; Meier and McFarlane 1993, 6n). Groups active in seeking the regulation of sexually explicit materials commonly have strong ties to Catholic or Protestant fundamentalist organizations (Kobylka 1991). The general argument is that large numbers will increase the ability of the group to use the political process to redistribute its values (Meier 1994). The expected relationship is that the higher the proportion of the population belonging to these groups, the greater is the likelihood of the adoption of tough obscenity laws and stringent enforcement.

Values opposing regulation. To gauge the strength of the opposing values agenda, I used the per capita circulation rate of *Playboy* magazine as certified by the Audit Bureau of Circulation (1991). This measure can be viewed in two ways. First, it is a measure of the demand for sexually explicit material within the population (although by now considered on the mild end of the pornography spectrum, *Playboy* remains explicit enough to be a frequent and large target for those favoring regulation of sexual expression). Second, it is a reasonable proxy of broader attitudes toward pornography within a state. *Playboy* takes a very liberal editorial stance on sexually explicit material, and this is taken to reflect its readers' attitudes. Higher circulation rates are thus expected to be associated with less harsh laws and laxer enforcement. As a surrogate of demand for and attitudes about sexually explicit material, this measure carries an important caveat. The rapid growth of the Internet porn business theoretically offers a much more accurate way to tap into these concepts, but as far as I am aware, no reliable state-by-state comparative measures exist (especially because in 1994, the cyber-porn business was in its relative infancy).

Social harm.   The most obvious measure of social harm associated with sexual violence toward women is a state's rape rate, as reported in the FBI's (1995) *Uniform Crime Reports* contained in *Crime in the United States.* The problem with this measure is that rape is notoriously underreported. By how much and with what result on its validity as a measure of social harm is an unresolved debate. Rape rates are positively correlated with other measures of social harm (assault rates and divorce rates, for example). If nothing else, as law enforcement authorities record higher rates of sexually related crimes that are seen as at least a partial product of pornographic materials, proponents of regulation can (and do) use such statistics to pressure governments to adopt and enforce tough obscenity laws as a response to perceived social harm.[5]

Women's political status.   For this I used a composite measure constructed by the Institute for Women's Policy Research (1996), which includes female voter registration and turnout, the number of women holding political office, and the number of institutional resources available to women in the political process. A positive relationship is taken to support the inference that increased female political power leads to tougher regulation of sexual material. If pornography can be construed as a mechanism to keep women second-class citizens, as some of its feminist critics suggest, it makes sense that as women gain more political power, female policymakers will move to shackle the avenues of sexual repression. A negative relationship would support the counterhypothesis that increased female political power is more likely to reduce state attempts to regulate pornography.

Political context.   Other factors need to be included to properly specify the model, thus offering a solid test of my core hypotheses. Values are filtered through political institutions, and the responsiveness of these institutions to citizen values and demands plays an obvious role in the official affirmation of these values. Theory predicts that in states with greater political competition, political elites will be more attuned and responsive to demands from citizen groups (Meier 1994). Of course, it is important to consider to whom they are responsive. To model this effect, I included an interaction term of political competition (Holbrook and Van Dunk 1993) and *Playboy* circulation.[6] The expectation is that higher levels of competition coupled with greater demand for sexually explicit materials will lead to laxer regulation. As a final control, I also included the state's per capita income (Hovey 1996). Previous studies have shown that morality policy (especially implementation or enforcement) is often a function of slack resources in society and that this possibility can be picked up using an income measure (Meier 1994; Haider-Markel and Meier 1996).

Three basic regression models were estimated using OLS to predict obscenity fines, the arrest rate for sex crimes, and the enforcement rate of obscenity laws. Diagnostics revealed few problems except a handful of outlier states in the fine and enforcement rate models as discussed later. Whenever appropriate, state dummies were included to prevent undue bias of the regression line.

Results

The results of these analyses presented in Table 12.1 (p. 196) are generally consistent with the expectations of morality policy theory but not with the expectations of female political power. The most consistent predictor is the proportion of a state's population affiliated with a Protestant fundamentalist denomination. Larger fundamentalist populations are positively associated with punishment in Model 1 (obscenity fines) and with enforcement in Models 2 (sex arrests) and 3 (enforcement rate). This fits with the redistributive notion of morality policy theory: Groups sharing basic moral codes will attempt to use the state to force these values onto others.

In contrast to the fundamentalist variable, larger Catholic populations seem to have no impact on the regulation of sexually explicit material. The value agenda that drives this issue seems to be anchored in the mores of the Christian right, not a broader movement of religion-based morality. Higher *Playboy* readership is a fairly weak predictor, although the predicted negative relationship does show up in the enforcement rate model ($p < .10$). High rates of consumption thus seem to be only mildly associated with laxer regulation. Interestingly, the interaction between political competition and *Playboy* readership is positive and statistically significant (at $p < .10$) in both the obscenity fine and enforcement rate models. This is not the relationship hypothesized, although the finding is not without precedent. Previous studies have argued that as the demand or consumption of "sin" behaviors increase, they become more visible and more subject to scrutiny by the political system (Meier 1994). This attention is likely to result in increased regulation because there are few political costs in denouncing sin and few benefits in defending it.

The variable measuring female political power is consistently negative, but only significant in the enforcement rate model. The negative relationship con-

**TABLE 12.1   DETERMINANTS OF THE PRESENCE AND ENFORCEMENT OF OBSCENITY
LAWS**

VARIABLE	MODEL 1: OBSCENITY FINES	MODEL 2: SEX ARRESTS	MODEL 3: ENFORCEMENT RATE
Fundamentalists	509.14*	0.58*	.005*
	(192)	(0.28)	(.0009)
Catholics	57.20	−0.18	.0004
	(203)	(0.29)	(.001)
Playboy circulation	−1576.72	1.08	−.01**
	(1,236)	(1.73)	(.005)
Rape	−82.48	−0.09	−.001
	(160)	(0.21)	(.007)
Female political power	−953.22	−0.37	−.006*
	(615)	(0.99)	(.003)
Political competition*	24.62**	0.02	.0001**
Playboy	(14.8)	(0.02)	(.00007)
Income	1.79*	0.002**	.00001*
	(0.83)	(0.001)	(.000004)
Intercept	−26,488	−34.01	−.13
	(20,928)	(31)	(1.22
N	49	47	49
R^2	.84	.22	.97
Adj. R^2	.80	.08	.96

*$p < .05$
**$p < .10$
Unstandardized coefficients (standard errors) reported.
Note: Model 1 included dummies for Michigan and Arizona. Model 3 included dummies for
Alabama, Arkansas, North Carolina, and West Virginia.

tradicts the expectation that increasing political equity for women will translate
into stricter state attitudes toward sexual expression. This fits with the "liberal
feminist" hypothesis rather than the "radical feminist" one. The ability to make
generalizable inferences here is complicated by the failure of the variable to meet
thresholds of statistical significance in the other models. The general pattern
favors the argument that female political power does not lead to increased regulation of sexual expression, although the findings are mixed enough to warrant
a caution in this conclusion.

The social harm hypothesis is flatly contradicted by the findings on rape
rates. The coefficient is never statistically significant, and the slopes are uniformly
negative. Sexual violence against women seems to have no role in having tough
obscenity laws or in enforcing them. In contrast, the income variable is uniformly
positive and significant. It makes sense that enforcement will partially depend on

slack societal resources, although it is less clear why wealthier states have higher obscenity fines. It may be simply that the perceived price of deterrence is higher in wealthy states and fines are consequently higher across the board.

In both the obscenity fine and enforcement rate models, a series of state dummies is included to control for outliers. Two outlier states in the obscenity fine model have higher penalties due to quirks of statutory law. Michigan has a high fine by a specific statute, and in Arizona, a conviction may be classified as a Class 5 felony; the maximum fine for any felony is $150,000, although that seems unlikely to be levied in the offense used to construct the measure. In the enforcement rate model, outlier states uniformly reflect crackdowns by state and/or local authorities. For example, Alabama has an above average enforcement rate because a large number of cases were still percolating through the system as a result of an early crackdown in the 1990s by Attorney General Jimmy Evans. These crackdowns are not region specific, and they reflect the particular characteristics of morality politics in a specific state at a specific time. However, it is worth noting that three of the four outlier states (Arkansas, Alabama, and North Carolina) have fundamentalist populations two to three times above the national average.

Conclusion

The purpose of this chapter was to examine the regulation of sexually explicit materials by testing for relationships predicted by morality policy theory while controlling for competing explanations for such regulation. Morality policy theory argues that outcomes are driven by one group's attempt to use the state to force its values on others. Other explanations, especially those associated with a particular branch of feminism, argue that regulation is driven more by concerns over social harm and female political power. My analysis has shown that the politics of porn is indeed based in attempts at value redistribution—specifically from fundamentalist groups to everyone else.

In one sense, this analysis simply confirms the obvious: Many seeking the regulation of sexual expression make no secret of the moral or religious basis of their arguments. This research also provides a measure of systematic confirmation of the fear by expressed civil libertarians that groups can effectively use the coercive power of the state to arbitrarily force their values on others. For example, the findings on political competitiveness and *Playboy* readership seem to present a double-edged sword to those who see sexual expression as a political freedom: Exercising the right to view sexually explicit material appears to be one way to put that same right at risk. This is not surprising; as Meier (Chapter 2, this volume, 23) observes, "A striking phenomenon of morality politics is that no one is willing to stand up for sin." A responsive political system is likely to react to the salience of sin by regulating it, not by legitimating the behavior of the undoubtedly numerous sinners. This reflects the contradiction between public opinion (porn is a threat) and private behavior (widespread consumption of porn) noted earlier in the chapter. If we air our clean thoughts in public and keep our dirty minds to ourselves, it is not altogether surprising that government responds to the public condemnation of "sin" rather than its private embrace. As in other morality issues, there is a clear division between public pronouncement and private behavior. Although the sin may be committed in private by many, few are willing to invoke publicly the normal strengths of majoritarian processes on behalf of the sinners. The unwillingness to stand up for sin offers groups advocating the adoption of morality policies an important political advantage. Toss these factors into a political arena where there are groups actively advocating religious-based moral codes of behavior, and there are real opportunities to use the state to redistribute values, especially if this advocacy can be linked to concerns over social order.

While the findings clearly indicate that the politics of porn is the politics of morality, they have less to say about the feminist debate that has played an increasingly important role on this issue. The general pattern is that female political power is linked to less regulation of sexual expression and that sexual violence toward women plays no role. Some of my results are ambiguous and are unlikely to do anything more than add fuel to an already divisive debate. The results show, however, that there are grounds to question whether "feminist-fundamentalist" cooperation on this issue may be to some extent a "pact with the devil" for feminist groups favoring regulation. Cooperation is something of a narrow agreement of convenience between these groups. Although both want the state to set limits on sexual expression, there is clearly a difference over the whys, and perhaps the hows. Fundamentalist political concerns are driven by the "conservative Christian version of the public good," and this includes a set of cultural norms and practices often at odds with those sought by feminists (Kobylka 1991, 61–62). The demonstrated strength of fundamentalists in the arena of regulating sexual expression and the much more ambiguous role of female political power may be as much a concern as a cause for celebration for feminists who want greater state protection for women on sexual matters.

Appendix: Measures of Variables

Obscenity laws. Maximum fine possible for a conviction of selling or renting fifteen copies of a videotape found to be legally obscene. A list of all statutes consulted is available from the author.

Sex arrests. Reported arrests per 100,000 population for offenses against chastity, common decency, morals, and the like. The measure excludes forcible rape, prostitution, and commercialized vice but does include statutory rape.

Obscenity enforcement rate. Number of state obscenity enforcement actions per 100,000 population. The measure includes arrests, prosecutions, and convictions.

Religious group membership. Percentage of a state's population belonging to the Roman Catholic Church and percentage of a state's population belonging to a Protestant fundamentalist denomination.

Playboy *circulation.* Total circulation of *Playboy* magazine per 1,000 population. This measure includes subscriptions and single copy sales.

Rape rate. Number of rapes reported to police per 100,000 population.

Female political power. Composite measure of four basic indicators of female political activity: voter registration, voter turnout, women in elective office, and institutional resources available for women (e.g., a legislative caucus, a commission on the status of women).

Political competition. Measure based on district-level state legislative election results between 1982 and 1996.

Per capita income. Total disposable income per capita.

Notes

All data used in this analysis are available publicly from the sources cited in the text or from the author. I am grateful to Kenneth Meier for sharing his data on fundamentalist adherents.

1. Historically, most (especially repressive) regimes have sought to suppress sexual expression, and the division between public condemnation of pornography and its private consumption is long standing (Strossen 1995, 218–19). The 1973 *Miller v. California* decision prompted most states to begin revising and rewriting their obscenity statutes, a long, continuing, and iterative process that provides a prime arena for struggles over value redistribution, a process that is continually repeated in decisions on when and how to enforce these laws. That the public condemnation of pornography carries more weight in this arena than the empirical fact of high levels of demand and consumption of sexually explicit materials clearly sets up redistributive possibilities for those who wish to make private behavior comport with public pronouncement.

2. I agree with Justice Stewart. I use *pornography*, *obscenity*, and *sexually explicit* as generic terms to describe any and all sexually related material that prompts attempts at regulation or censorship. Technically, obscenity may have a different legal definition; the Supreme Court has ruled that it has no First Amendment protection, while in reality, making such terms conceptually distinct seems a lost cause. At the very least, it is an objective far beyond what is attempted here.

3. The evidence here is mixed; for a recent survey of research on the issue, see Scott and Cuvelier (1993).
4. As the director of the National Obscenity Law Center informed me, "The type of statistics you're looking for don't exist."
5. The causal argument here is that rape rates can and are used as evidence of social harm that is linked to pornography (Scott and Cuvelier 1993). Whether porn does indeed cause rape is another issue not directly addressed by the chapter.
6. I also attempted an interaction between competitiveness and fundamentalist and Catholic population. These terms introduced such high levels of multicollinearity into the model (auxiliary R^2 of .9 and above) that they were dropped.

CHAPTER THIRTEEN

Morality Politics and the Implementation of Abstinence-Only Sex Education: A Case of Policy Compromise

Sandra Vergari

POLITICAL SCIENTISTS HAVE often mistakenly viewed U.S. politics purely in terms of the "tug and haul of economic interests" and have largely neglected morality politics (Leege 1992, 1993). At its heart, morality politics involves conflict over the authoritative legitimization of one set of rights or values over another (Gusfield 1963; Page and Clelland 1978; Moen 1984; Hunter 1991; Meier 1994). Government has great power to define, legitimize, and reconcile disparate world views (Heymann 1988). Thus, morality policies can be the subject of impassioned political battles.

Can policy compromise occur in morality politics? According to many morality politics theorists, morality politics is a zero-sum game characterized by highly salient issues, clashes among absolute positions, and relatively low information requirements for participation. Thus, scholars have hypothesized that compromises on morality policy are unlikely (Moen 1984; Tatalovich and Daynes 1988; Hunter 1991; Hofrenning 1995; Mooney and Lee 1995; Haider-Markel and Meier 1996). However, a recently adopted federal grant for abstinence-only sex education suggests that this notion needs refinement. As demonstrated in this chapter, a significant morality policy victory at the federal level may be moderated into a compromise at the state and local levels.

Morality Politics and Compromise

Morality politics can be thought of as conflict between status interests (as distinguished from economic interests), in which opposing sides battle for the preservation of their respective values. Status politics develops out of a group's concerns about its loss of prestige or the elevation of values and mores deemed to be objectionable to it (Gusfield 1963; Edelman 1964; Page and Clelland 1978; Moen 1984; Tatalovich and Daynes 1988; Provenzo 1990; Rochefort and Cobb 1994). In the instrumental model of policymaking, policies are evaluated in terms of their consequences for the private interests of affected individuals. Citizens want more from government, however, than a collection of goods and services; they also want to live in a society that generally expresses their values. The instrumental view of policymaking fails to capture this expressive role of government in communicating and legitimizing values (Heymann 1988).

This instrumental model of public policy focuses on rational problem solving and objective evaluation of policy outcomes. The urgency of the public problem and the short-term practicality of the proposed solution overshadow moral or ideological considerations. For instance, in the case of sex education, instrumental arguments focus on the most effective ways to prevent pregnancy and sexually transmitted diseases among teens. In contrast, expressive approaches to public policy consider moral values and whether a policy promotes or detracts from these (Lowi 1988; Rochefort and Cobb 1994). Expressive arguments take a long-term perspective and focus on the moral implications of a policy. An expressive analysis of sex education focuses on the moral principles that public schools should encourage students to uphold.

In some cases, morality politics involves competing expressive arguments about the policy in question. In the politics of assisted suicide, for example, activists who assert that individuals should be guaranteed the right to die on their own terms battle activists who argue that such a guarantee would be immoral (Glick and Hutchinson, Chapter 4, this volume). The expressive arguments offered for the two positions are rooted in different moral frameworks. Morality politics may also involve contending instrumental and expressive arguments. In controversies over sex education, instrumental arguments about reducing teen pregnancy and sexually transmitted diseases come up against compelling expressive arguments about values and moral sexual behavior (Bosso 1994).

Moral considerations and status interests may overshadow empirical evidence regarding the instrumental effects of a given policy. Even a policy that has been shown to produce a widely desired goal may be rejected on the basis of an assertion that the policy is an immoral, unacceptable means to an end.[1] Policy compromise may be thwarted due to the difficulty of overcoming powerful symbolic and emotional appeals with empirically based arguments about the instrumental benefits of a policy. As noted by Rochefort and Cobb (1994, 178), "Only those policies that are widely perceived as doing both 'what's right' and 'what will work' will cross untroubled political waters." Indeed, values-laden disagreements on "what's right" and "what works" impede morality policy compromise. Morality policy activists seek to protect and promote ideals and principles that are not merely attitudes but fundamental commitments and beliefs (Hunter 1991). Therefore, controversies over basic values and the regulation of social norms are likely to be more divisive than discussions of government action couched in instrumental terms (Mooney and Lee 1995; Heymann 1988).

While holding strongly to their beliefs, morality activists may try to engineer compromise when it is in their interest to do so. If one side in a morality conflict is about to (or does) gain a policy victory and this victory is deemed to be detrimental to the status interests of the losing side, the losing side can be expected to take all possible steps to diminish the impact and significance of the victory. If the values of the losing side are in line with public opinion, it is more likely to be successful in engineering such policy compromise. As demonstrated by Mooney and Lee (Chapter 11, this volume), when the majority has a minority-favored policy thrust upon it, it will attempt to moderate that policy to be more in line with majority values. The result may be a policy that reflects some degree of compromise between two absolute positions. As indicated later, key factors that facilitate the development of compromise on morality policy include public opinion and policy salience, bureaucratic discretion, and political culture and federalism.

A New Federal Grant for Abstinence-Only Sex Education

Public schools bear a special responsibility for preparing children for adult life in the United States, since nearly 90 percent of all K–12 students in the United States attend public schools (National Center for Education Statistics 1997). Public education plays an important role not only in helping students to acquire knowledge and develop technical skills but also in socializing students according to the norms and mores of society. The moral values expressed by the public schools can be interpreted as the expected values for all members of society (Benninga 1991; Wynne and Ryan 1993; De Roche and Williams 1998). Given the scope of its critical functions in society, it is not surprising that public education is a frequent target of morality policy activists. Recurring morality controversies in public education include debates over teaching evolutionism and creationism, school prayer, censorship of reading materials, and other curricula issues (Provenzo 1990; Gaddy, Hall, and Marzano 1996).

In a significant case of an attempt to encourage the states to adopt a morality policy, Title V of the federal Personal Responsibility and Work Opportunity Reconciliation Act of 1996 (PRWORA) initiated a five-year, $250 million block grant to be used by the states to promote abstinence-only sex education. The abstinence-only grant was advocated by conservative morality groups such as the Heritage Foundation and the Family Research Council.[2] To qualify for the grant, states must match every $4 from Washington with $3 of their own.[3] Since the states' portion of the match may be composed of in-kind contributions from state, local, and/or private sources, this was a very attractive source of federal grant money.

When advocates of policy change are unable to secure agenda status for a proposal, they frequently attempt to link it to a problem already on the decision agenda (Polsby 1984; Kingdon 1995). Given that young unwed mothers often draw on welfare programs, the welfare reform debate provided a convenient opportunity for conservative morality activists to frame the abstinence-only grant as an instrumental response to a compelling economic problem. Senator Lauch Faircloth (R-N.C.), the leading sponsor of the abstinence-only grant, explained its inclusion in the welfare reform package as follows:

> Most welfare reform proposals try to pick up the pieces after an out-of-wedlock birth has occurred. It is much more effective to prevent young women from getting pregnant in the first place. And teaching young people to abstain from sexual activity is one of the best ways to accomplish that. (Healy 1997, 1)

The federal rules require that the new grant be used for programs that deliver the message of abstinence only. As stated in the legislation, a program eligible for the funds must have "as its exclusive purpose, teaching the social, psychological, and health gains to be realized by abstaining from sexual activity." None of the funds may be used to discuss birth control or indicate tacit approval of sexual activity among teenagers. The funds need not be used for classroom instruction.

According to Carmen Pate, vice president of communications for Concerned Women for America (CWA), her organization had an expressive as opposed to instrumental intent in its support of the abstinence-only grant. She explains:

> Well, quite honestly, it's not that we're wanting states to apply for the money. It has nothing to do with that. We would prefer that people not go after federal money because then you have all the rules and regulations involved. Our fight and our voice was simply that if you're going to be talking about sex education in schools—which we don't think should be

done, we think we should be empowering our parents to teach kids about sex—but if it is going to be in the schools, then it needs to be abstinence-only. So that was our message, not so much "yes, we need these federal funds." We're not pushing that states get those federal funds. But we definitely wanted to make sure that the stipulation was there that the funds were for abstinence-only.[4]

Thus, CWA sought to advance the official status of the value of sexual abstinence in the social order through this authoritative legitimization of its moral framework. Conservative morality activists note that the abstinence-only grant makes federal funding more fair since the U.S. government funds birth control counseling in family planning clinics and for teens receiving Medicaid.[5] As noted in a report from the Heritage Foundation (Piccione and Scholle 1995, 25):

The goal of government-supported abstinence campaigns is not necessarily to make it possible for every adolescent to be in a government-funded abstinence program. Rather, the idea is to make communities aware that government tangibly supports the idea of adolescent development rooted in abstinence, risk avoidance, and the attainment of positive life goals.

Public Opinion and Policy Salience

Title V of PRWORA provides eight precise guidelines for abstinence education.[6] Significantly, at least two of the guidelines—establishing marriage as the "expected standard" of human sexual activity and that "sexual activity outside of marriage is likely to have harmful physical and psychological effects"—are not presently backed by societal consensus. Public opinion polls indicate that Americans support more comprehensive forms of sexuality education in the public schools. For instance, a recent poll on a range of education issues found broad support for giving students information about the biological aspects of sex and pregnancy, the dangers of sexually transmitted diseases, and, for older students, information about birth control (Public Agenda 1994).

Haider-Markel and Meier (1996) specify two models of the policymaking process: (1) the model of quiet, insider interest group politics and (2) the morality politics model exemplified by high salience and broad public participation. With the encouragement of the conservative morality lobby, the abstinence program was quietly slipped into the welfare reform package at a late stage in the legislative process, thus fitting the interest group model (Daley 1997; Haskins and Bevan 1997). With the implementation of the program, however, morality politics took shape as the new grant became salient and evoked much debate.

Groups such as Planned Parenthood (PP) and the Sexuality Information and Education Council of the United States (SIECUS) voiced strong opposition to the program and attempted to discourage states from applying for the funds.[7] Daniel Daley, public policy director of SIECUS, denounced the program as the broadest attack ever on the provision of comprehensive sexuality education to young people in the United States (Mathews 1997).

In contrast, several conservative morality groups advised members at the grass-roots level to contact state agencies and urge them to apply for the abstinence funds. For example, in the 13 June 1997 edition of its weekly facsimile and e-mail publication, *Ed Facts*, the Family Research Council provided a list of four actions for its supporters to take. These steps included contacting the Medical Institute for Sexual Health to obtain a list of state agencies eligible to handle the abstinence funding.[8] Supporters were advised to make phone calls to the agencies and to contact their governor and "favorable" state legislators, urging support for the abstinence money. In addition, groups "involved or interested in becoming involved in abstinence" were told to contact their state agency about how to apply for funds under the grant. Colorado-based Focus on the Family (FOF) encouraged similar activities.

During the state application period, the California health department received more than 100 calls urging the department to apply for the $5.8 million it was eligible to receive in the first year of the grant program. Catherine Camacho, a deputy director in the department, remarked that "some pretty passionate people were urging us not to miss this opportunity" (Ritter 1997, 1). In New Jersey, supporters and opponents of the program sent hundreds of letters to officials. Similarly, in Maine, the state health director was inundated with proposals on how to spend the federal funds ("Maine Leans toward Applying for Federal 'Abstinence Only' Funds" 1997; "States Set to Spend Millions" 1997). A number of states seriously considered abstaining from the abstinence funds.[9] Thus, the new federal grant became a highly salient and expressive issue for both advocates and opponents of abstinence-only sex education.

Local Control, Bureaucratic Discretion, and Federalism

There are strong cultural predispositions toward local control in the United States (Bosso 1994), and this value has long been applied to public education. Yet states rarely turn down federal money. In some states, the new abstinence grant made state health administrators uncomfortable. They risked offending groups such as PP and SIECUS, with whom they had long-standing working relationships. Nira Bonner, director of Children's Health for the Maryland Department of Health, remarked, "Because of the highly contentious nature of the debate, there are some people in my office who would not touch that program with a 10-foot pole"

(Mathews 1997, A1). Given the amount of funds available, however, state officials might have suffered severe criticism had they not applied for the abstinence grant.

In exercising their discretionary powers, administrators shape access to resources that are highly prized (Rourke 1984; Ripley and Franklin 1986). The federal application guidelines for the abstinence grant, devised by the Maternal and Child Health Bureau, include reference to the fact that "many states receive relatively modest funding under the legislative formula which will result in the development of programs with significant variation." Thus, the application rules for the grant advise that states need not place equal emphasis on each element of the eight-pronged abstinence education definition as long as the proposed project is not inconsistent with any aspect of the definition. As a result, although no state has abandoned comprehensive sex education in favor of abstinence education, the states vary widely as to how they use the grant money ("States Set to Spend Millions" 1997). Some states, such as Virginia, will use the grant for sex education in the public schools (Mathews 1997). In contrast, New Jersey will not channel any of the money to its public schools because the New Jersey public school curriculum standard for sex education requires that students receive instruction about both abstinence and contraception, in violation of the federal guidelines for the abstinence grant.

Significantly, many of the fifty state applications for the first year of the abstinence grant reflect a loose rather than strict interpretation of the law's guidelines. Many states plan to ignore parts of the law they do not support, with most states viewing the grant as an opportunity to supplement teen pregnancy prevention efforts already underway. As indicated in Table 13.1 (p. 208), about forty states plan to give grants to youth and community-based organizations. More than half of the states have applied to use the federal funds for mass media campaigns promoting abstinence; some states plan after-school recreation programs to keep teens occupied during hours when homes are empty. Some will use the funds for mentoring programs on the dangers of drugs and alcohol in reducing inhibitions to engage in sexual activity. Such uses of the funds mean that birth control can still be discussed in the classroom while the value of abstinence is promoted in other contexts. This represents an unmistakable form of compromise on abstinence-only education.

Focus on the Family has publicized its dissatisfaction with this situation through interviews and guest editorials in the mass media (Hoskins 1997; Mathews 1997). Spokespersons for FOF have argued that some states are subverting the legislative intent of the abstinence program. Similar expressions of discontent have emerged from other sources. Two leading members of the House of Representatives who were involved in drafting the abstinence provision, House Commerce Committee Chairman Thomas Bliley (R-Va.) and Ways and Means Committee Chairman Bill Archer (R-Tex.) have expressed concerns that states may be dodging the requirement that the new grant be used for abstinence-only

TABLE 13.1   STATE PLANS FOR THE ABSTINENCE-ONLY EDUCATION GRANT (FY 1998)

PROPOSED USE OF PROGRAM FUNDS	STATES
Mass media campaigns (30 states)	Ala., Ark., Ariz., Calif., Colo., Conn., Del., Ga., Idaho, Ind., Ky., Maine, Md., Mass., Mich., Minn., Mont., Nebr., N.M., N.Y., Nev., Okla., Pa., Tenn., Tex., Vt., Va., Wash., Wisc., Wyo.
Grants to youth and/or community-based groups[a] (41 states)	Alaska, Ala., Ark., Ariz., Calif., Colo., Conn., Del., Fla., Ga., Hawaii, Idaho, Ill., Ind., Iowa, Kans., Ky., La., Md., Mich., Minn., Miss., Mo., Nebr., N.J., N.M., N.Y., N.C., N.D., Ohio, Okla., Ore., R.I., S.C., S.D., Tenn., Tex., Utah, Va., Wash., Wisc.
Mentoring and/or after-school programs[b] (5 states)	Ky., Md., N.Y., R.I., Tex.
Other (2 states)	N.H.[c], W.V.[d]

Source: Abstinence education grant abstracts for FY 1998 submitted by each state to the Maternal and Child Health Bureau, U.S. Department of Health and Human Services.

a. Most states in this category did not specify that the grants would be directed toward public schools in particular. However, the North Carolina proposal specifies that grants will be provided to local school boards, and the Mississippi proposal notes that grants will be given to local schools and other community based organizations.

b. These grant proposals made specific reference to after-school and/or mentoring programs. This does not preclude the possibility that other states will channel funds to community organizations that will establish such programs.

c. New Hampshire proposed to use the grant to develop a statewide abstinence education training site; however, it returned its grant for FY 1998.

d. West Virginia planned to use the FY 1998 grant for planning and developing an abstinence-only program aimed at 10–14-year-olds.

programs (Portner 1997; "Abstinence-Only Plans Questioned" 1998). This criticism from the proponents of this policy is a strong indication that there has been slippage, or compromise, in the expressive contest of its implementation.

Conclusion

Why did compromise occur in this case of morality policy? It was not because any of the stakeholders desired compromise from the outset. Advocates of abstinence-only sex education wanted their status interests respected as states implemented the grant. They wanted the states to affirm the moral values embodied in the eight-pronged definition of abstinence education contained in PRWORA. Opponents of abstinence-only sex education, however, were dismayed that such a grant had been approved. Only in the implementation of the grant was this minority-favored policy modified to be more in line with majority values.

A combination of factors explains the outcome of compromise on this morality policy. As the abstinence grant became salient during the implementation phase, its opponents sought to engineer a policy compromise. They were aided in their efforts by several factors. First, they had majority opinion on their side. Second, the tradition of local control was evident when officials in some states initially considered forgoing their share of the federal abstinence-only funds. Third, the Maternal and Child Health Bureau exercised its discretionary power when declaring that projects eligible for the new grant need not uphold all components of the abstinence-only definition specified in PRWORA.

The federal abstinence grant provided bold guidelines and a financial incentive for states to promote a significant minority-held value. To date, the states have not embraced the program and the values it represents with the enthusiasm desired by its proponents. Instead, events in many states reflect obvious compromise on the issue. It will be useful to track whether this pattern of events continues in subsequent years of the grant and how any new data on the instrumental value of alternative sex education programs impact the morality politics in this policy area.

The case of the federal abstinence-only sex education grant presents several insights for morality politics theorists. Given their strongly held views, morality policy activists typically avoid policy compromise. However, morality politics can result in policies that reflect compromises between absolute positions. Morality legislation that apparently signals a victory for one side can take a different form during the implementation phase. In particular, the exercise of bureaucratic discretion can serve as a moderating force in morality politics. When morality politics involves federalism, the abstinence case suggests that state-level responses may favor the values of state autonomy and local control over one or more federally prescribed moral values. These dynamics favoring the moderation of a morality policy are most likely to occur when the originally adopted policy becomes salient and is also counter to majority opinion.

Notes

I am grateful to Chris Mooney for his many helpful comments on previous drafts of this chapter.

1. For example, evidence indicating that government-sponsored needle exchange programs are effective in reducing the spread of AIDS has been overshadowed by powerful expressive arguments. According to an instrumental analysis, needle exchange programs constitute a pragmatic response to a serious social problem. For activists who analyze needle exchange programs from a purely expressive orientation, such programs undermine respect for the law and condone drug use, and not even alleviating the challenge of AIDS is an end justified by such means (Anderson 1991; Rochefort and Cobb 1994).

2. For further information on the passage of the legislation, see Haskins and Bevan (1997) and Daley (1997).
3. The federal grant is awarded based on a formula of the ratio of low-income children in a state to the total of low-income children in all states. States must reapply each year. For the first round (FY 1998), all states applied and were awarded federal funds. New Hampshire returned its allocation.
4. Author interview with Ms. Pate, 11 July 1997. CWA is a conservative organization based in Washington, D.C.
5. See the Family Planning program specified in Title X of the Public Health Service Act and Medicaid. The Adolescent Family Life (AFL) program, enacted in 1981 as Title XX of the Public Health Service Act, develops and tests programs with an abstinence component. The AFL program was directed to spend $9 million of its $14.2 million FY 1997 budget on abstinence education in accordance with the eight abstinence guidelines established in PL 104–193.
6. The eight guidelines specified in Title V of PRWORA follow:
   (1) Abstinence from sexual activity has social, psychological, and health gains.
   (2) Abstinence from sexual activity outside marriage is the expected standard for all school-age children.
   (3) Abstinence from sexual activity is the only certain way to avoid out-of-wedlock pregnancy, sexually transmitted diseases, and other associated health problems.
   (4) A mutually faithful monogamous relationship in the context of marriage is the expected standard of human sexual activity.
   (5) Sexual activity outside of marriage is likely to have harmful psychological and physical effects.
   (6) Childbearing out of wedlock is likely to have harmful consequences for the child, the child's parents, and society.
   (7) Alcohol and drug use increases vulnerability to sexual advances.
   (8) It is important to attain self-sufficiency before engaging in sexual activity.
7. SIECUS is a New York–based organization that promotes comprehensive sex education.
8. The Medical Institute for Health, based in Texas, is a conservative morality organization formed in 1992. It aims to counter the activities of the liberal morality group SIECUS.
9. Officials in Wyoming and Connecticut chose to apply only after learning that they could use staff time and office supplies as their matching contributions and thus not have to divert funds from other programs aimed at preventing teen pregnancy ("States Set to Spend Millions" 1997).

PART SEVEN

Morality Policymaking in Parliamentary Systems

CHAPTER FOURTEEN

Morality Policy without Politics? The Case of Britain

Philip Cowley

BRITISH POLITICS HAS been described as "postparliamentary," with public policy being formulated in segmented consensus-seeking policy communities, each community consisting of the relevant organized interests and executive units (Richardson and Jordan 1979, 191). Policy thus constructed is presented to a legislature that, as a result of high levels of party cohesion and an electoral system that tends to give exaggerated parliamentary majorities to the governing party, almost unquestioningly agrees to it. It is extremely rare for governments to see their measures defeated within Parliament; even minor amendments are very unlikely unless supported by the government. As Michael Mezey (1979) puts it, the British Parliament is a reactive rather than an active legislature. Even by comparison with many other reactive legislatures, the British Parliament's influence on legislation is low (Norton 1990). Parliament is "at best a proximate—at worst, a marginal—actor in determining the content of measures of public policy" (Norton 1993, 88). In Britain, therefore, the government may not necessarily govern well, but govern it most certainly does.

However, in the formulation of morality policy in Britain, this pattern does not appear to hold. The key difference between morality politics and "normal" politics in Britain is that the former is often described and treated as issues of "conscience." That is, it is usually treated as issues on which it would be wrong for the political parties to adopt stances. As a result, the executive remains neutral, and the issues are left to parliamentarians to decide according to their own consciences. Legislators are accordingly not given instructions on how to vote by their parties, and such votes are therefore known as "free votes." As a result, rather than being peripheral, the legislature—and the legislators within it—becomes central to morality policy politics. If the formulation of British public policy as a whole is postparliamentary, when dealing with issues of conscience, it remains most firmly parliamentary.

The politics of morality in Britain, therefore, appears to be atypical. This chapter examines the consequences of this for the British political system, focusing on the way moral issues are removed from the electoral domain. The chapter also argues, however, that despite the different way in which morality politics is handled, there are more similarities with "normal" policy than immediately appear evident. Although parliamentarians are not issued instructions on how to vote, party remains the key determinant of vote outcomes. Although the executive usually declares itself neutral, it remains an important political actor.

Issues of Conscience

Although there is no unequivocal definition of what constitutes an issue of conscience, topics usually considered to be so defined include corporal and capital punishment, abortion and embryo research, hunting, contraception, euthanasia, the punishment of war criminals, Sunday entertainment and trading, homosexuality, prostitution, censorship, divorce, and (somewhat incongruously) the compulsory wearing of car seatbelts (Jones 1995). With the exception of the last, therefore, most issues of conscience are also issues of morality politics, as that term is defined and understood in the United States and as that term is used in the other chapters in this volume.

However, there are prima facie issues of morality that have generally not been issues of conscience in the British Parliament. For example, the majority of animal welfare issues go through the normal legislative procedure. The government takes a stance and then expects its MPs to follow. Hunting is the exception, for reasons that are difficult to identify (Garner 1998). Issues such as single parents, while being acknowledged as having a moral dimension, are not treated as issues of conscience (Isaac 1994). The Conservative government took special care that the policy on AIDS was to be treated more as a medical issue than one of morality (Durham 1991; Fowler 1991).

Even with those issues that are normally seen as being issues of conscience, there is nothing automatic about MPs having free votes. There have been occasions in recent years when MPs were not granted free votes on issues in the preceding list, including capital punishment, censorship, homosexuality, and Sunday trading (see Cowley 1998, 180–81). Free votes on issues of conscience may be the norm, but they are not the rule.

The congruence between "morality issues" and "conscience issues" therefore is not perfect. However, the heading of conscience issues subsumes nearly all the major morality issues. It normally covers, for example, all the topics discussed in the other chapters in this volume. For this reason, this chapter concentrates on those issues of morality politics that are viewed as issues of conscience while recognizing that this definition does not include each and every morality issue if that latter term is broadly defined.

Dogs That Do Not Bark

Treating most morality issues as issues of conscience removes them almost entirely from the electoral domain. British elections rarely include more than a passing mention (if that) of such issues. This exclusion works on several levels. First, and most formally, because the parties do not take stances on these issues, the issues are rarely mentioned in their manifestos, the documents issued by the parties stating what they intend to do if elected (Budge, Robertson, and Hearl 1987). Second, the issues are largely absent from the national campaign. Table 14.1 (p. 216) lists the ten most frequently mentioned topics in the broadcast media in the five general elections from 1979 to 1997. Although the prominent issues vary somewhat from election to election, there is one commonality: the striking absence of issues of morality. Table 14.2 (p. 217) gives similar data for the national print media for the last four elections.[1] Again, while the issues vary from election to election, the exclusion of morality issues is a constant. Third, morality issues are not mentioned by the public as being important, either in terms of the needs of the nation as a whole or in terms of determining their own vote (see, for example, Crewe 1993, 113; Sanders 1997, 50).

Given the free votes that the parties have on these issues, this low electoral salience for morality policy should not be surprising. It is, after all, difficult for a party to campaign on, or to be attacked on, an issue to which its official stance is to be neutral. What happens at the local level? Given that the free vote leaves the decision up to the individual candidates, we might expect candidates to raise morality issues as part of their campaigns and for pressure groups to target individual candidates.

Table 14.3 (p. 218) shows the percentage of candidates of the three main parties to mention morality issues in their election addresses—that is, the statements issued by candidates to their electors—between 1979 and 1987.[2] Although election addresses "would not normally figure highly in a list of voters' sources of information about politics" (Denver and Hands 1997, 103), they give us an idea of the type of issues that candidates *think* are important and/or might endear them to voters. Of all morality issues, capital punishment was the most frequently mentioned, but it was almost exclusively mentioned by Conservatives.

TABLE 14.1   TOP TEN ISSUES IN NATIONAL BROADCAST MEDIA IN GENERAL ELECTIONS, 1979–97

ORDER	1979	1983	1987	1992	1997
1	Leaders' tours	Employment	Defense	Economic policy	Europe
2	Prices/ inflation	Defense	Employment	Taxes	Constitution
3	Law and order	Foreign affairs	Education	Constitution	Sleaze
4	Unions/ industrial relations	Economy	National Health Service (NHS)	NHS	Education
5	Taxes	General attacks or self-praise	Economy	"Jennifer's Ear"	Taxes
6	Jobs/ unemployment	Social services	Attacks, self-praise, and exhortation	Education	NHS
7	Cost of Tory tax cuts	Inflation, prices, and wages	Taxes	Proportional representation (PR)	Pensions
8	Industry and new technology	Constitution	Hung Parliament	Hung Parliament	Economy
9	Ills of socialism	Public expenditure	Law and order	Employment	Employment
10	Northern Ireland	Europe	Ireland	Public expenditure	Law and order

Source: Adapted from Pilsworth 1980 and Harrison 1984, 1988, 1992, 1997.

No Labour Members of Parliament (MP) and only a handful of Center Party MPs did so. This is, of course, not surprising: Labour and Center Party MPs vote against capital punishment, which is favored heavily by the public, whereas Conservative MPs tend to vote in favor of its restoration.[3] Animal welfare was also mentioned by candidates of all parties in 1983 and 1987. Other morality issues, however, receive scant attention: abortion is mentioned by less than 5 percent of candidates (mostly Conservatives), AIDS only in 1987 and then by just 1 percent of Conservatives and 2 percent of Social Democratic Party (SDP) candidates, and family or moral issues more generally were mentioned by just slightly more candidates.[4] It is also striking that some issues, such as homosexuality and divorce, were not mentioned at all.

Even at the local level, then, where one might have thought candidates would be able to make some play of these issues, morality politics plays a distinctly lim-

TABLE 14.2   TOP TEN FRONT-PAGE LEAD STORIES IN NATIONAL PRESS IN GENERAL ELECTIONS, 1983–97

ORDER	1983	1987	1992	1997
1	Defense	Opinion polls	Opinion polls	Europe
2	Opinion polls	Defense	Taxes/spending	Party strategies/ prospects
3	Party strategies	Scandal	Party strategies/ prospects	Party election broadcasts
4	Summits	Party strategies/ prospects	Party election broadcasts	Manifestos
5	Manifestos	Taxes	PR/hung Parliament	Opinion polls
6	Healy/Kinnock on Falklands	Health	Exhortation to vote	Northern Ireland
7	Thatcher's speeches	Education	Fitness to govern	Taxes/public spending
8	Election announcement	Manifestos	Challenge of Liberal Democrats	Exhortation to vote/advice on voting
9	IRA threat	Editorials	Budget/shadow budget	Health
10	Alliance progress	Divided Britain	Health	Other

Source: Adapted from Harrop 1984, 1988; Harrop and Scammell 1992; and Scammell and Harrop 1997.

ited role in the electoral process: Even capital punishment, at its peak, was mentioned in just one-third of constituencies. Some organizations, such as the Movement for Christian Democracy (Bell 1997; Graffius 1997), try to publicize the stances of candidates on specific issues, but they are hampered by the 1983 Representation of the People Act, which prohibits the expenditure by groups of more than a total of £5 (less than $10) during the election period to convey information to electors with a view to promoting the election of a candidate (Read 1998). The evidence we have about the activity of such groups at election time suggests that it is very limited (Butler and Kavanagh 1997, 220–21).

As a result, the knowledge of electors about the stances taken by candidates on morality issues is low (Crewe 1985; Cowley 1995, 107–8). There is some limited evidence that positions taken by MPs on free votes—most notably the death penalty—can affect their electoral fortunes (Pattie, Fieldhouse, and Johnston 1994, 378–79), but any such "personal" vote remains extremely marginal (Gaines 1998). What personal vote does exist is usually assumed to be caused by constituency-based work rather than resulting from MPs' stances on issues (Norton and Wood 1993). British elections remain primarily national-level events. As we have seen, morality issues play but a small part at the national level. Thus, the

TABLE 14.3   PERCENTAGE OF CANDIDATES MENTIONING MORALITY ISSUES
IN THEIR ELECTION ADDRESSES, 1979–87

	LABOUR	CENTER	CONSERVATIVE
Abortion			
1979	3	4	3
1983	1	0	2
1987	0	0	2
Capital Punishment			
1979	0	0	35
1983	0	0	13
1987	0	0/3	19
Animal Welfare			
1983	26	4/30	10
1987	2	0	3
AIDS			
1987	0	2/0	1
Family/Moral Issues			
1987	3	0	6
"Victorian Values"			
1983	14	0/2	0

Source: Butler and Kavanagh 1980, 298–301; 1984, 258–61; 1988, 222–26.

Note: Center parties were the Liberals (in 1979) and the Liberal/SDP Alliance in 1983 and 1987. Figures for 1983 and 1987 give SDP first, followed by Liberals.

most striking feature about morality policy in general elections in Britain is its lack of importance. With one or two minor exceptions, morality issues simply do not register during elections.

The Centrality of Party

One of the main justifications for treating issues of morality as free votes and removing them from the partisan fray is that they are said to "cut across party lines," to be nonparty, "above" party, cross-party, or to be not "issues of party politics" (see Cowley 1998, 187). This belief is understandable. When these issues come before Parliament, they tend to be supported (or opposed) by a range of MPs from all parties. MPs bringing forward an amendment or bill are usually supported by MPs from other parties, on both sides of the House (that is, government and opposition), and often stress the cross-party nature of their support. This is not the norm in British politics, in which the majority of votes see complete party cohesion, with no MPs cross-voting (Cowley and Norton 1998, n.d.). As a result, the issues are usually reported differently in the media. The free vote (notable because it is not the norm) is highlighted, as (for the same reason) is the extent of cross-party support; the focus of reporting is not (as it usually is) the split between government and opposition.

However, regardless of this perception, conscience issues *are* party issues, at least as measured by the behavior of parliamentarians voting on them. The media and politicians tend to concentrate on the exceptions (those MPs voting against the majority of their party) and overlook the norm (that the majority of MPs are not doing so). For example, when two Labour MPs voted against banning hunting and eight Conservatives voted in favor of such a ban, *The Times* (29 November 1997) said that they had "defied conventional wisdom about the politics of hunting." Yet 374 Labour MPs (99 percent of those voting) voted in favor of a ban, while 128 Conservatives (94 percent) voted against it.

I test this proposition with a measure known as the *Index of Party Unity* (IPU), which is calculated by subtracting the minority percentage on a vote from that of the majority (excluding all nonvoters) and then expressing the outcome as a proportion (Read, Marsh, and Richards 1994, 375; Rice 1925). The IPU ranges from 0.0 to 1.0. An IPU of zero indicates that the party is totally split, with half voting in one lobby and half in the other lobby. An IPU of 1.0 indicates that the party is totally cohesive, with all voting MPs voting in the same lobby. As defined by Lowell (1908), a party vote with 90 percent of a party voting in one lobby and 10 percent in the other yields a value of 0.80. A split that sees one-third of a party's MPs faced by two-thirds yields an IPU of 0.33.

Table 14.4 (p. 220) shows the IPUs for the three main British party groups for a range of free votes between 1979 and 1998. In each case, one key vote per issue has been selected to use for this analysis.[5] The votes are as follows:

1. A vote to restore the death penalty for murder (Death) (21 February 1994).

2. A vote to introduce a bill allowing euthanasia (Euthan) (10 December 1997).

3. A vote to tighten the divorce laws (Divorce) (24 April 1996).

4. The Second Reading of the 1990 War Crimes Bill, which would have allowed war criminals now living in Britain to be tried for crimes committed overseas when not British subjects (Warcrms) (19 March 1990).

5. A vote to lower the age of consent for male homosexual acts to sixteen (Gay16) (22 June 1998).

6. A vote to introduce a bill prohibiting so-called Page Three Girls (naked or partially naked women in sexually provocative poses in newspapers) (Page3) (13 April 1988).

7. The Second Reading of the 1986 Obscene Publications (Protection of Children Etc.) (Amendment) Bill, which tightened the 1959 Obscene Publications Act (Obscene) (24 January 1986).

8. The Second Reading of the 1997 Wild Mammals (Hunting with Dogs) Bill, which would have prohibited hunting with hounds (Hunting) (28 November 1997).

9. The Third Reading of the 1994 Sunday Trading Bill, which partially deregulated Sunday trading (Sunday) (23 February 1994).

10. A vote to reduce the time limit for abortion to twenty-four weeks (Abort) (24 April 1990).

11. A vote to ban the ownership of all handguns (Guns) (11 June 1997).

12. A vote to legalize (under certain restrictions) embryo research (Embryo) (23 April 1990).

In each case, the Conservative Party's IPU is in bold type, as are those parties for which the majority of the voting MPs vote with the majority of the Conservatives. This enables the reader to see whether or not parties are voting together.[6]

First, note how the majority of each of the two main parties vote in opposite lobbies on most occasions. Only three of the votes see a majority of Labour

TABLE 14.4   IPU FOR SELECTED FREE VOTES, 1979–98

	CONSERVATIVE	CENTER	LABOR
Death	**0.09**	1.00	1.00
Euthan	**0.90**	**0.34**	**0.20**
Divorce	**0.17**	0.45	0.82
Warcrms	**0.48**	**0.75**	**0.92**
Gay16	**0.70**	0.82	0.90
Page3	**0.57**	0.60	1.00
Obscene	**0.94**	**0.75**	0.19
Hunting	**0.88**	0.32	0.98
Sunday	**0.78**	**0.12**	0.51
Abort	**0.89**	**0.50**	0.30
Guns	**1.00**	**0.22**	0.96
Embryo	**0.12**	**0.67**	**0.68**

Note: The IPU of the Conservatives and of those parties for which the majority of the voting MPs vote with the majority of the Conservatives is in bold type.

and Conservative MPs in the same lobby—Euthan, Warcrms, and Embryo—and these are issues on which the majority of the center parties join them. These three issues, then, are examples of the main division not being between the parties, but these are the exceptions. On all the other issues, the majority of Labour MPs face the majority of Conservative MPs.

Second, note how the parties split internally. Table 14.5 shows the party splits for the two main parties. The Conservatives split on three issues—Embryo, Death, and Divorce—but on all three issues, Labour is either completely unified, party voting, or, at most (e.g., on Embryo), just slightly divided. Conversely, when Labour is split, the Conservatives are united. This is true of Obscene, Abort, and Euthan. There is not one situation of these selected votes for which both parties have IPUs of less than 0.33. The nearest we get to a situation in which both main parties split is on Embryo, for which the Labour IPU is 0.68 and that for the Conservatives is 0.12. Even this represents a situation in which some 84 percent of the Labour Party's voting MPs were in the same lobby.

If we move from macroanalysis—examining how the parties behave en bloc—to microanalysis—examining how individual MPs behave when voting—party remains preeminent. Studies of MPs' voting on these issues find party to be the only consistent force affecting the way MPs vote (see Richards 1970; Pattie, Fieldhouse, and Johnston 1994; Pattie, Johnston, and Stuart 1998; Hibbing and Marsh 1987; Marsh and Read 1988; Mughan and Scully 1997; for a parallel finding in the Canadian Parliament, see Overby, Tatalovich, and Studlar 1998). To be sure, other factors do influence the votes. Taking all other factors into account, Roman Catholic MPs are more likely to vote in favor of restrictions on abortion and embryo research and are less likely to support euthanasia (Pattie, Johnston, and Stuart 1998). Women are less likely than men to vote in favor of restrictions on

TABLE 14.5   **LABOR AND CONSERVATIVE DIVISIONS ON FREE VOTES, 1979–98**

	CONSERVATIVE		
LABOUR	Split (IPU<0.33)	Divided (0.33≤IPU≤0.80)	Cohesive (IPU≥0.80)
Split (IPU<0.33)			Obscene Abort Euthan
Divided (0.33≤IPU≤0.80)	Embryo	Sunday	
Cohesive (IPU≥0.80)	Death Divorce	Warcrms Page3 Gay16	Hunting Guns

abortion. Age and education also have a limited effect, both tending to be liber-
alizing influences (Richards 1970). Constituency factors can also play a small role
(Hibbing and Marsh 1987; Pattie, Johnston, and Stuart 1998). These are sporadic
influences, however; for the most part, party dominates. Even when freed from
the supposed constraints of the party whips, the "MPs' first instinct is still to vote
with their fellow party members. They are like creatures of habit: like salmon
crossing the ocean to spawn in the river where they hatched, MPs tend to follow
pre-set routes, even when there is nothing to force them to do so" (Pattie, Johnston, and Stuart 1998, 172).

Given this micro- and macrolevel analysis, it is difficult to argue that morality politics is nonpartisan in Britain. It is rare to find an issue on which both of
the major parties are significantly split. Conscience issues may split some of the
parties some of the time, but they do not split all of the parties all of the time.
The outcome of votes on these issues, therefore, owes much—although not every-
thing (Mughan and Scully 1997, 647)—to the party composition of the Commons. Given the current behavior of MPs, a House of Commons with a respectable
Conservative majority would very likely not vote to lower the age of consent for
homosexual men to sixteen, to ban handgun ownership, or to prohibit hunting
with hounds. Yet, because of the current Labour majority, all three of these issues
are likely to be resolved in this way by the end of the Parliament. To talk of issues
of morality being nonparty issues, therefore, hides the importance of party.

The Importance of the Executive

Just as party remains important even when issues are described as nonparty, so
the executive remains important even when the decision is left to the legislature.
On occasions, this is because the executive declares itself neutral but applies pressure behind the scenes (Bromhead 1956, 13–14). As one cabinet minister wryly
admitted in March 1996, there are "free votes and free votes" (HC Debs, 25
March 1996, 742). Even when the executive is not applying such pressure, it is
not divorced from the policymaking process. Rather, it remains an actor, playing an important role in facilitating the discussion and resolution of the issues.
It does so in two principal ways: either by lending assistance to private members'
bills—that is, bills introduced by backbench MPs—or by bringing forward government bills on which it then adopts a neutral stance, either in full or in part.

The former used to be the norm. In the 1960s, a series of private members'
bills that affected significant changes in morality policy in Britain was passed:
the de facto abolition of capital punishment in Great Britain, the legalization of
male homosexuality in England and Wales, and the liberalization of laws relating to censorship, divorce, and abortion (Richards 1970; Pym 1974). The

avowed neutrality of the government on these issues (i.e., allowing free votes on the bills) and the fact that the bills emanated from backbench MPs combined to give the impression that the government was neutral.

In fact, far from being a neutral bystander, the then-Labour government had been central to the passage of these bills. This is so because the rules of the British legislature do not make it easy for private members' bills to succeed. Such bills are frail creatures, easily killed by the rigors of Westminster (Marsh and Read 1988; Norton 1997). It is easy for those who object to their content to obstruct and kill private members' bills, whatever the size of the bill's majority. Indeed, the ease with which private members' bills can be stopped is demonstrated by the fact that not since 1959 has such a bill opposed by even a single MP at either Second or Third Reading passed into law without the government of the day lending its support by granting the bill additional parliamentary time (Marsh and Read 1988). In the 1960s, in particular, the Labour government gave considerable time to the various private members' bills dealing with conscience issues (Richards 1970; Short 1989). Had it not done so, all would most certainly have failed. The attitude of the government, therefore, was vital.

Governments since the 1960s have been more possessive of their control of the parliamentary timetable; such government time that has been given since then has been minor, mainly used to tidy up bills as when amendments made by the House of Lords threaten an otherwise uncontroversial bill (Marsh and Read 1988). By their very nature, issues of morality are usually controversial, and, as a result, governments have been unwilling to allow the bills to benefit from extra parliamentary time. As a result, a series of backbench measures backed by the Commons has failed to become law, most notably those concerning hunting and abortion (Garner 1998; Millns and Sheldon 1998).

Parliamentarians continue to use private members' bills to enact uncontentious pieces of legislation and to attract publicity for a topic (Cowley and Stace 1996; Berry 1996; Brown 1996), but it is now more usual for conscience issues to be *resolved* through pieces of legislation introduced by the government (Cowley 1998, 177–78). The precise details vary from issue to issue, but we can usefully identify three methods by which conscience issues are now resolved. The first two are initiated by the executive and the last by individual MPs, but they all involve government bills.

The first method is when the government introduces a bill into Parliament but then adopts a neutral stance from the beginning. This was done, for example, on the Human Fertilization and Embryology Act 1990, the War Crimes Act 1991, and the Sunday Trading Act 1993. In such cases, the government believes that it is important for a morality issue to be resolved and introduces a bill to expedite the process. The resolution of the issue is more important for the government than any particular policy outcome in these cases. The second method is when the government introduces a bill on which it intends to take a stance but on which it subsequently is forced to adopt a position of neutrality. This happened, for example, with the Family Law Act 1996, for which the government offered free votes on key parts once it became clear that it would face a sizable rebellion if it did not. The third method is when backbench MPs move amendments to government bills, inserting clauses dealing with morality issues into bills primarily concerned with nonmorality issues. This has happened, for example, to many criminal justice bills into which backbench MPs have attempted (sometimes successfully) to insert amendments dealing with the age of homosexual consent or capital punishment. As long as the subject matter is deemed appropriate for that bill, and as long as the executive is not hostile to the amendment, a free vote may be granted. If the amendment is carried, the government bill then proceeds through Parliament carrying a morality-related amendment.

Just because the executive adopts a neutral stance on these issues does not mean that it does not play an important role. The very act of introducing a bill enables the legislature to come to a decision (something that might be difficult otherwise) and, once a decision has been reached, it is usual for the government to apply the whips to the rest of the bill's passage to pilot the bill onto the statute book (something that would be practically impossible otherwise). In the case of the War Crimes Act, this involved invoking the Parliament Act to force the issue past a hostile upper chamber (Ganz 1992, 1998; Richardson 1992).

It could be argued that in doing this, the executive is just enabling the will of the legislature to prevail. However, the government plays an important role by choosing *which* issues it will facilitate in this way. Since 1992, for example, it is likely that there has been a majority in the Commons in favor of abolishing hunting with hounds. Yet it is notable that the Conservative government— the majority of whose members supported hunting—did not bring a bill forward to facilitate the legislature in making its decision. As a result, hunting continued to be legal. The decision of the executive, therefore, while appearing to be neutral, was not neutral in its effect on policy.

Conclusion

If the fundamental question that this volume attempts to resolve is whether the politics of morality policy is fundamentally different from that of nonmorality policy (cf. Lowi 1972, 1998; Smith 1969), the answer from Britain appears to be "yes, but . . . ."

The "yes" part of that conclusion is clear and self-evident. The majority of issues of morality—certainly nearly all that excite scholars and observers in other polities—are treated in Britain as a breed apart. In a political system dominated by party and executive, the issues are treated as nonpartisan and are dealt with by the legislature.

The "but . . ." part of the conclusion is less obvious but equally important. It has two components. First, some issues that could be defined as issues of morality are not seen as issues of conscience. These go through the normal executive-dominated policy process. Both Smith (1969, 1975) and Studlar (1996) argue that when this happens, morality issues will lead to higher levels of rebellion against the party whips. This certainly happened in the case of the 1986 Shops Bill, which was defeated at Second Reading when seventy-two Conservative MPs voted against their own government (Bown 1990; Regan 1988). This was the only government bill in the entire twentieth century to be defeated at Second Reading when the government enjoyed a parliamentary majority. However, this case aside, there is as yet no evidence that suggests that the higher level of rebellion applies to other nonconscience moral issues as well. Second, and more significantly, despite the perception that conscience issues are nonpartisan, party appears to remain key in determining the outcome of votes and the resolution of public policy, just as it does in "normal" policy. Similarly, just as in nonmorality policy, the stance of the executive is important in determining the outcome. The difference between morality and nonmorality politics, then, is not quite as stark as it first seems.

The British case gives one additional comparative insight into the nature of morality politics. It demonstrates that nothing is inevitable about morality issues having high salience. In Britain, the issues may have high salience when a measure is passing through Parliament, at which point they can attract significant letter-writing campaigns and/or external protests (Cowley 1998, 190).[7] In turn, this can lead to increased media coverage of the issue (Cowley and Stace 1996). However, because the political elites tend to view these issues as nonpartisan, their salience remains limited to these narrow points in time. For most of the time—and particularly during elections—the salience of these issues is low. Morality issues, therefore, may not enjoy high salience if—as in Britain—the political environment neutralizes them. As a result, for most of the time in Britain, the politics has been taken out of morality policy.

Notes

1. Unfortunately, comparable data for the 1979 election are not available. Capital punishment did feature briefly in the newspapers' editorial columns during that election as a result of the assassination of the Conservative MP Airey Neave at the beginning of the campaign. However, most of the coverage focused on the rights and wrongs of the issue per se or on the promise of a free vote rather than as a force that should make electors back one or other of the parties (Bilton and Himelfarb 1980).

2. Again, unfortunately, problems of data comparability prevent analysis of a longer timeframe. Before 1979, the Nuffield studies of the election did not print the data in tabulated form, and from 1992 onward advances in publishing meant that candidates rarely issued just one election address, preferring instead to target their message, making such analysis of the election addresses difficult. The data reported in Table 14.3 are drawn from a sample of addresses rather than from all addresses (see Butler and Kavanagh 1980, 298–301; 1984, 258–61; 1988, 222–26).

3. The data do not reveal what each candidate said about capital punishment, merely that he or she said something. However, given the figures for Labour and the Center Parties, it is plausible to assume that those Conservative MPs mentioning the subject were in favor of its restoration.

4. "Victorian values," a phrase of Mrs. Thatcher, was mentioned solely by Opposition MPs in 1983, and so we can assume that they were doing so pejoratively.

5. For more detailed analysis of the votes than is possible here, see Cowley and Stuart (1997).

6. An alternative measure would be to indicate whether the parties voted in a "liberal" or a "conservative" fashion. However, this is difficult to do. Take the cases of Page3 and Obscene. Both are issues of censorship. Yet, as Table 14.4 indicates, the two issues see the parties behave in a different way. Which position is the "liberal" position?

7. As one Labour MP said, "God writes an awful lot of letters" (MP to author, December 1998).

CHAPTER FIFTEEN

Avoiding the Issue Down Under: The Politics of Legalizing Abortion in Australia

Ian Mylchreest

LIKE MOST WESTERN DEMOCRACIES, Australia legalized medical abortion in the 1970s. In comparison with other countries, this process was undertaken with a minimum of legal formality. Political leaders refused to repeal criminal abortion restrictions (e.g., the N.S.W. Crimes Act 1900, ss. 82–84; the Victorian Crimes Act 1958, ss. 65–66), but they acquiesced in de facto legalization. This process generated neither the prolonged controversy that characterized the *Roe* v. *Wade* (410 U.S. 113 [1973]) decision in the United States (Garrow 1994), nor the grand compromises that brought the issue to closure in Western Europe (Outshoorn 1996). In effect, Australian policymakers were able to avoid the abortion issue.

When abortion regulation reform first became a realistic possibility, the issue seemed destined to follow the typical pattern of morality politics (Luker 1984; Goggin 1993). A progressive coalition of academics, law reformers, doctors, and, in later years, feminists promoted legalization during the 1960s, and the threat of reform spawned a religion-based conservative coalition that opposed reform. The uncompromising moral arguments replicated the controversy in other countries. For one side, safe medical abortion was the only humane option; for the other, the fetus was a life that could not be sacrificed. These arguments implied very different views of sexual morality and the role of the state in policing that morality. These arguments did not play themselves out fully in Australia, however, because a series of judicial decisions allowed the major political parties to pretend that they had maintained the status quo (in the criminal statutes) even as abortion was effectively legalized. This episode illustrates the limited possibilities of pursuing morality issues in Australia because they threaten the basis of ordinary partisan politics and their pragmatic political culture.

The First Reform Statute

The Australian states derived their criminal abortion laws from the British Offences against the Person Act of 1861. These laws permitted abortions only to save the life of the mother, and this provision was interpreted fairly strictly until the 1960s. Informal networks of medical abortionists and "backyard" operators provided abortions outside the law, and police prosecuted such providers on the odd occasion when a patient's death forced them to investigate.

In the 1960s, reform emerged as a serious possibility. The discovery in Australia that exposure to rubella damaged the fetus greatly increased the number of therapeutic abortions in the late 1950s and early 1960s. The thalidomide scandal in Britain further dramatized the need for reform. Public opinion accepted fetal deformity as grounds for abortion, even though the legal basis for such abortions was only the doctor's belief that the birth would make the mother suicidal. Few doctors performed abortions, but those who did relied on this therapeutic exception, which was consequently stretched beyond recognition. The rhetoric for reform initially focused on the need of poor, usually married, women to limit family size and the medical necessity of abortion to protect the mother's health. Reformers argued consistently that abortion would reduce poverty because the poor were particularly burdened with unwanted children. Reformers campaigned for a broadly worded set of exceptions, not repeal, and made no mention of women's autonomy or rights (Mylchreest 1995). They hoped to make abortion a matter of health and social justice rather than moral right.

Only one state, South Australia in 1969, enacted such a reform statute, which was modeled on the British Abortion Act of 1967 (Section 82A, Criminal Code Consolidation Act). Under the South Australian statute, two doctors were required to certify that an abortion was necessary for medical reasons, and the procedure was to be performed in a public hospital. Some of the opposition was mollified because the medical profession gatekeepers were seen as preventing "abortion on demand." The measure was supported by a combination of progressives on both sides of politics in a nonpartisan vote, although key members of Don Dunstan's Labor government, including the premier himself, actively supported the legislation, which was very unusual for a conscience vote on a private member's bill.

The novelty of the South Australian situation in the 1960s made it the exception to the pattern of informal legalization in Australia. The Dunstan government had been elected as the modern, educated, and middle-class face of the

Labor Party—"trendy" in the view of its critics—after three decades of conservative, rural-oriented state government under Sir Thomas Playford's Liberal-Country League[1] (Blewett and Jaensch 1971). In that context, the reform of abortion
law appeared to be one of a number of reforms that would allow South Australia
to catch up with the modern world. Once enacted, the state's politicians have
consistently refused to revisit the issue, leaving South Australia in the anomalous
situation of now having the most restrictive laws in the country because doctors
must still formally approve the procedure.

Pressure Groups, Splinter Parties, and Police Protection

The passage of the South Australian law put reform on the agenda elsewhere. In
Australia's two largest cities, Sydney and Melbourne, abortion clinics had been
operating with police protection during the 1960s. Neither the Abortion Law
Reform Association nor the Right to Life Association was happy with this situation. At a minimum, reformers wanted the law amended along the lines of the
South Australian law. They used the obvious corruption of the police force as a
major argument to discredit a law that was routinely flouted and deprived
women of professional medical services. They often likened abortion to Prohibition, arguing that both were unenforceable laws that dictated morality to an
unwilling populace. Pro-life groups, closely allied with the Roman Catholic
Church and the mainstream Protestant churches, insisted that the criminal abortion statute should be enforced as it was originally written. They wanted police
to prosecute, not protect, the private clinics.

Conservative (Liberal-Country Party) coalitions were in power in both New
South Wales and Victoria in the 1960s when these pressure groups were trying
to push abortion policy in opposite directions. Both governments decided to
take a firm symbolic stand against the signs of moral and cultural change. Conservative politicians rarely had strong views on the morality of abortion itself, but
they conflated it with what they saw as a concerted attack on traditional values,
including student protests against the Vietnam War, efforts to relax film censorship standards, and even the advent of oral contraceptives. They pictured
themselves as standing in the breach against every sign of "permissiveness." Abortion reform was one of several serious threats to the values they wanted to defend,
and they believed that formally defending the status quo would reassure their
core constituencies. They were most active in curtailing war protests (which
threatened the anticommunist foundations of conservative foreign policy),
making the moral regulation of abortion a secondary issue.

To understand why the conservatives took this stand, it is necessary to know
some of the technicalities of Australian electoral law. The preferential voting system

that has operated in Australia since World War I has given third-party and independent candidates more influence than their parliamentary representation would otherwise justify. Minor candidates do not play the spoiling role that they would in first-past-the-post elections, as in the United States and Britain. A vote for a third-party candidate is not wasted because even in single-member constituencies (under which the lower houses of the federal Parliament and all but one state Parliament are elected), close contests are decided on the distribution of minor party preferences to the major parties. That is, a voter can choose any candidate and still express a preference for one of the two major party groups. Both the coalition and Labor must therefore try to attract the preferences of the third parties.

In the 1960s and early 1970s, the Democratic Labor Party (DLP) was the largest third party. It had splintered from the Australian Labor Party (ALP) in the 1950s when right-wing Catholics formed "industrial groups" within the trade unions to organize against communists and then tried to force the Labor party to break with all unions influenced by communists. By the time of the abortion controversies, the DLP had become a conservative and mainly Catholic rump of former Labor supporters whose votes were effectively delivered to the conservatives. The Liberal-Country Party coalitions could not have remained in power during the 1950s and 1960s without DLP preferences (Jaensch 1994). The price of this electoral alliance was a staunchly anticommunist foreign policy and strict adherence to traditional moral values on issues such as abortion and censorship.

Abortion reform did not, however, divide easily along partly lines. Some reform leaders belonged to or sympathized with the ALP, but the party also had a significant constituency of working-class Catholics. To maintain unity, the ALP consistently refused to take any position on abortion. The party was acutely aware of the price of sectarian division because of the DLP split and a prolonged and debilitating struggle over government aid to parochial schools. It steadfastly refused to allow abortion to become another occasion on which socially conservative Catholics in the party would be pitted against social liberals. By the 1960s, however, a few conservatives thought that the time was approaching when they would have to countenance some liberalization on social policies to broaden their base.

Meanwhile, the Abortion Law Reform Association and some medical abortionists publicized the existence of abortion clinics in Sydney and Melbourne because they wanted to force the state governments to legalize abortion. Reformers hoped to rid the clinics of police protection and to reduce the highly inflated cost of the procedure. The Askin government in New South Wales and the Bolte government in Victoria were forced to show their socially conservative constituencies that they were genuinely enforcing the laws and that they were not turning a blind eye to the lucrative protection racket. Neither government had much enthusiasm for the task, however, which provided ammunition for critics who charged that the DLP tail often wagged the coalition dog.

Only a small minority of voters, firmly tied to the conservative side of politics, strongly favored retaining an abortion ban. However, the publicity generated by the reform groups energized these voters and their groups, forcing policymakers to act. Police in both states began charging doctors known to perform abortions. Paradoxically, it was the judicial rulings in these very trials that unraveled the criminal abortion statutes as they read broad professional discretion into the criminal laws.

De Facto Legalization

The first such judicial "reform" came in Victoria in 1969, when Justice Clifford Inch Menhennitt dramatically reinterpreted the criminal statute against procuring an abortion to the advantage of the accused doctor (*R. v. Davidson* V.R. 667). Expanding on a 1939 British case, *R. v. Bourne* (1 K.B. 687), the judge focused on the word *unlawfully* in the statute to surmise that some abortions had to be lawful. He then read the statute in the light of the doctrine of necessity, whereby some criminal actions might be lawful if legally necessary. This usually meant self-defense, but Justice Menhennitt extended it to include the honest belief of the doctor that the abortion was necessary to prevent a greater mischief, such as damage to the patient's mental health. With these instructions, the jury acquitted Dr. Davidson on all counts.

This creative use of the necessity doctrine opened a very broad loophole. The conservative government paid lip service to enforcing the law, but it did not try to overturn this decision in either the courts or Parliament. In effect, it acquiesced in this legalization of "therapeutic" abortion for "social" reasons. Doctors relied on their professional status to legitimize abortion as necessary for the health of the mother. The interpretation of a trial judge alone did not settle the matter, however. Under government direction, the police continued prosecuting and acted as if Davidson's acquittal were of little moment. Despite this pretense, the police knew that the criminal law was now limited to the so-called backyard butchers.

The Victorian government did not appeal Menhennitt's judgment but initially took the position that the *Davidson* ruling was narrow. So long as this remained a lower court ruling, the law could remain on the books, and the government would make token efforts to enforce it. The government argued that the ruling did not amount to abortion on demand, even though it plainly gave doctors such wide discretion that medical abortion was legalized. This tacit compromise allowed the government to pay lip service to its socially conservative constituents and at the same time quietly make abortion available in city clinics, thus undermining a key demand of social liberals.

However, Victorian reform advocates still hoped to amend the law. To force the government's hand, the leading reformer, Dr. Bertram Wainer, publicized the protection rackets, and the government was obliged to appoint a special board to investigate (Wainer 1972). The inquiry resulted in months of tabloid revelations about the corrupt abortion trade. Headlines such as "Ex-policeman ran crime syndicate" and "Inspector tells of lunch with abortionist" appeared regularly, even in the quality press. The inquiry revealed that police had warned doctors of pending raids, advised them on how to prepare bogus medical records that would make prosecution impossible, and coached them on diverting police suspicion (Winneke 1970). The inquiry dramatically illustrated the claims of abortion reformers: Doctors charged large fees for illegal abortions, the law was unenforceable, and abortion had become a thriving but sordid business. Reformers hoped that this information would persuade politicians and the public of the need to legalize medical abortion. Getting rid of an outdated law that made decent women criminals, they argued, was only common sense. In retreating to a "common sense" position, however, the reformers destroyed their best chance of pursuing full repeal of the old laws.

A similar, if less dramatic, turn of legal events nullified the New South Wales (N.S.W.) abortion laws. The conservative Askin government would have happily left the issue alone, but it too had to pay lip service to enforcing the law. A squad of thirty police was formed to investigate abortionists. Few prosecutions resulted, but in September 1971, three doctors were tried for procuring abortions. The press characterized the prosecution as a novelty for the state because police had never charged a doctor with procuring an abortion to which the patient consented. The prosecution was designed to rein in medical abortions, but the trial judge again ambushed the prosecutors.

The defense used two strategies. Jim Staples, representing the owners of the clinic, argued that at common law, abortion was not a crime unless the woman were harmed. He asked the court to overrule *Bourne* and *Davidson* and read the statute as an addendum to the ancient common law, articulated by Blackstone, which treated abortion very leniently until "quickening." Judge Levine replied that he would not "indulge in any judicial legislation" but would simply construe the statute ("NSW Courts and the Law on Abortion" 1971b, 3). Staples was asking the court to interpret the statute out of existence, and the judge refused to do so.

Sir Jack Cassidy, representing Dr. Wald, employed a different strategy. He relied on the modern cases to assert that abortion was lawful if performed skillfully by a qualified practitioner, with the woman's consent, and on reasonable grounds. Echoing the litany of social causes, he argued ("Word 'Unlawful' Is Vital—Defence" 1971a, 1) that the women

> had exhibited the social, economic and domestic factors that contributed to mental and physical health—uncertainty as to the future, financial hardship, trouble with past pregnancies, disgrace attending an illegitimate child and fear of an unwanted pregnancy. The doctors stood well within the law for they honestly believed beyond a reasonable doubt that in each particular case a termination of pregnancy was necessary for the health of the woman.

The defense emphasized the clinic's scrupulously high medical standards. Patients testified about their distressed circumstances and personal anguish. Sir Jack also reminded the jury that the Crown had to prove that the abortion was unlawful.

Judge Levine construed the law very favorably for the defendants. Society, he asserted, had an interest in "the preservation of the human species," and the word *unlawfully* in the statute might "well afford a safeguard to implement the society interest." But he fully accepted the reading of the statute offered by the doctors' lawyers (*R. v. Wald* 3 NSWDCR 25 [1971], 29):

> In my view it would be for the jury to decide whether there existed in the case of each woman any economic, social or medical ground or reason which in their view could constitute reasonable grounds upon which an accused could honestly and reasonably believe there would result a serious danger to her physical or mental health.

The judge still sent the case to the jury because prosecution evidence suggested that the clinic's business was not general practice but abortion. Fees were paid in cash without receipts, and the account books contained irregularities. One defendant had referred a constant stream of patients to the clinic who invariably received abortions. In the end, however, the doctors were acquitted. Like the Melbourne case, this verdict left abortion to the discretion of the medical profession because juries were unwilling to condemn doctors performing procedures on consenting patients.

The N.S.W. state government responded much like its Victorian counterpart. It pretended that the law was unchanged. Premier Robert Askin immediately announced that his administration would not amend the abortion laws to accommodate more liberal attitudes. "I am against legalized abortion. My Cabinet doesn't believe in it and, while we are in Cabinet, we will not alter the present law," he declared. The police, Askin told Parliament, would investigate all abortionists ("Askin: No 'Open Go' on Abortion" 1971, 1). But "the present law" was a duplicitous phrase because Judge Levine had given that law a very liberal interpretation.

The police tried to revivify the law by charging a specialist gynecologist. The police targeted Dr. George Smart, who was known to offer abortion services as a central part of his practice. Twenty-three separate charges were filed, which in itself suggested that Smart was a professional abortionist. Again Sir Jack Cassidy led the defense; again he wove the threads of abortion reform, social justice, and medical expertise into his argument.

Cassidy wanted to persuade the jurors that his client was more than a mercenary and exploitative abortionist. The legal test, he told the court, was the "belief of the medical practitioner" ("Word 'Unlawful' Is Vital—Defence" 1971, 1). Smart's academic credentials were impeccable. Cassidy reminded the jury that the patients, whatever their present demeanor, had all been troubled women when they first consulted his client, and performing an abortion had been an integral part of their treatment. He highlighted Smart's professionalism by reminding the jury that the doctor had treated many women whose lives had been threatened by amateur backyard providers. Smart was portrayed as a good doctor deeply concerned about the welfare of his patients.

The prosecution case attempted to discredit the doctor. Smart, the Crown alleged, had no real interest in the women's health. He had told police "cold-blooded, deliberate lies" about his appointments schedule and about checks in his possession ("Word 'Unlawful' Is Vital—Defence" 1971, 1). The Crown alleged that Smart charged three to five times the standard fee for a therapeutic abortion, which automatically cast doubt on the doctor's integrity.

The jury could not reach a unanimous verdict, and Judge Goran blamed the mistrial on the long and complicated case. "The issues were such," he commented, "that it affected different people with different opinions" ("Abortion Jury Can't Decide" 1972, 3). This meant that the jury was hung because its members could not agree to convict a specialist gynecologist who was performing abortions for consenting women. Smart had performed the acts with which he was charged, but some jurors simply believed that these acts should not be illegal. With two such strikes, the attorney general dropped all charges (Fisher and Buckingham 1985). For political purposes, the government continued to pay lip service to the law, but those sections of the Crimes Act had become a dead letter. Within a few months, clinics were operating unhindered in Sydney and in other major cities in New South Wales.

Abortion was thus legalized in the two most populous states in Australia by a combination of political pressure for reform from the Abortion Law Reform Association and other progressive groups and the bipartisan consensus among political elites that nothing was to be gained from agitating this issue. A few individual members in both major parties tried to act on their moral convictions in Parliament, but most of their colleagues refused to accept the challenge and sought to dispose of the issue as quietly as possible. Even conservative governments accepted that trial courts could provide the definitive interpretation of the old statute, relieving parliaments of the responsibility of coming to a definitive legislative compromise. Their inaction was a deliberate calculation that the coalition needed to win moderate voters who probably considered abortion a necessary evil and would be alienated if the coalition became too closely identified with the DLP's crusade against a permissive society. It illustrated Woodrow Wilson's classic analysis that parliamentary systems focus on issues that build a party majority and ignore issues that confuse that process (Wilson 1885).

By the early 1970s, police in New South Wales and Victoria had stopped prosecuting doctors for performing abortions. Other states, with more socially conservative, less urban populations, clung to the traditional interpretation of their criminal abortion statutes, but women in these states could fly to Sydney or Melbourne, and many drove from Brisbane or other parts of southern Queensland to clinics in the resort towns on the other side of the border for abortion services. Gradually, without any formal process, doctors performed abortions in these states for indications that police and prosecutors did not examine very closely. Within a decade, even the more conservative, rural states of Queensland and Western Australia had quietly stopped prosecuting doctors who performed abortions. To conform with the criminal law, doctors adopted the legal fiction that the procedure was necessary to preserve the health of the mother. Therefore, by the early 1980s, every state had freely available abortion, although one would never be able to tell this from the statute books.

Ignoring the Pro-Life Lobby

This informal legalization has proved remarkably stable and enduring. Right-to-life groups began to press state governments to enforce the law in the 1970s, but they were steadfastly ignored. Politicians and judges in all states were very reluctant to revisit the issue of abortion. Legal and political elites doggedly insisted that abortion be treated as a separate issue divorced even from larger issues of personal morality and permissiveness. The Australian campaign to keep abortion legal appealed to the rights of women, scorned priests, and moralizers who insisted that conception obligated women to bear children. Stories of the desperate measures to which women would resort to procure an abortion were said to prove that criminal prohibitions were unenforceable. Opponents of legalized abortion, in contrast, invoked traditional religious values and called abortion the legalized murder of the "unborn child." Easy access to abortion, in their view, necessarily weakened moral standards. The issue has remained unimportant in the public's consciousness, however, and there has been very little skirmishing over the legacy of the new cultural freedoms. Political parties have paid no price for ignoring this and most other moral issues; right-to-life politicians have tried but failed to convince their colleagues that they should deal with the issue.

Australian public opinion has remained remarkably constant since the 1960s. A small minority has always been adamantly opposed to abortion for any reason, while a large majority has been divided between allowing women a free choice or specifying legal grounds, such as a threat to the mother's health or a deformed fetus, to justify the procedure. Religious affiliation is only moderately related to opinion here (Ray 1984). Numerical majorities have not decided this issue.

Australian politicians ostensibly sided with the pro-life movement in the early 1970s, but once the de facto legalization of abortion had taken place, the pro-life lobby was powerless to reverse it because mainstream politicians would not upset the compromise implicit in retaining the formal statute law while acquiescing in de facto legalization of medical abortion. Elected officials from both parties began to distance themselves from either side in the abortion debate as early as 1973. The Labor Party would have been badly divided and had long refused to take sides. The Liberal Party was split between social conservatives who more or less supported traditional moral values and social moderates who favored some concession to reform. The conservative coalition had to placate the mainly Catholic DLP to remain in power, thus keeping the moderates in check. This policy was primarily shaped by the coalition's need to maintain its political base without provoking a popular reaction to the draconian enforcement that the activists sought.

In the early 1970s, some Liberal leaders flirted briefly with identifying their party with traditional values. They imitated the politics of Richard Nixon's "silent majority" as they painted Labor as the party of "permissiveness." This complemented their pretense that abortion remained illegal at the very time the courts were nullifying the statute. N.S.W. Premier Askin and the DLP pursued this strategy during the federal election in 1972, hoping that morality issues would override a damning critique of the government's competence that seemed likely to elect a Labor government in Canberra for the first time since the 1940s. The hierarchy of the Catholic Church and the DLP had both attacked the Labor leader, Gough Whitlam, because he had personally advocated the right to choose. The hierarchy instructed Catholics that they should not vote for any candidate who would legalize abortion. The DLP's national leader, Senator Jack Kane, painted Labor as the destroyer of traditional values because it was "soft" on the "permissive" society of drugs, antiwar protest, communist subversion, and promiscuity. Trying to shore up the federal Liberal-Country Party government, Askin unabashedly appealed to the pro-life vote when he told an election rally that only his party would protect the unborn. This commitment to fetal rights was a campaign conversion, unsupported by the policy of ignoring judicial decisions legalizing abortion. The "permissive society," particularly abortion, dominated the last days of the 1972 election campaign but did not stop the widely anticipated Labor victory.

This last-minute conversion of the conservatives to moral issues in 1972 was a transparent attempt to stave off defeat. After years of playing down these issues, conservatives embraced them aggressively only in the last days of the campaign, and few voters took them seriously. The DLP had played very heavily on traditional religious values during this campaign, and the 1972 election marked the beginning of its end. In the intensely polarized atmosphere of the Whitlam Labor governments between 1972 and 1975, the DLP disappeared entirely as an electoral force. Partisan competition finally brought the party's supporters to vote directly for the mainstream conservatives. Neither major party in Australia has overtly embraced morals campaigners since that time because they believed it would alienate moderate voters whom they need to win government. Neither have the major parties actively supported legalizing abortion, which might also trouble moderate voters.

In 1973, the national Parliament debated the Medical Practice Clarification Bill, which would have legalized early term medical abortion in federal territories. Its sponsor, David McKenzie, likened the proposal to the Anglo-American practice of using viability as the point at which the law should take over from professional medical decisions. Opponents argued that, as the liberalized laws in New York and Britain showed, this bill would simply create abortion on demand. Both sides saw the vote as a crucial test of larger battles over abortion looming in the states, and both sides lobbied ferociously. Letters, telegrams, and petitions poured into parliamentary offices, and pressure groups sent busloads of their supporters to make a show of strength outside Parliament House as the vote was being taken.

Very soon it became clear that most members would vote against the bill. They reasoned that the churches had mobilized their very committed supporters, while the reform lobby lacked a broad support. To forestall a total rout, Race Mathews, a Victorian member of the House of Representatives, proposed an inquiry akin to the Lane Committee in Britain. He urged the honorable members to become "accustomed again to reasoning with one another" (*Commonwealth Parliamentary Debates* 1973, 1987), but this was precisely the deliberative model that the activists rejected. Pro-life members argued that the committee would simply pave the way to liberalization, and large bipartisan majorities defeated the bill and the proposed commission. Since public opinion did not fully support the status quo or complete repeal, many members saw political safety in voting to retain the existing laws.

Four months later, Mathews proposed a national inquiry into all aspects of sexual relations. This idea won more support, but pro-life groups again condemned the inquiry as a Trojan horse. The focus on sexuality doomed it. The terms were then amended to include all aspects of human relationships! Having thus diluted the contentious issues, it received broad bipartisan support. As this parliamentary charade was being played out, clinics continued to perform abortions unhindered in Sydney and Melbourne.

Australian politicians typically shunned reform efforts because legislative action would have required choosing sides. They took the pragmatic view that they should pay lip service to the criminal statute but should not interfere with choice. To this end, a broad parliamentary consensus endorsed an ineffective inquiry to placate abortion opponents while still keeping abortion freely available, even if it was not formally legal. Political safety shaped such decisions much more than moral principle. Australian politicians saw no advantage in formalizing the informal compromise that the courts had fortuitously given them, nor did they see any advantage in coopting the small number of activists who wanted the existing laws to be either actively enforced or completely repealed.

The Politics of Abortion Funding

The funding issue illustrates the determination of politicians on all sides to maintain the existing party cleavages rather than have them disrupted by morality policy. Members of the pro-life caucus in the federal Parliament tried to devise a measure similar to the Hyde Amendment that had severely restricted federal funding of abortion in the United States after 1976 (*Harris* v. *McRae* 448 U.S. 297 [1980]). Stephen Lusher, a backbench member of the National Party, argued that taxpayers should not have to subsidize what they found morally repugnant.

The Hyde Amendment provided symbolic opposition to abortion without contravening the constitutional rights articulated in *Roe* v. *Wade*, but it did not threaten the stability of the U.S. political system. The Lusher amendment, however, was proposed in a different political system, one that demands party cohesion and in which parties constantly appeal to the middle ground to win office. While as late as 1973, as we have seen, a huge parliamentary majority had refused to recognize that abortion had been effectively legalized, in 1979, a bare six years later, a bipartisan majority rejected a proposal to eliminate national health insurance benefits for elective abortions (which was officially still a crime). Proponents of continuing to fund abortions with national health insurance focused on the doctor-patient relationship and protecting equitable treatment for women in all states. Only a couple of left-wing Labor members denounced it as an attack on women's rights. This indicated how reluctant mainstream politicians were to embrace feminist rhetoric lest they appear too extreme. Former Prime Minister William McMahon, who had tried to find a silent majority to save his faltering government in 1972, typified the pragmatic political approach in 1979. He still claimed to oppose abortion on demand, but he spoke against cutting abortion funds because it was not "in the best interests of a tolerant and concerned society" (Mylchreest 1995, 57).

However, many of those who opposed the funding restrictions did not want to have a pro-choice vote on their record. They found refuge in a compromise that provided that abortion would be funded "in accordance with state law." These words deliberately disguised the informal way that abortion had been legalized. If the Lusher amendment had passed, it would have revisited the fundamental question of abortion's legality because doctors and eventually the courts would have had to decide when the mother's life required that a pregnancy be terminated. Instead, the federal Parliament left the fiction that abortion was a crime untouched and rescued state legislators from having to repeal or reaffirm criminal statutes that had been a dead letter for nearly a decade. The form and purpose of the Lusher Amendment seemed much the same as the Hyde Amendment, but *Roe v. Wade* had preempted state laws in the United States, while the Lusher Amendment would have succeeded only in smoking out those informal arrangements by which Australian states had allowed doctors to provide abortion.

The Politics of Inertia

Abortion opinion cut across the main party divisions in Australia, but it was not important enough to disrupt the existing party divisions. In these circumstances in which party discipline was the dominant value, pro-life groups eventually tired of being paid lip service. They wanted to put teeth back into the moribund criminal statutes. In Queensland and Victoria, these issues were settled within the parties, and they maintained the status quo, but in New South Wales, the issue became public because minor parties were able to win token and temporary representation in Parliament through electoral quirks.

Even in New South Wales, the bipartisan compromise to ignore abortion was breached only once. In 1982, Kevin Stewart, the N.S.W. minister responsible for state wards, refused one of his charges (identified as K) routine permission for an abortion. Her mother sued to overturn this decision and created the bizarre spectacle of the attorney general, Frank Walker, encouraging legal aid lawyers to sue another government minister. Stewart claimed that the old criminal statute authorized abortion only if the mother's health were in danger. K's social workers had argued that bearing a child would be detrimental to her mental health and future prospects. This case pitted the two interpretations of the criminal law against each other. Premier Neville Wran quickly convened a private meeting to resolve the dispute within his cabinet; Walker agreed not to join the suit if Stewart agreed not to challenge the de facto legalization of abortion. To dispose of the case, the court revived an ancient judicial power of royal courts to overrule the minister and grant the permission. This slightly exotic decision upheld the status quo on de facto legalization of abortion. Stewart remained defiant that his Catholic, pro-life convictions had not threatened the ward's best interests, but he was removed from the cabinet at the first opportunity. The abortion controversy had again been defused.

Out of frustration with the existing compromise, pro-life activists turned to litigation. The courts offered little hope to these groups who had to rely on obscure common law rights or on returning to strict construction of criminal abortion laws to make their case. For example, courts refused to grant injunctions to fathers seeking to prevent abortions. One plaintiff, Kerr, sought an injunction in 1983 to prevent a woman (identified as T) from aborting a child he had fathered in an isolated act of intercourse. T told the court that an abortion would be "best for everybody," an argument that illustrated how thoroughly routine abortion had become even though the criminal statute had never been repealed (*Queensland Attorney General [ex. rel. Kerr]* v. *T* 57 A.L.J.R. 285, 265). Kerr was asking the court to revert to a literal reading of the law when he argued that T's abortion was illegal. The trial judge asked the government to provide some policy guidance on the ambiguous legal status of abortion, but the conservative attorney general withdrew from the suit entirely to avoid giving government backbenchers the opportunity to press their pro-life beliefs.

The trial judge and two appellate courts refused T's application on procedural grounds, but they did not disguise their discomfort at being asked to provide increasingly intricate interpretations of the old statute to limit the availability of abortion. Chief Justice Gibbs of the High Court, Australia's final court of appeal, noted that there were "limits" to legal intrusions on "personal liberty and personal privacy in the pursuit of moral and religious aims" (*Queensland Attorney General [ex rel. Kerr]* v. *T*, 287). Unlike the U.S. court action on the right to privacy, which invited legislatures to probe its meaning and led in turn to new litigation, Australian courts followed their traditions of formalist construction and deference to Parliament and the executive (Atiyah and Summers 1987). Thus, Gibbs, a political conservative, deferred to the government's policy of not prosecuting medical abortions and so refused to grant an injunction to a private plaintiff.

Another instance of the courts upholding the de facto legalization occurred in 1994 when a Sydney mother sued for "wrongful birth" when her doctors had failed to detect her impending motherhood until very late in the pregnancy. The basis of her claim was that if she had been notified early enough, she would have been able to have an abortion and so avoid the cost and stress of raising the child. The doctors defended the action by arguing that there was no cause of action because this putative abortion would have been illegal. The trial judge agreed with the defense and dismissed the action. The mother appealed this decision, and the court of appeal decided in a 2-to-1 decision that the abortion might have been lawful because a doctor might have reasonably decided that the pregnancy threatened the woman's health. The action was reinstated but soon settled out of court. The courts had again protected de facto legalization.

Senior police officials and politicians in Western Australia tried to head off another recent challenge to the status quo, but it has led to the first codification of the policy. In 1996, Drs. Victor Chan and Ho Peng Lee performed an abortion on a Maori woman who requested that the fetal remains be saved for traditional burial in New Zealand. The doctors complied, but the story of a baby stored in the refrigerator reached the director of Public Prosecutions, who brought charges in early 1998. Lobbyists on both sides sprang into action. Press reports suggested that senior police were unhappy about the prosecution and believed that the prosecutor had taken advantage of inexperienced officers when he took this case to court. The police commissioner told a press conference that the current law was "outmoded and inadequate in addressing the concerns of the medical profession and the community" (*Victory at Midnight* 1998, 28). For a while, however, doctors in the state stopped performing abortions.

Soon government leaders tried to calm fears that policy had changed or would change. The prosecutor denied that he was seeking evidence to prosecute other doctors. Richard Court, the conservative premier, argued that the current laws were working well, and he tried to quarantine the Chan/Lee prosecution as a singular case. He also told the press that disgruntled doctors would not force him to amend the abortion statute. The government clearly wanted to avoid a parliamentary debate on reform or repeal and simultaneously to obviate the renewed pressure from pro-life forces who saw this prosecution as the first of many that would again make the old law effective.

Some members of Parliament saw this case as an opportunity finally to speak out on the personal convictions that they had previously had to suppress. After three months of intense lobbying and drafting, a majority coalesced around a private member's bill that codified the de facto legalization that had existed for almost two decades. Again, the politicians' rhetoric avoided women's rights (although that could be found on demonstrators' placards) and focused on abortion as a public health issue. Some conservatives called their pro-choice colleagues "murderers" but only in the privacy of a party meeting ("Victory at Midnight" 1998, 29). The government tried to structure its own bill, allowing members a free vote on a series of exceptions to a general prohibition on abortion, hoping to minimize the reforms that would be enacted. However, a majority of members did not want to provide pro-life activists the opportunity to split so many legal hairs. They enacted a bill that legalized medical abortion. The only real concession was a series of measures to seek to reduce the number of abortions with contraceptive education and health department research.

On the surface, this legislation may seem to be a radical departure from the previous pattern of abortion politics. In fact, however, it took years and a chance prosecution, which threatened chaos in the hospital system, to make the politicians act. When they acted, they did so in a way that obviated the possibility that they will have to revisit the issue. They simply codified the status quo.

Conclusion

Australia does not fit clearly into any of the existing patterns of abortion law reform observed in other industrial countries. After the initial battle in the early 1970s, abortion became as widely and easily available as it was anywhere. The rulings of some trial courts, the occasional hung jury, and the tacit cooperation of political elites to ignore the issue as much as possible produced this situation of de facto legalization. This echoes Rosenberg's (1991) hypothesis about the hollow hope of a litigation strategy without the active cooperation of other political actors. Political elites in Australia have cooperated in legalizing abortion by acting with studied indifference. They have mostly avoided the issue and acted to defuse it whenever it threatened to become a divisive problem.

This consistent pattern of cooperation illustrates the dominance of established political parties in Australia and their reluctance to step outside that fixed pattern even when an issue seems clearly to demand it. Politics in Australia concentrates on the "hip-pocket nerve": economic management, welfare benefits, tax cuts, improving the standard of living, and mortgage rates are the issues that have driven Australian politics since World War II. A political culture dominated by such utilitarian issues has little room for the type of prolonged moral debate that came in the wake of *Roe* v. *Wade*. Without a language to discuss moral issues or a political culture that can accommodate them, it is little wonder that there have been so many silences even as abortion has been legalized in Australia.

Note

1. Despite its name, the Liberal Party is the more conservative of the two major parties. In general, its policies are more hawkish on defense and favor lower taxes and government spending. In government, it invariably forms a coalition with the National Party (known as the Country Party until the 1970s). This is a more conservative rural party that has been the political advocate of agricultural and mining interests. The Liberal Party has been the dominant partner in such coalitions everywhere except in Queensland, where the National Party has been the dominant partner.

References

"A French Debate about Death," 1998. *Economist*, 15 August.

"Abortion Jury Can't Decide." 1972. *Daily Telegraph* (Sydney), 13 October.

"Abstinence-Only Plans Questioned." 1998. AP news wire, 5 January.

Adam, Barry D. 1995. *The Rise of a Gay and Lesbian Movement.* Rev. ed. New York: Twayne.

Adams, Greg D. 1997. "Abortion: Evidence of Issue Evolution." *American Journal of Political Science* 41:718–38.

Adler, Margot. 1998. *All Things Considered,* "Abortion in Buffalo." National Public Radio, 23 November.

Allen, Edward J. 1967. "Capital Punishment: Your Protection and Mine." In *The Death Penalty in America,* ed. Hugh Adam Bedau. Garden City, N.Y.: Anchor.

Allison, Paul D. 1984. *Event History Analysis.* Beverly Hills, Calif.: Sage.

Alvarez, R. Michael, and John Brehm. 1995. "Americans' Ambivalence Towards Abortion Policy: Development of a Heteroskedastic Probit Model of Competing Values." *American Journal of Political Science* 39:1055–82.

American Public Opinion Index. Various years. Bethesda, Md.: Opinion Research Service.

Anderson, Warwick. 1991. "The New York Needle Trial: The Politics of Public Health in the Age of AIDs." *American Journal of Public Health* 81:1506–17.

Arnold, R. Douglas. 1990. *The Logic of Congressional Action.* New Haven, Conn.: Yale University Press.

Asher, Herbert B., and Donald S. Van Meter. 1973. *Determinants of Public Welfare Policies: A Causal Approach.* Beverly Hills, Calif.: Sage.

"Askin: No 'Open Go' on Abortion." 1971. *Sydney Morning Herald,* 3 November.

Atiyah, P. S., and R. S. Summers. 1987. *Form and Substance in Anglo-American Law: A Comparative Study of Legal Reasoning, Legal Theory, and Legal Institutions.* New York: Oxford University Press.

Au, William. 1985. *The Cross, The Flag, and The Bomb: American Catholics Debate War and Peace, 1960–1980* Westport, Connecticut: Greenwood Press.

Audit Bureau of Circulation. 1991. *Magazine Publisher's Statement: Playboy, For 6 Months Ended December 31, 1990.* Shaumburg, Ill.: ABC.

Ayer, Douglas, Roy E. Bates, and Peter F. Herman. 1970. "Self-Censorship in the Movie Industry: An Historical Perspective on Law and Social Change." *Wisconsin Law Review* 1970:791–838.

Bachrach, Peter. 1963. "Decisions and Nondecisions: An Analytical Framework." *American Political Science Review* 57:632–42.

————, and Morton S. Baratz. 1962. "Two Faces of Power." *American Political Science Review* 56:947–52.

Baldus, David, and James W. Cole. 1975. "A Comparison of the Work of Sellin and Ehrlich on the Deterrent Effect of Capital Punishment." *Yale Law Journal* 85:170–86.

Bashevkin, Sylvia. 1994. "Confronting Neo-Conservatism: Anglo-American Women's Movements under Thatcher, Reagan and Mulroney." *International Political Science Review* 15:275–96.

Bates, Robert H., Rui J. P. de Figueiredo Jr., and Barry R. Weingast. 1998. "The Politics of Interpretation: Rationality, Culture, and Transition." *Politics and Society* 26:221–56.

Bauer, Raymond A., Ithiel de Sola Pool, and Lewis Anthony Dexter. 1963. *American Business and Public Policy.* New York: Atherton.

Baumgartner, Frank R. 1989. *Conflict and Rhetoric in French Policymaking.* Pittsburgh, Penn.: University of Pittsburgh Press.

————, and Bryan D. Jones. 1993. *Agendas and Instability in American Politics.* Chicago: University of Chicago Press.

Beauchamp, Dan E. 1980. *Beyond Alcoholism.* Philadelphia: Temple University Press.

Becker, Gary S. 1996. *Accounting for Taste.* Cambridge, Mass.: Harvard University Press.

Bedau, Hugh Adam. 1967. *The Death Penalty in America.* Garden City, N.Y.: Anchor.

————. 1977. *The Courts, the Constitution, and Capital Punishment.* Lexington, Mass.: Lexington Books.

"Beer Can Be Far Away in Most of West Texas." 1997. *New York Times,* 25 August.

Bell, G. 1997. "Is Your Politician Moral? Dial 0898 . . ." *Independent,* 19 January.

Bennett, Stephen. 1989. "'Know-Nothings' Revisited: The Meaning of Political Ignorance Today." *Social Science Quarterly* 69:476–90.

Benninga, Jacques S., ed. 1991. *Moral Character and Civic Education in the Elementary School.* New York: Teachers College Press.

Benson, Peter L., and Dorothy L. Williams. 1982. *Religion on Capitol Hill: Myths and Realities.* San Francisco: Harper & Row.

Berkman, Michael B., and Robert E. O'Connor. 1993. "Do Women Legislators Matter? Female Legislators and State Abortion Policy" in *Understanding the New Politics of Abortion,* ed. Malcolm Goggin. Newbury Park, Calif.: Sage.

Berns, Walter. 1979. *For Capital Punishment: Crime and the Morality of the Death Penalty.* New York: Basic Books.

Berry, Frances Stokes, and William D. Berry. 1990. "State Lottery Adoptions as Policy Innovations: An Event History Analysis." *American Political Science Review* 84:395–416.

————. 1992. "Tax Innovation in the States: Capitalizing on Political Opportunity." *American Journal of Political Science* 36:715–42.

Berry, R. 1996. "A Case Study in Parliamentary Influence: The Civil Rights Disabled Persons Bill." *The Journal of Legislative Studies* 2:135–44.

Bianco, William T., and Robert H. Bates. 1990. "Cooperation by Design: Leadership, Structure, and Collective Dilemmas." *American Political Science Review* 84:133–47.

Bilton, M., and S. Himelfarb. 1980. "Fleet Street," in *The British General Election of 1979,* ed. D. Butler and D. Kavanagh. London: Macmillan.

Birch, Anthony H. 1973. *The British System of Government*, 2d ed. Boston: Allen and Unwin.

Black, Charles L., Jr. 1974. *Capital Punishment: The Inevitability of Caprice and Mistake.* New York: Norton.

Black, Gregory D. 1994. *Hollywood Censored: Morality Codes, Catholics, and the Movies.* Cambridge, Eng.: Cambridge University Press.

———. 1998. *The Catholic Crusade Against the Movies, 1940–1975.* Cambridge: Cambridge University Press.

Blalock, Hubert M., Jr. 1979. *Social Statistics.* 2d ed. New York: McGraw-Hill.

Blewett, Neal, and Dean Jaensch. 1971. *Playford to Dunstan: Politics of Transition.* Melbourne: Cheshire.

Blondel, J., et al. 1970. "Legislative Behaviour: Some Steps towards a Cross-National Measurement." *Government and Opposition* 5:67–85.

Boggan, Amy L. 1998. "The Right to Die Movement: An Examination of a Unique Coalition for Constitutional Change." Paper presented at the annual meeting of the American Political Science Association, Boston.

Bosso, Christopher. 1994. "The Contextual Bases of Problem Definition," in *The Politics of Problem Definition,* ed. David A. Rochefort and Roger W. Cobb. Lawrence: University of Kansas Press.

Bowers, William J. 1984. *Legal Homicide: Death as Punishment in America, 1864–1982* Boston: Northeastern University Press.

Bown, F. A. C. S. 1990. "The Shops Bill," in *Parliament and Pressure Politics,* ed. M. Rush. Oxford: Oxford University Press.

Boyer, Patrick. 1992. *Direct Democracy in Canada.* Toronto: Dundurn Press.

Bradley, Martin, Norman Green, Dale E. Jones, Mac Lynn, and Lou McNeil. 1992. *Churches and Church Membership in the United States.* Atlanta, Ga.: Glenmary Research Center.

Bragg, Rick. 1998. "End Video Poker Gambling, Carolina Chief Urges," *New York Times,* 22 January.

Branch, Taylor. 1988. *Parting the Waters: America in the King Years 1954–63.* New York: Simon & Schuster.

———. 1998. *Pillar of Fire: America in the King Years 1963–65.* New York: Simon & Schuster.

Bromhead, P. 1956. *Private Members Bills in the British Parliament.* London: Routledge and Kegan Paul.

Brown, Clifford, Lynda Powell, and Clyde Wilcox. 1995. *Serious Money: Fundraising and Contributing in Presidential Nomination Campaigns.* New York: Cambridge University Press.

Brown, M. 1996. "The Age of Consent: The Parliamentary Campaign in the UK to Lower the Age of Consent for Homosexual Acts." *Journal of Legislative Studies* 2:1–7.

Brown, Norman O. 1959. *Life Against Death: The Psychoanalytical Meaning of History.* Middletown, Conn.: Wesleyan University Press.

———. 1966. *Love's Body.* New York: Random House.

Browne, William P. 1995. *Cultivating Congress: Constituents, Issues, and Agricultural Policymaking.* Lawrence: University of Kansas Press.

Bruce, John M., and Clyde Wilcox. 1998. *The Changing Politics of Gun Control.* Lanham, Md.: Rowman and Littlefield.

Buchanan, Robert J., and Robert L. Ohsfeldt. 1993. "The Attitudes of State Legislators and State Medicaid Policies Related to AIDS." *Policy Studies Journal* 21:651–71.

Budge, I., D. Robertson, and D. Hearl, eds. 1987. *Ideology, Strategy and Party Change.* Cambridge, Eng.: Cambridge University Press.

Butler, D. and D. Kavanagh. 1980. *The British General Election of 1979.* London: Macmillan.

———. 1984. *The British General Election of 1983.* London: Macmillan.

———. 1988. *The British General Election of 1987.* London: Macmillan.

———. 1997. *The British General Election of 1997.* London: Macmillan.

Butler, David, and Austin Ranney, eds. 1978. *Referendums.* Washington, D.C.: AEI Press.

———. eds. 1994. *Referendums around the World.* Washington, D.C.: AEI Press.

Button, James W., Barbara A. Rienzo, and Kenneth D. Wald. 1997. *Private Lives, Public Conflicts: Battles over Gay Rights in American Communities.* Washington, D.C.: CQ Press.

Byrnes, Timothy A. 1991. *Catholic Bishops in American Politics.* Princeton, N.J.: Princeton University Press.

———. 1993. "The Politics of the American Catholic Hierarchy." *Political Science Quarterly* 108:497–514.

Calvert, Randall L. 1985. "The Value of Biased Information: A Rational Choice Model of Political Advice." *Journal of Politics* 47:530–55.

———. 1992. "Leadership and Its Basis in Problems of Social Coordination." *International Political Science Review* 13:7–24.

Camus, Albert. 1961. "Reflections on the Guillotine." In *Resistance, Rebellion, and Death,* trans. Justin O'Brien. New York: Alfred A. Knopf.

Cannon, A. Peter. 1995. "Capital Punishment in Wisconsin and the Nation." Madison, Wisc.: State of Wisconsin Legislative Reference Bureau, Informational Bulletin 95-1.

Canon, Bradley C., and Lawrence Baum. 1981. "Patterns of Adoption of Tort Law Innovations." *American Political Science Review* 75:975–87.

Cantril, Hadley. 1951. *Public Opinion, 1935–1946.* Princeton, N.J.: Princeton University Press.

Carmen, Ira H. 1966. *Movies, Censorship, and the Law.* Ann Arbor: University of Michigan Press.

Carmines, Edward G., and James A. Stimson. 1980. "The Two Faces of Issue Voting." *American Political Science Review* 74:78–91.

———. 1989. *Issue Evolution: Race and the Transformation of American Politics.* Princeton, N.J.: Princeton University Press.

Carson, Rob. 1992. "Washington's I-119." *Hastings Center Report,* March–April.

Carter, Donald D. 1998. "Employment Benefits for Same Sex Couples: The Expanding Entitlement." *Canadian Public Policy* 24:107–17.

Cassady, Ralph, Jr. 1958. "Impact of the Paramount Decision on Motion Picture Distribution and Price Making." *Southern California Law Review* 31:150–97.

Castles, Francis G., ed. 1993. *Families of Nations.* Aldershot, N.H.: Dartmouth.

———. 1994a. "On Religion and Public Policy: Does Catholicism Make a Difference?" *European Journal of Political Research* 25:19–40.

————. 1994b. "On Religion and Public Policy: The Case for Covariance." *European Journal of Political Research* 26:111–15.

————, and Michael Flood. 1993. "Why Divorce Rates Differ: Law, Religious Belief and Modernity," in *Families of Nations,* ed. Francis G. Castles. Aldershot, N.H.: Dartmouth.

Chandler, David B. 1976. *Capital Punishment in Canada.* Toronto: McClelland and Stewart.

Childress, Steven A. 1992. "Pornography, 'Serious Rape,' and Statistics: A Reply to Dr. Kutchinsky." *Law & Society Review* 26:457–60.

Chressanthis, George A., Kathie S. Gilbert, and Paul W. Grimes. 1991. "Ideology, Constituent Interests, and Senatorial Voting: The Case of Abortion." *Social Science Quarterly* 72:588–600.

Christian Coalition. 1995. " The Contract with the American Family." Washington, D.C.: Christian Coalition. Typescript.

Christoph, James B. 1962. *Capital Punishment and British Politics.* Chicago: University of Chicago Press.

Clark, Jill. 1985. "Policy Diffusion and Program Scope: Research Directions." *Publius* 15: 61–70.

Clausen, Aage R. 1973. *How Congressmen Decide.* New York: St. Martin's Press.

"Clean Air Bill Fails to Move." 1999. In *1998 CQ Almanac,* Vol. 64. Washington, D.C.: CQ Press.

Cobb, Roger W., and Charles D. Elder. 1983a. *Participation in American Politics: The Dynamics of Agenda-Building.* 2d ed. Baltimore, Md.: Johns Hopkins University Press.

————. 1983b. *The Political Uses of Symbols.* New York: Longman.

————, Jennie Ross, and Marc Howard Ross. 1976. "Agenda Building as a Comparative Political Process." *American Political Science Review* 70: 126–38.

Cobin, Herbert L. 1967. "Abolition and Restoration of the Death Penalty in Delaware." In *The Death Penalty in America,* ed. Hugh Adam Bedau. Garden City, N.Y.: Anchor.

Cohan, Alvin. 1986. "Abortion as a Marginal Issue: The Use of Peripheral Mechanisms in Britain and the United States," in *The New Politics of Abortion,* ed. Joni Lovenduski and Joyce Outshoorn. London: Sage.

Cohen, Jeffrey E., and Charles Barrilleaux. 1993. "Public Opinion, Interest Groups, and Public Policy Making: Abortion Policy in the American States," in *Understanding the New Politics of Abortion,* ed. Malcolm Goggin. Newbury Park, Calif.: Sage.

Combs, Michael W., John R. Hibbing, and Susan Welch. 1984. "Black Constituents and Congressional Roll Call Votes." *Western Political Quarterly* 37:424–34.

Commonwealth Parliamentary Debates (Australia) (House of Representatives) 83, New Series, 10 May 1973, 1963–2001.

Conant, Michael. 1960. *Antitrust in the Motion Picture Industry.* Berkeley: University of California Press.

Congressional Quarterly. Various years. *Congressional Quarterly Almanac* Washington, D.C.: CQ Press.

Converse, Philip. 1964. "The Nature of Belief Systems in Mass Publics." In *Ideology and Discontent,* ed. David Apter. New York: Free Press.

————. 1975. "Public Opinion and Voting Behavior." In *Handbook of Political Science,* ed. Fred Greenstein and Nelson Polsby. Reading, Mass.: Addison-Wesley.

Cook, Elizabeth Adell. 1993. "Catholicism and Abortion Attitudes in the American States: A Contextual Analysis." *Journal for the Scientific Study of Religion* 32: 223–31.

————. 1994. "Issue Voting in Gubernatorial Elections: Abortion and Post-Webster Politics." *Journal of Politics* 56:187–99.

————, Frederick Hartwig, and Clyde Wilcox. 1993. "The Abortion Issue Down Ticket: The Virginia Lieutenant Governor's Race of 1989." *Women and Politics* 12:5–18.

————, Ted G. Jelen, and Clyde Wilcox. 1992. *Between Two Absolutes: Public Opinion and the Politics of Abortion.* Boulder, Colo.: Westview Press.

Cook, Timothy. 1998. *Governing with the News: The News Media as a Political Institution.* Chicago: University of Chicago Press.

Cooney, John. 1984. *The American Pope: The Life and Times of Francis Cardinal Spellman.* New York: Times Books.

Coriden, James A., Thomas J. Green, and Donald E. Heintschel. 1985. *The Code of Canon Law: A Text and Commentary.* New York: Paulist Press.

Council of State Governments. Various years. *The Book of the States.* Lexington, Ky.: Council of State Governments.

Cowley, Philip. 1995. "Parliament and the Poll Tax." *The Journal of Legislative Studies* 1:94–115.

————. 1998. "Conclusion," in *Conscience and Parliament,* ed. P. Cowley. London: Frank Cass.

————, ed. 1998. *Conscience and Parliament.* London: Frank Cass.

————. n.d. "Rebels and Rebellions: Conservative MPs in the 1992 Parliament." *British Journal of Politics and International Relations,* forthcoming.

————, and P. Norton. 1998. "Rebelliousness in the British House of Commons." Paper presented to the Third Workshop of Parliamentary Scholars and Parliamentarians, Wroxton, Oxfordshire.

————, and N. Stace. 1996. "The Wild Mammals (Protection) Bill: A Parliamentary White Elephant?" *The Journal of Legislative Studies* 2:339–55.

————, and M. Stuart. 1997. "Sodomy, Slaughter, Sunday Shopping and Seatbelts." *Party Politics* 3:119–30.

Cox, Gary M., and Mathew McCubbins. 1993. *Legislative Leviathan: Party Government in the House.* Berkeley: University of California Press.

Craig, Barbara Hinkson, and David M. O'Brien. 1993. *Abortion and American Politics.* Chatham, N.J.: Chatham House.

Crain, Robert L. 1966. "Fluoridation: The Diffusion of Innovation among Cities." *Social Forces* 44:467–76.

Crewe, I. 1985. "MPs and Their Constituents in Britain: How Strong Are the Links?," in *Representatives of the People,* ed. V. Bogdanor. Aldershot: Gower.

————, I. 1993. "Voting and the Electorate," in *Developments in British Politics 4,* ed. P. Dunleavy, A. Gamble, I. Holliday, and G. Peele. London: Macmillan.

Culver, John, and April Smailes. 1999. "Abortion Politics and Policies in California." Paper presented at the annual meeting of the Western Political Science Association, Seattle.

d'Emilio, John B., and Estelle B. Freedman. 1988. *Intimate Matters: A History of Sexuality in the United States.* New York: Harper & Row.

Dahl, Robert A. 1956. *A Preface to Democratic Theory.* Chicago: University of Chicago Press.

Daley, Daniel. 1997. "Exclusive Purpose: Abstinence-Only Proponents Create Federal Entitlement in Welfare Reform." Report 25:4. New York: Sexuality Information and Education Council of the United States.

Dann, Robert H. 1967. "Abolition and Restoration of the Death Penalty in Oregon." In *The Death Penalty in America,* ed. Hugh Adam Bedau. Garden City, N.Y.: Anchor.

Davies, Kimberly A. 1997. "Voluntary Exposure to Pornography and Men's Attitudes Toward Feminism and Rape." *The Journal of Sex Research* 34:131–37.

Day, Christine L. 1994. "State Legislative Voting Patterns on Abortion Restrictions in Louisiana." *Women & Politics* 14:45–63.

Daynes, Byron W. 1988. "Pornography: Freedom of Expression or Societal Degradation?" in *Social Regulatory Policy,* ed. Raymond Tatlovich and Byron Danes. Boulder, Colo.: Westview Press.

———, and Raymond Tatalovich. 1992. "Presidential Politics and Abortion, 1972–1988." *Presidential Studies Quarterly* 22:545–62.

De Vaus, David, and Ian McAllister. 1989. "The Changing Politics of Women: Gender and Political Alignment in 11 Nations." *European Journal of Political Research* 17:241–62.

Deering, Christopher J., and Steven S. Smith. 1997. *Committees in Congress.* 3d ed. Washington, D.C.: CQ Press.

Delli Carpini, Michael X., and Scott Keeter. 1996. *What Americans Know about Politics and Why It Matters.* New Haven, Conn.: Yale University Press.

Denver, D., and G. Hands. 1997. *Modern Constituency Electioneering.* London: Frank Cass.

DeRoche, Edward F., and Mary M. Williams. 1998. *Educating Hearts and Minds: A Comprehensive Character Education Framework.* Thousand Oaks, Calif.: Corwin Press.

Derthick, Martha, and Paul J. Quirk. 1985. *The Politics of Deregulation.* Washington, D.C.: Brookings Institution.

Diamond, Sara. 1995. *Roads to Dominion: Right-Wing Movements and Political Power in the United States.* New York: Guilford Press.

Doan, Alesha. 1998. "Agenda Setting on the Abortion Issue." College Station: Texas A&M University. Typescript.

———, and Kenneth J. Meier. 1998. "Violence as a Political Strategy: The Case of Anti-Abortion Activists." Paper presented at the annual meeting of the Midwest Political Science Association, Chicago.

Doherty, Thomas. 1999. *Pre-Code Hollywood: Sex, Immorality, and Insurrection in the Movies.* New York: Columbia University Press.

Dolan, Jay P. 1978. *Catholic Revivalism: The American Experience 1830–1900.* Notre Dame, Ind.: University of Notre Dame Press.

———. 1985. *The American Catholic Experience: A History from Colonial Times to the Present.* Garden City, N.Y.: Doubleday & Company.

Donnison, David, and Caroline Bryson. 1996. "Matters of Life and Death: Attitudes to Euthanasia," in *British Social Attitudes: The 13th Report,* ed. Roger Jowell, John Curtice, Alison Park, Lindsay Brook and Katarina Thomson. Aldershot: Gower.

Dority, Barbara. 1992. "The Justice Department's Morality Brigade." *The Humanist* 52:39–42.

Downs, Anthony. 1957. *An Economic Theory of Democracy.* New York: Harper & Row.

———. 1967. *Inside Bureaucracy.* Boston: Little, Brown.

Duggan, Lisa and Nan D. Hunter. 1995. *Sex Wars: Sexual Dissent and Political Culture.* New York: Routledge.

Duncan, Phil, ed. Various years. *Politics in America.* Washington, D.C.: CQ Press.

Durham, M. 1991. *Sex and Politics: The Family and Morality in the Thatcher Years.* Basingstoke: Macmillan.

Durham, Martin. 1998. "Censorship," in *Parliament and Conscience,* ed. Philip Cowley. London: Frank Cass.

Dye, Thomas R. 1984. *Understanding Public Policy.* Englewood Cliffs, N.J.: Prentice Hall.

———. 1990. *American Federalism.* Lexington, Mass.: D.C. Heath.

———. 1966. *Politics, Economics and the Public: Policy Outcomes in the American States.* Chicago: Rand McNally.

Dyer, Gwynne. 1998. "The Last Days of the War on Drugs," *Globe and Mail,* 26 September.

Edelman, Murray. 1964. *The Symbolic Uses of Politics.* Urbana: University of Illinois Press.

———. 1967. *The Symbolic Uses of Politics,* 2d ed. Urbana: University of Illinois Press.

Ellis, John Tracy. 1969. *American Catholicism.* 2d ed., rev. Chicago: University of Chicago Press.

Ellis, Margaret. 1998. "Gay Rights: Lifestyle or Immorality?" in *Moral Controversies in American Politics,* ed. Raymond Tatalovich and Byron W. Daynes. Armonk, N.Y.: M.E. Sharpe.

Emanuel, Ezekiel J. 1999. "The End of Euthanasia? Death's Door." *New Republic,* 17 May.

Emerson, Thomas I. 1963. *Toward a General Theory of the First Amendment.* New York: Vintage Books.

———. 1970. *The System of Free Expression.* New York: Vintage Books.

Emrey, Jolly Ann, and Elizabeth Anne Stiles. 1998. "Playing the Symbolic Policy Game: A Game Theoretic Analysis of the Communications Decency Act and the Flag Burning Bill/Amendment." Paper presented at the annual meeting of the American Political Science Association, Boston.

———, Paige Schneider, and Elizabeth Ann Stiles. 1998. "Cultural Politics: Legislating Morality in the States." Paper presented at American Political Science Association, Boston.

Epp, Charles R. 1998. *The Rights Revolution: Lawyers, Activists, and Supreme Courts in Comparative Perspective.* Chicago: University of Chicago Press.

Epstein, Lee, and Joseph F. Kobylka. 1992. *Supreme Court and Legal Change: Abortion and the Death Penalty.* Chapel Hill: University of North Carolina Press.

Erikson, Robert S. 1978. "Constituency Opinion and Congressional Behavior: A Reexamination of the Miller-Stokes Representation Data." *American Journal of Political Science* 22: 511–35.

———, Gerald C. Wright, and John P. McIver. 1993. *Statehouse Democracy: Public Opinion and Policy in the American States.* New York: Cambridge University Press.

"Euthanasia in Australia." 1996. *New England Journal of Medicine* 334:1668–69.

Fairbanks, J. David. 1977. "Religious Forces and 'Morality' Policies in the American States." *Western Political Quarterly* 30:411–17.

Farber, Stephen. 1972. *The Movie Rating Game*. Washington, D.C.: Public Affairs Press.

Farr, James. 1985. "Situational Analysis: Explanation in Political Science." *Journal of Politics* 47:1085–1107.

Farrell, Joseph, and Matthew Rabin. 1996. "Cheap Talk." *Journal of Economic Perspectives* 10:103–18.

Federal Bureau of Investigation. 1995. *Crime in the United States*. Washington, D.C.: U.S. Department of Justice.

Feller, Irwin, and Donald C. Menzel. 1978. "The Adoption of Technological Innovations by Municipal Governments." *Urban Affairs Quarterly* 13:469–90.

Fenno, Richard. 1978. *Home Style: House Members in Their Districts*. Boston: Little, Brown.

Field, Marilyn J. 1979. "Determinants of Abortion Policy in Developed Nations." *Policy Studies Journal* 9:771–81.

Filer, John E., Donald L. Moak, and Barry Uze. 1988. "Why Some States Adopt Lotteries and Others Don't." *Public Finance Quarterly* 16:259–83.

Fishbein, Paul, ed. 1995. *AVN 1995 Adult Entertainment Guide*. Los Angeles, Calif.: AVN.

Fisher, Anthony, and Jane Buckingham. 1985. *Abortion in Australia: Answers and Alternatives*. Melbourne, Dove Press.

Fleisher, Richard. 1993. "Explaining the Change in Roll-Call Voting Behavior of Southern Democrats." *Journal of Politics* 55:327–41.

Foster, John L. 1978. "Regionalism and Innovation in the American States." *Journal of Politics* 40:179–87.

Fowler, N. 1991. *Ministers Decide*. London: Chapmans.

Fox, Kraig. 1992. "Note: *Paramount* Revisited: The Resurgence of Vertical Integration in the Motion Picture Industry." *Hofstra Law Review* 21:505–36.

Franklin, Charles H., and Liane C. Kosaki. 1989. "Republican Schoolmaster: The U.S. Supreme Court, Public Opinion, and Abortion." *American Political Science Review* 83:751–71.

Frant, Howard, Frances Stokes Berry, and William Berry. 1991. "Specifying a Model of State Policy Innovation." *American Political Science Review.* 85:571–80.

Freeman, Gary P. 1985. "National Styles and Policy Sectors: Explaining Structural Variation." *Journal of Public Policy* 5:467–95.

Freeman, Patricia K. 1985. "Interstate Communications Among State Legislators Regarding Energy Policy Innovation." *Publius* 15:99–111.

Freud, Anna. [1938] 1946. *The Ego and the Mechanism of Defence,* trans. Cecil Barnes. Reprint, New York: International Universities Press.

Freud, Sigmund. [1923] 1960. *The Ego and the Id,* trans. Joan Rivere and James Strachey. Reprint, New York: W. W. Norton.

———. [1933] 1961. *Civilization and Its Discontents,* ed. James Strachey. Reprint, New York: W. W. Norton.

Gaddy, Barbara B., T. William Hall, and Robert J. Marzano. 1996. *School Wars: Resolving Our Conflicts over Religion and Values*. San Francisco: Jossey-Bass.

Gaines, G. J. 1998. "The Impersonal Vote?" *Legislative Studies Quarterly* 23:167–96.

Gamble, Barbara. 1994. "Measuring State Opinion on Policy Issues." Ann Arbor: University of Michigan. Typescript.

Gamble, Barbara S. 1997. "Putting Civil Rights to a Popular Vote." *American Journal of Political Science* 41:245–69.

Ganz, G. 1992. "The War Crimes Act 1991—Why No Constitutional Crisis?" *Modern Law Review* 55:87–95.

————. 1998. "War Crimes," in *Conscience and Parliament,* ed. P. Cowley. London: Frank Cass.

Gardiner, Harold C. 1958. *Catholic Viewpoint on Censorship.* Garden City, N.Y.: Hanover House.

Gardner, Gerald. 1987. *The Censorship Papers: Movie Censorship Letters from the Hays Office, 1934 to 1968.* New York: Dodd, Mead.

Garner, Robert. 1998. "Animal Welfare," in *Conscience and Parliament,* ed. Philip Cowley. London: Frank Cass.

Garrow, David J. 1986. *Bearing the Cross: Martin Luther King, Jr., and the Southern Christian Leadership Conference.* New York: Vintage Books.

————. 1994. *Liberty and Sexuality: The Right to Privacy and the Making of* Roe v. Wade. New York: Macmillan.

Gees, Sally B. 1992. "The Meaning of Death: Time to Talk." *Christianity and Crisis,* 3 February.

George, Alexander L. 1979. "Case Studies and Theory Development: The Method of Structured-Focused Comparison," in *Diplomacy: New Approaches in History, Theory, and Policy,* ed. Paul Gordon Lauren. New York: Free Press.

Glendon, Mary Ann. 1987. *Divorce and Abortion in Western Law.* Cambridge, Mass.: Harvard University Press.

Glick, Henry R. 1992. *The Right to Die.* New York: Columbia University Press.

————, and Scott P. Hays. 1991. "Innovation and Reinvention in State Policymaking: Theory and Evolution of Living Will Laws." *Journal of Politics* 53:835–50.

Goggin, Malcolm L. 1986. "The 'Too Few Cases/Too Many Variables' Problem in Implementation Research." *Western Political Quarterly* 38:328–47.

————, ed. 1993. *Understanding the New Politics of Abortion.* Newbury Park, Calif.: Sage.

————. 1995. "Congressional Redesign of Public Policy." Paper presented at the annual meeting of the American Political Science Association, Chicago.

————, and Jung-Ki Kim. 1992. "Interest Groups, Public Opinion, and Abortion Policy in the American States." Paper presented at the annual meeting of the Western Political Science Association, San Francisco.

————, James P. Lester, Ann O'M. Bowman, and Lawrence O'Toole Jr. 1990. *Implementation Theory and Practice: Toward a Third Generation.* Glenview, Ill.: Scott, Foresman/Little, Brown.

————, and Christopher Wlezien. 1993. "Abortion Opinion and Policy in the American States," in *Understanding the New Politics of Abortion,* ed. Malcolm Goggin. Newbury Park, Calif.: Sage.

Gohmann, Stephan F. 1994. "Voting in the U.S. House on Abortion Funding Issues: The Role of Constituents' and Legislators' Ideology before and after the Webster Decision." *American Journal of Economics and Sociology* 53:455–74.

————, and Robert L. Ohsfeldt. 1990. "Predicting State Abortion Legislation from U.S. Senate Votes: The Effects of Apparent Ideological Shirking." *Policy Studies Review* 9:749–64.

Goldberg, Carey. 1997. "Oregon Braces for New Fight on Helping the Dying to Die." *New York Times,* 17 June.

Gomery, Douglas. 1991. "Who Killed Hollywood?" *The Wilson Quarterly* 15:106–12.

Gormley, William T. 1986. "Regulatory Issue Networks in a Federal System." *Polity* 18:595–620.

Gould, Arthur, Andrew Shaw, and Daphne Ahrendt. 1996. "Illegal Drugs: Liberal and Restrictive Policies," in *British Social Attitudes: The 13th Report,* ed. Roger Jowell, John Curtice, Alison Park, Lindsay Brook and Katarina Thomson. Aldershot: Dartmouth.

Graber, Mark A. 1991. *Transforming Free Speech: The Ambiguous Legacy of Civil Libertarianism.* Berkeley: University of California Press.

Graffius, C. 1997. *Election '97 A Christian View of the Major Issues.* London: Hodder and Stoughton.

Gray, Virginia. 1973. "Innovation in the States: A Diffusion Study." *American Political Science Review* 67:1174–85.

———, and David Lowery. 1996. *The Population Ecology of Interest Representation: Lobbying Communities in the American States.* Ann Arbor: University of Michigan Press.

Greeley, Andrew M. 1977. *The American Catholic: A Social Portrait.* New York: Basic Books.

Green, John C., and James L. Guth. 1991. "Religion, Representatives, and Roll Calls." *Legislative Studies Quarterly* 16:571–84.

Greenberg, George D., Jeffrey A. Miller, Lawrence B. Mohr, and Bruce C. Vladeck. 1977. "Developing Public Policy Theory: Perspectives from Empirical Research." *American Political Science Review* 71:1532–43.

Greene, William H. 1997. *Econometric Analysis.* 3d ed. Upper Saddle River, N.J.: Prentice Hall.

Grenzke, Janet M. 1989. "PACs and the Congressional Supermarket: The Currency Is Complex." *American Journal of Political Science* 33:1–24.

Guillot, Ellen Elizabeth. 1967. "Abolition and Restoration of the Death Penalty in Missouri." In *The Death Penalty in America,* ed. Hugh Adam Bedau. Garden City, N.Y.: Anchor.

Gusfield, Joseph R. 1963. *Symbolic Crusade: Status Politics and the American Temperance Movement.* Urbana: University of Illinois Press.

Hagerstrand, Torsten. 1965. "A Monte Carlo Approach to Diffusion." *European Journal of Sociology* 6:43–67.

Hagle, Timothy M., and Glenn E. Mitchell II. 1992. "Goodness-of-Fit Measures for Probit and Logit." *American Journal of Political Science* 36:762–84.

Haider-Markel, Donald P. 1997. "From Bullhorns to PACs: Lesbian and Gay Politics, Interest Groups, and Policy." Ph.D. dissertation University of Wisconsin-Milwaukee.

———. 1998. "The Politics of Social Regulatory Policy: State and Federal Hate Crime Policy and Implementation Effort." *Political Research Quarterly.* 51:69–88.

———, and Kenneth J. Meier. n.d. "Legislative Victory, Electoral Uncertainty: Explaining Outcomes in the Battles Over Lesbian and Gay Rights." *Policy Studies Review,* forthcoming.

———, and Alesha M. Doan. 1998. "Bonfire of the Righteous: Geographically Expanding the Scope of the Conflict over Same-Sex Marriage." Paper presented at the annual meeting of the Midwest Political Science Association, Chicago.

————, and Kenneth J. Meier. 1996. "The Politics of Gay and Lesbian Rights: Expanding the Scope of the Conflict." *Journal of Politics* 58:332–50.

Hale, Nathan G., Jr. 1971. *Freud and the Americans: The Beginnings of Psychoanalysis in the United States, 1876–1917.* New York: Oxford University Press.

————. 1995. *The Rise and Crisis of Psychoanalysis in the United States: Freud and the Americans 1917–1985.* New York: Oxford University Press.

Hall, Richard L. 1998. *Participation in Congress.* New Haven, Conn.: Yale University Press.

Halva-Neubauer, Glen. 1993. "The States after *Roe*: No 'Paper Tigers,' " in *Understanding the New Politics of Abortion,* ed. Malcolm Goggin. Newbury Park, Calif.: Sage.

Hanna, Mary T. 1979. *Catholics and American Politics.* Cambridge, Mass.: Harvard University Press.

Hansen, Susan. 1993. "Differences in Public Policies toward Abortion: Electoral and Policy Context," in *Understanding the New Politics of Abortion,* ed. Malcolm Goggin. Newbury Park, Calif.: Sage.

Hanushek, Eric A., and John E. Jackson. 1977. *Statistical Methods for Social Scientists.* San Diego, Calif.: Academic Press.

Harris v. McRae. 1980. 448 U.S. 297.

Harrison, M. 1984. "Broadcasting," in *The British General Election of 1983,* ed. D. Butler and D. Kavanagh. London: Macmillan.

————. 1988. "Broadcasting," in *The British General Election of 1987,* ed. D. Butler and D. Kavanagh. London: Macmillan.

————. 1988. "Press," in *The British General Election of 1987,* ed. D. Butler and D. Kavanagh. London: Macmillan.

————. 1992. "Politics on the Air," in *The British General Election of 1992,* ed. D. Butler and D. Kavanagh. London: Macmillan.

————. 1997. "Politics on the Air," in *The British General Election of 1997,* ed. D. Butler and D. Kavanagh. London: Macmillan.

Harrop, M. 1984. "Press," in *The British General Election of 1983,* ed. D. Butler and D. Kavanagh. London: Macmillan.

————, and M. Scammell. 1992. "A Tabloid War," in *The British General Election of 1992,* ed. D. Butler and D. Kavanagh. London: Macmillan.

Haskins, Ron, and Carol Statuto Bevan. 1997. "Abstinence Education Under Welfare Reform." *Children and Youth Services Review* 19 (5/6):465–84.

Hayes, Michael T. 1978. "The Semi-Sovereign Pressure Groups: A Critique of Current Theory and an Alternative Typology." *Journal of Politics* 40:134–61.

Hays, Scott P., and Henry R. Glick. 1997. "The Role of Agenda Setting in Policy Innovation: An Event History Analysis of Living Will Laws." *American Politics Quarterly* 53:497–516.

Healy, Melissa. 1997. "Clinton Frees $250 Million for Sex Abstinence Teaching," *Los Angeles Times,* 1 March.

Heck, Edward V. 1982. "Justice Brennan and the Development of Obscenity Policy by the Supreme Court." *California Western Law Review* 18:410–41.

Hennesey, James, S.J. 1981. *American Catholics: A History of the Roman Catholic Community in the United States.* New York: Oxford University Press.

Hertzke, Allen D. 1988. *Representing God in Washington: The Role of Religious Lobbies in the American Polity.* Knoxville: The University of Tennessee Press.

Heymann, Philip B. 1988. "How Government Expresses Public Ideas," in *The Power of Public Ideas,* ed. Robert B. Reich. Cambridge, Mass.: Harvard University Press.

Hibbing, J. R., and D. Marsh. 1987. "Accounting for the Voting Patterns of British MPs on Free Votes." *Legislative Studies Quarterly* 12:275–97.

Hill, Kim Quaille, Jan E. Leighley, and Angela Hinton-Andersson. 1995. "Lower-Class Mobilization and Policy Linkage in the U.S. States." *American Journal of Political Science* 39:75–86.

Hirschman, Albert O. 1970. *Exit, Voice, and Loyalty: Responses to Decline in Firms, Organizations, and States.* Cambridge, Mass.: Harvard University Press.

———. 1977. *The Passions and the Interests: Political Arguments for Capitalism before Its Triumph.* Princeton, N.J.: Princeton University Press.

Hochberg, Adam. 1999. *All Things Considered,* "Southern Lotteries." National Public Radio, 14 April.

Hofrenning, Daniel J. B. 1995. *In Washington, but Not of It: The Prophetic Politics of Religious Lobbyists.* Philadelphia: Temple University Press.

Holbrook, Thomas M., and Emily Van Dunk. 1993. "Electoral Competition in the American States." *American Political Science Review* 87:955–62.

Holmes, Stephen. 1995. *Passions and Constraints: On the Theory of Liberal Democracy.* Chicago: University of Chicago Press.

Hoskins, Carla Mockaitis. 1997. "Finally, Abstinence Support." *Milwaukee Journal Sentinel,* 9 August.

Hovey, Harold A. 1996. *State Fact Finder.* Washington, D.C.: CQ Press.

Humphry, Derek. 1992. *Final Exit.* New York: Dell.

Hunter, James Davidson. 1983. *American Evangelicalism: Conservative Religion and the Quandary of Modernity.* New Brunswick, N.J.: Rutgers University Press.

———. 1991. *Culture Wars: The Struggle to Define America.* New York: Basic Books.

Hwang, Sung-Don, and Virginia Gray. 1991. "External Limits and Internal Determinants of State Public Policy." *Western Political Quarterly* 44:277–99.

Inglehart, Ronald. 1977. *The Silent Revolution: Changing Values and Political Styles Among Western Publics.* Princeton, N.J.: Princeton University Press.

Institute for Women's Policy Research. 1996. *The Status of Women in the States.* Washington, D.C: Author.

Isaac, J. 1994. "The Politics of Morality in the UK." *Parliamentary Affairs* 47:175–89.

Iyengar, Shanto, and Donald R. Kinder. 1987. *News That Matters.* Chicago: University of Chicago Press.

Izod, John. 1988. *Hollywood at the Box Office, 1895–1986.* New York: Columbia University Press.

Jackman, Jennifer L. 1997. "Blue Smoke, Mirrors, and Mediators: The Symbolic Contest over RU 486," in *Cultural Strategies of Agenda Denial,* ed. Roger W. Cobb and Marc Howard Ross. Lawrence: University of Kansas Press.

Jackson, John E., and John W. Kingdon. 1992. "Ideology, Interest Group Scores, and Legislative Votes." *American Journal of Political Science* 36:805–23.

Jackson, John S., III, and Nancy L. Clayton. 1996. "Leaders and Followers: Major Party Elites, Identifiers, and Issues, 1980–92," in *The State of the Parties,* 2d ed., ed. John C. Green and Daniel M. Shea. Lanham, Md.: Rowman and Littlefield.

Jacob, Herbert. 1988. *Silent Revolution: The Transformation of Divorce Law in the United States.* Chicago: University of Chicago Press.

Jaensch, Dean. 1994. *Power Politics: Australia's Party System.* Sydney: Allen & Unwin.

Jasper, James M., and Dorothy Nelkin. 1992. *The Animal Rights Crusade.* New York: Free Press.

Jensen, Robert. 1995. "Pornography and Affirmative Conceptions of Freedom." *Women & Politics* 15:1–18.

Johnson, Douglas, et al. 1974. *Churches and Church Membership in the United States.* Washington, D.C.: Glenmary Research Center.

Jones, Bradford S., and Barbara Norrander. 1996. "The Reliability of Aggregated Public Opinion Measures." *American Journal of Political Science* 40:295–309.

Jones, P. 1995. "Members of Parliament and Issues of Conscience," in *Party, Parliament and Personality,* ed. P. Jones. London: Routledge.

Jowett, Garth. 1996. " 'A Significant Medium for the Communication of Ideas': The *Miracle* Decision and the Decline of Motion Picture Censorship," in *Movie Censorship and American Culture,* ed. Francis G. Couvares. Washington, D.C.: Smithsonian Institution Press.

Kalman, Laura. 1986. *Legal Realism at Yale, 1927–1960.* Chapel Hill: University of North Carolina Press.

Katz, Elihu, Martin L. Levin, and Herbert Hamilton. 1963. "Traditions of Research on the Diffusion of Innovations." *American Sociological Review* 28:237–52.

Kazis, Israel J. 1967. "Judaism and the Death Penalty," in *The Death Penalty in America,* ed. Hugh Adam Bedau. Garden City, N.Y.: Anchor.

Kelman, Steven. 1987. *Making Public Policy.* New York: Basic Books.

Kennedy, Peter. 1994. *A Guide to Econometrics.* 3d ed. Cambridge, Mass.: MIT Press.

Key, V. O., Jr. 1949. *Southern Politics.* New York: Vintage.

Kinder, Donald, and David Sears. 1985. "Public Opinion and Political Action," in *Handbook of Social Psychology,* 4th ed., ed. G. Lindzey and E. Aronson. New York: Random House.

King, Paula J. 1988. "Policy Entrepreneurs: Catalysts in the Policy Innovation Process." Ph.D. dissertation. University of Minnesota.

Kingdon, John W. 1973. *Congressmen's Voting Decisions.* New York: Harper & Row.

———. 1984. *Agendas, Alternatives, and Public Policies.* Boston: Little, Brown.

———. 1989. *Congressmen's Voting Decisions.* 3d ed. Ann Arbor: University of Michigan Press.

———. 1995. *Agendas, Alternatives and Public Policies.* 2d ed. New York: HarperCollins.

Klingman, David, and William W. Lammers. 1984. "The 'General Policy Liberalism' Factor in American State Politics." *American Journal of Political Science* 28:598–610.

Knight, Jack. 1992. *Institutions and Social Conflict.* Cambridge, Eng.: Cambridge University Press.

Kobylka, Joseph F. 1987. "A Court-Created Context for Group Litigation: Libertarian Groups and Obscenity." *Journal of Politics* 49:1061–78.

———. 1991. *The Politics of Obscenity: Group Litigation in a Time of Legal Change.* New York: Greenwood Press.

Kovenock, David. 1973. "Influence in the U.S. House of Representatives: A Statistical Analysis of Communications." *American Politics Quarterly* 1:407–64.

Krehbiel, Keith. 1991. *Information and Legislative Organization.* Ann Arbor: University of Michigan Press.

Kutchinsky, Berl. 1973. "The Effect of Easy Availability of Pornography on the Incidence of Sex Crimes: The Danish Experience." *Journal of Social Issues* 29:163–81.

Layman, Geoffrey C., and Edward G. Carmines. 1997. "Cultural Conflict in American Politics: Religious Traditionalism, Postmaterialism, and U.S. Political Behavior." *Journal of Politics* 59:751–77.

———, and Thomas M. Carsey. 1998. "Why Do Party Activists Convert? An Analysis of Individual-Level Change on the Abortion Issue." *Political Research Quarterly* 51:723–50.

Leege, David C. 1992. "Coalitions, Cues, Strategic Politics, and the Staying Power of the Religious Right, or Why Political Scientists Ought to Pay Attention to Cultural Politics." *PS: Political Science & Politics* 25:198–204.

———. 1993. "Religion and Politics in Theoretical Perspective," in *Rediscovering the Religious Factor in American Politics,* ed. David C. Leege and Lyman A. Kellstedt. Armonk, N.Y.: M.E. Sharpe.

Leff, Leonard J., and Jerrold L. Simmons. 1990. *The Dame in the Kimono: Hollywood, Censorship, and the Production Code from the 1920s to the 1960s.* New York: Grove Weidenfeld.

Licari, Michael J. 1997. "Smoke Gets in Your Eyes: The Politics of Tobacco Policy." Ph.D. dissertation, University of Wisconsin-Milwaukee.

Lichbach, Mark. 1995. *The Rebel's Dilemma.* Ann Arbor: University of Michigan Press.

Lijphart, Arend. 1975. "The Comparative Case Strategy in Comparative Research." *Comparative Political Studies* 8:158–77.

Lindblom, Charles E. 1959. "The Science of 'Muddling Through.'" *Public Administration Review* 19:79–88.

Lowell, A. Lawrence. 1908. *The Government of England.* London: Macmillan.

Lowery, David, and Virginia Gray. 1993. "The Density of State Interest Group Systems." *Journal of Politics* 55:191–206.

Lowi, Theodore J. 1969. *The End of Liberalism.* New York: W.W. Norton.

———. 1972. "Four Systems of Policy, Politics, and Choice." *Public Administration Review* 32:298–310.

———. 1988. "Foreword: New Dimensions in Policy and Politics," in *Social Regulatory Policy: Moral Controversies in American Politics,* ed. Raymond Tatalovich and Byron W. Daynes. Boulder, Colo.: Westview Press.

———. 1998. "New Dimensions in Policy and Politics," in *Moral Controversies in American Politics: Cases in Social Regulatory Policy*, ed. Raymond Tatalovich and Byron Daynes. Armonk, N.Y.: M.E. Sharpe.

Luker, Kristin. 1984. *Abortion and the Politics of Motherhood.* Berkeley: University of California Press.

Lupia, Arthur, and Mathew D. McCubbins. 1994. "Who Controls? Information and the Structure of Legislative Decision Making." *Legislative Studies Quarterly* 19:361–84.

Luskin, Robert. 1987. "Measuring Political Sophistication." *American Journal of Political Science* 31:856–99.

Lyons, Charles. 1997. *The New Censors: Movies and the Culture Wars.* Philadelphia: Temple University Press.

MacKinnon, Catharine A. 1984. "Not A Moral Issue." *Yale Law & Policy Review* 2: 321–45.

Magleby, David B. 1984. *Direct Legislation.* Baltimore: Johns Hopkins University Press.

"Maine Leans Toward Applying for Federal 'Abstinence Only' Funds." 1997. *The Boston Globe,* 2 July.

March, James G., and Herbert A. Simon. 1958. *Organizations.* New York: Wiley.

Marcuse, Herbert. 1955. *Eros and Civilization: A Philosophical Inquiry in Freud.* Boston: Beacon Press.

Marsh, David, and Melvyn Read. 1988. *Private Members' Bills.* New York: Cambridge University Press.

Mathews, Jay. 1997. "Sex-Ed Funds Worry States: Lessons on Teen Abstinence Stir Debate." *The Washington Post,* 8 July.

Matthews, Donald R., and James A. Stimson. 1975. *Yeas and Nays: Normal Decision Making in the U.S. House of Representatives.* New York: Wiley.

Maynard-Moody, Steven. 1995. *The Dilemma of the Fetus.* New York: St. Martin's Press.

McArthur, John, and Stephen V. Marks. 1988. "Constituent Interest vs. Legislator Ideology: The Role of Political Opportunity Cost." *Economic Inquiry* 36:461–70.

McBrien, Richard P. 1987. *Caesar's Coin: Religion and Politics in America.* New York: Macmillan.

McDonagh, Eileen L. 1989. "Issues and Constituencies in the Progressive Era: House Roll-Call Voting on the Nineteenth Amendment, 1913–1919." *Journal of Politics* 51:119–36.

McElroy, Wendy. 1995. *XXX: A Woman's Right to Pornography.* New York: St. Martin's Press.

McGuire, Kevin T., and Gregory A. Caldiera. 1993. "Lawyers, Organized Interests, and the Law of Obscenity: Agenda Setting in the Supreme Court." *American Political Science Review* 87:717–26.

Meier, Diane E., et. al. 1998. "A National Survey of Physician-Assisted Suicide and Euthanasia in the United States." *New England Journal of Medicine* 338:1193–1201.

Meier, Kenneth J. 1994. *The Politics of Sin.* Armonk, N.Y.: M.E. Sharpe.

———. 1997. "Drugs, Sex, Rock and Roll: Two Theories of Morality Politics." Paper presented at the annual meeting of the American Political Science Association, Washington, D.C.

———, and Cathy Johnson. 1990. "The Politics of Demon Rum." *American Politics Quarterly* 18:404–29.

———, and Michael J. Licari. 1997. "Public Policy Design: Combining Policy Instruments." Paper presented at the annual meeting of the American Political Science Association, Washington, D.C.

———, and Deborah R. McFarlane. 1992. "State Policies on Funding Abortions: A Pooled Time Series Analysis." *Social Science Quarterly* 73:690–98.

———, and Deborah R. McFarlane. 1993. "Abortion Politics and Abortion Funding Policy" in *Understanding the New Politics of Abortion,* ed. Malcolm Goggin. Newbury Park, Calif.: Sage.

———, and Deborah R. McFarlane. 1993. "The Politics of Funding Abortion: State Responses to the Political Environment." *American Politics Quarterly* 21:81–101.

Menzel, Donald C., and Irwin Feller. 1977. "Leadership and Interaction Patterns in the Diffusion of Innovations Among the American States." *Western Political Quarterly* 30:528–36.

Mezey, M. 1979. *Comparative Legislatures.* Durham, N.C.: Duke University Press.

Milbrath, Lester W. 1970. "Lobbyists Approach Government," in *Interest Group Politics in America,* ed. Robert Salisbury. New York: Harper & Row.

Miller, Danny, and Jamal Shamsie. 1996. "The Resource-Based View of the Firm in Two Environments: The Hollywood Film Studios from 1936 to 1965." *Academy of Management Journal* 39:519–43.

Miller, Frank. 1994. *Censored Hollywood: Sex, Sin, and Violence on the Screen.* Atlanta, Ga.: Turner.

Miller, Warren E., Donald R. Kinder, Steven J. Rosenstone, and the National Election Studies. 1993a. *American National Election Study, 1992: Pre- and Post-Election Survey.* Ann Arbor, Mich.: Inter-University Consortium for Political and Social Research.

Miller, Warren E., Donald R. Kinder, Steven J. Rosenstone, and the National Election Studies. 1993b. *American National Election Study: Pooled Senate Election Study, 1988, 1990, 1992.* Ann Arbor, Mich.: Inter-university Consortium for Political and Social Research. [Computer file].

———, and Donald E. Stokes. 1963. "Constituency Influence in Congress." *American Political Science Review* 57:45–57.

Millns, S., and S. Sheldon. 1998. "Abortion," in *Conscience and Parliament,* ed. P. Cowley. London: Frank Cass.

Mintrom, Michael. 1997. "Policy Entrepreneurs and the Diffusion of Innovation." *American Journal of Political Science* 41:738–70.

Moen, Matthew C. 1984. "School Prayer and the Politics of Life-style Concern." *Social Science Quarterly* 65: 1065–71.

Mohr, James C. 1978. *Abortion in America: The Origins and Evolution of National Policy, 1800–1900.* New York: Oxford University Press.

Mohr, Lawrence B. 1969. "Determinants of Innovation in Organizations." *American Political Science Review* 63:111–26.

Moley, Raymond. 1945. *The Hays Office.* Indianapolis, Ind.: Bobbs-Merrill.

Monaco, James. 1984. *American Film Now: The People, the Power, the Money.* New York: Zoetrope.

Mooney, Christopher Z. 1991. "Information Sources in State Legislative Decision Making." *Legislative Studies Quarterly* 16:445–55.

———. 1993. "Strategic Information Search in State Legislative Decision Making." *Social Science Quarterly* 74:185–98.

———. 1997. "Social Learning or Political Threat: Is the Regional Effect on the Diffusion of State Policy Always Positive and Unidirectional?" Paper presented at the annual meeting of the Southern Political Science Association, Norfolk, Va.

———, and Mei-Hsien Lee. 1995. "Legislating Morality in the American States: The Case of Pre-*Roe* Abortion Regulation Reform." *American Journal of Political Science* 39:599–627.

———, and Mei-Hsien Lee. 1996 "Why Not Swing? The Diffusion of Death Penalty Legislation in the American States Since 1838." Paper presented at the annual meeting of the American Political Science Association, San Francisco.

———, and Mei-Hsien Lee. 1997. "Morality Policy in Distinctive Political Contexts: The Determinants of Death Penalty Reform in the U.S. States, 1956–1983." Paper presented at the XVII World Congress of the International Political Science Association, Seoul, Korea.

————, and Mei-Hsien Lee. 1998. "Morality Policy Re-invention and Evolution in the American States: The Case of Death Penalty Policy." Paper presented at the annual meeting of the American Political Science Association, Boston, Mass.

————, and Mei-Hsien Lee. 1999. "Morality Policy Reinvention: State Death Penalities." *Annals of the American Academy of Political and Social Sciences* 566:80–92.

————, and Mei-Hsien Lee. 2000. "The Influence of Values on Consensus and Contentious Morality Policy: U.S. Death Penalty Reform, 1956–83." *Journal of Politics,* forthcoming.

Morgan, David R., and Kenneth J. Meier. 1980. "Politics and Morality: The Effect of Religion on Referenda Voting." *Social Science Quarterly* 61:144–48.

Morris, Charles R. 1997. *American Catholic: The Saints and Sinners Who Built America's Most Powerful Church.* New York: Times Books.

Motion Picture Association of America. 1997. "March 27, 1997. Joan Graves Made Co-Chairman of Movie Rating System." Location: www.mpaa.org/.

————. n.d. "A Look at Jack Valenti." Location: www.mpaa.org/valenti.html.

Mughan, A., and R. M. Scully. 1997. "Accounting for Change in Free Vote Outcomes in the House of Commons." *British Journal of Political Science* 27:640–47.

Murray, John Courtney. 1956. "Literature and Censorship." *Books on Trial* 14:393–95, 444–46.

Mylchreest, Ian. 1995. " 'Sound Law and Undoubtedly Good Policy': *Roe* v. *Wade* in Comparative Perspective." *Journal of Policy History* 7:53–71.

NARAL. 1992. *Who Decides: A State-By-State Review of Abortion Rights.* Washington, D.C.: NARAL Foundation.

NASPL (National Association of State and Provincial Lotteries). n.d. *Lottery Facts and Background Information.* Cleveland, Ohio: NASPL.

National Center for Education Statistics. 1997. *Digest of Education Statistics 1996.* Washington, D.C.: U.S. Department of Education.

Navarro, Mireya. 1997. "Assisted Suicide Decision Looms in Florida." *New York Times,* 2 July.

Nelson, Barbara J. 1984. *Making an Issue of Child Abuse.* Chicago: University of Chicago Press.

Nice, David C. 1988. "State Deregulation of Intimate Behavior." *Social Science Quarterly* 69:203–11.

————. 1992. "The States and the Death Penalty." *Western Political Quarterly* 45:1037–48.

Nolan, Hugh, ed. 1983. *Pastoral Letters of the United States Catholic Bishops. Vol. 3: 1962–1973.* Washington, D.C.: National Conference of Catholic Bishops, United States Catholic Conference.

————. 1984a. *Pastoral Letters of the United States Catholic Bishops. Vol. 1: 1792–1940.* Washington, D.C.: National Conference of Catholic Bishops, United States Catholic Conference.

————. 1984b. *Pastoral Letters of the United States Catholic Bishops. Vol. 2: 1941–1961.* Washington, D.C.: National Conference of Catholic Bishops, United States Catholic Conference.

————. 1984c. *Pastoral Letters of the United States Catholic Bishops. Vol. 4: 1975–1983.* Washington, D.C.: National Conference of Catholic Bishops, United States Catholic Conference.

————. 1989. *Pastoral Letters of the United States Catholic Bishops. Vol. 5: 1983–1988.* Washington, D.C.: National Conference of Catholic Bishops, United States Catholic Conference.

Norrander, Barbara. 1997. "State Public Opinion and Capital Punishment Laws." University of Arizona, Department of Political Science. Typescript.

————, and Clyde Wilcox. 1993. "Sources of State Abortion Policy." Paper presented at the annual meeting of the Midwest Political Science Association, Chicago.

Norris, Pippa. 1987. *Politics and Sexual Equality.* Boulder, Colo.: Lynne Rienner.

North, Douglass C. 1990. *Institutions, Institutional Change, and Economic Performance.* Cambridge, Eng.: Cambridge University Press.

Norton, P., ed. 1990. *Parliaments in Western Europe.* London: Frank Cass.

————. 1993. *Does Parliament Matter?* London: Harvester Wheatsheaf.

———— with C. Beaumont. 1997. "The Provision of Government Time for Private Members' Bills in the House of Commons." University of Hull, Department of Politics. Typescript.

————, and D. M. Wood. 1993. *Back from Westminster.* Lexington: University Press of Kentucky.

"NSW Courts and the Law on Abortion." 1971. *Sydney Morning Herald,* 30 October.

O'Brien, Robert M. 1990. "Estimating the Reliability of Aggregate-Level Variables Based on Individual-Level Characteristics." *Sociological Methods and Research* 18:473–504.

"Ohio Minister Urges Charlotte to Fight Local Pornography." 1995. Greensboro, N.C. *News & Record,* 10 June.

Olson, Mancur, Jr. 1965. *The Logic of Collective Action.* Cambridge, Mass.: Harvard University Press.

Outshoorn, Joyce. 1986. "The Rules of the Game: Abortion Politics in the Netherlands," in *The New Politics of Abortion,* ed. Joni Lovenduski and Joyce Outshoorn. London: Sage.

————. 1996. "The Stability of Compromise: Abortion Politics in Western Europe," *Abortion Politics: Public Policy in Cross-Country Perspective,* ed. Marianne Githens and Dorothy McBride Stetson. London: Routledge.

Overby, L. Marvin. 1996. "Free Voting in a Provincial Parliament: The Case of 'Same Sex' Legislation in Ontario, 1994." *Journal of Legislative Studies* 2:172–83.

————, Raymond Tatalovich, and Donley T. Studlar. 1998. "Party and Free Votes in Canada—Abortion in the House of Commons." *Party Politics* 4:381–92.

Page, Ann L., and Donald A. Clelland. 1978. "The Kanawha County Textbook Controversy: A Study of the Politics of Life Style Concern." *Social Forces* 57:265–81.

Page, Benjamin I., and Robert Y. Shapiro. 1992. *The Rational Public.* Chicago: University of Chicago Press.

————, Robert Y. Shapiro, Paul W. Gronke, and Robert M. Rosenberg. 1984. "Constituency, Party, and Representation in Congress." *Public Opinion Quarterly* 48:741–56.

Pattie, C., E. Fieldhouse, and R. J. Johnston. 1994. "The Price of Conscience: The Electoral Correlates and Consequences of Free Votes and Rebellions in the British House of Commons 1987–92." *British Journal of Political Science* 24:359–80.

————, R. J. Johnston, and M. Stuart. 1998. "Voting without Party?," in *Conscience and Parliament,* ed. P. Cowley. London: Frank Cass.

Patton, Dana J. 1998. "Strip Club Regulation: Economic Competition or Morality Politics?" Paper presented at the annual meeting of the American Political Science Association, Boston.

Pauly, Thomas H. 1983. *An American Odyssey: Elia Kazan and American Culture.* Philadelphia: Temple University Press.

Piccione, Joseph J., and Robert A. Scholle. 1995. "Combatting Illegitimacy and Counseling Teen Abstinence: A Key Component of Welfare Reform." Backgrounder #1051, 31 August. Washington, D.C.: Heritage Foundation.

Pilsworth, M. 1980. "Balanced Broadcasting," in *The British General Election of 1979,* ed. D. Butler and D. Kavanagh. London: Macmillan.

Polsby, Nelson. 1984. *Political Innovation in America.* New Haven, Conn.: Yale University Press.

Porter, H. Owen. 1974. "Legislative Experts and Outsiders: The Two-Step Flow of Communication." *Journal of Politics* 36:703–30.

Portner, Jessica. 1997. "Funding to Urge Sexual Abstinence Ignites Debate." *Education Week,* 11 June.

Posner, Richard A. 1992. *Sex and Reason.* Cambridge, Mass.: Harvard University Press.

Provenzo, Eugene F., Jr. 1990. *Religious Fundamentalism and American Education: The Battle for the Public Schools.* Albany: State University of New York Press.

Public Agenda. 1994. "First Things First: What Americans Expect from the Public Schools." A Public Agenda Survey. New York: Public Agenda.

Purcell, Edward A., Jr. 1973. *The Crisis of Democratic Theory: Scientific Naturalism and the Problem of Value.* Lexington: University Press of Kentucky.

Pym, B. 1974. *Pressure Groups and the Permissive Society.* Newton Abbot: David and Charles.

Queensland Attorney-General (ex rel. Kerr) v. *T.* 57 A.L.J.R. (1983) 285.

Quinn, Bernard, Herman Anderson, Martin Bradley, Paul Goetting, and Peggy Shriver. 1982. *Churches and Church Membership in the United States, 1980.* Atlanta, Ga.: Glenmary Research Center.

Randall, Richard S. 1968. *Censorship of the Movies: The Social and Political Control of a Mass Medium.* Madison: University of Wisconsin Press.

————. 1976. "Censorship: From *The Miracle* to *Deep Throat,*" in *The American Film Industry,* ed. Tino Balio. Madison: University of Wisconsin Press.

Ray, J. J. 1984. "Attitude to Abortion, Attitude to Life and Conservatism in Australia." *Sociology and Social Research* 68(1):236–46.

Read, M. 1998. "The Pro-Life Movement." *Parliamentary Affairs* 51:445–57.

————, D. Marsh, and D. Richards. 1994. "Why Did They Do It? Voting on Homosexuality and Capital Punishment in the House of Commons." *Parliamentary Affairs* 47:374–86.

Reese, Thomas J. 1992. *A Flock of Shepherds: The National Conference of Catholic Bishops.* Kansas City, Mo.: Sheed & Ward.

————. 1996. "Catholic Voters: Pulled in Two Directions." *America,* 2 November.

Regan, P. 1988. "The 1986 Shops Bill." *Parliamentary Affairs* 41:218–35.

Reich, Wilhelm. 1971. *The Invasion of Compulsory Sex-Morality.* New York: Farrar, Straus, Giroux.

————. 1983. *Children of the Future: On the Prevention of Sexual Pathology.* Edited by Mary Higgins and Chester M. Raphael. New York: Farrar, Straus, Giroux.

Rhode, Deborah L., and Martha Minow. 1990. "Reforming the Questions, Questioning the Reforms: Feminist Perspectives on Divorce Law." In *Divorce Reform at the Crossroads,* ed. Stephen D. Sugarman and Herma Hill Kay. New Haven: Yale University Press.

Rice, S. A. 1925. "The Behavior of Legislative Groups." *Political Science Quarterly* 40:60–72.

Richards, P. G. 1970. *Parliament and Conscience.* London: George Allen and Unwin.

Richardson, A. T. 1992. "War Crimes Act 1991." *Modern Law Review* 55:73–87.

Richardson, J., and G. Jordan. 1979. *Governing Under Pressure: The Policy Process in a Post-Parliamentary Democracy.* Oxford: Martin Robertson.

Riker, William. 1986. *The Art of Political Manipulation.* New Haven, Conn.: Yale University Press.

Ripley, Randall B., and Grace A. Franklin. 1986. *Policy Implementation and Bureaucracy.* 2d ed. Chicago: Dorsey Press.

————. 1987. *Congress, the Bureaucracy, and Public Policy.* 4th ed. Chicago: Dorsey.

————. 1991. *Congress, the Bureaucracy, and Public Policy.* 5th ed. Pacific Grove, Calif.: Brooks/Cole.

Ritter, John. 1997. "States Battle over Sex Ed Guidelines." *USA Today,* 14 July.

Rochefort, David A., and Roger W. Cobb. 1994. "Instrumental versus Expressive Definitions of AIDS Policymaking," in *The Politics of Problem Definition,* ed. David A. Rochefort and Roger W. Cobb. Lawrence: University of Kansas Press.

Rogers, Everett. 1983. *Diffusion of Innovations.* 3d ed. New York: Free Press.

————. 1995. *Diffusion of Innovations.* 4th ed. New York: Free Press.

Rolston, Bill, and Anna Eggert, eds. 1994. *Abortion in the New Europe.* Westport: Greenwood.

Rose, Richard. 1993. *Lesson-Drawing in Public Policy.* Chatham, N.J.: Chatham House.

————, and Derek Urwin. 1969. "Social Cohesion, Political Parties and Strains in Regimes." *Comparative Political Studies* 2:7–67.

Rosenberg, Gerald N. 1991. *The Hollow Hope: Can Courts Bring About Social Change?* Chicago: University of Chicago Press.

Rourke, Francis E. 1984. *Bureaucracy, Politics and Public Policy.* 3d ed. Boston, Mass.: Little, Brown.

Rozell, Mark, and Clyde Wilcox. 1996. *Second Coming: The New Christian Right in Virginia Politics.* Baltimore, Md.: Johns Hopkins University Press.

Sabatier, Paul A. 1997. "The Status and Development of Policy Theory: A Reply to Hill." *Policy Currents* 7:1–10.

————, and Hank Jenkins-Smith. 1993. *Policy Change and Learning: An Advocacy Coalition Approach.* Boulder, Colo.: Westview.

————, and David Whiteman. 1985. "Legislative Decision Making and Substantive Policy Information." *Legislative Studies Quarterly* 10:395–91.

Sanders, D. 1997. "Voting and the Electorate," in *Developments in British Politics 5,* ed. P. Dunleavy, A. Gamble, I. Holliday, and G. Peele. London: Macmillan.

Savage, Robert L. 1985. "Diffusion Research Traditions and the Spread of Policy Innovations in a Federal System." *Publius* 15:1–27.

Scammell, M., and M. Harrop. 1997. "The Press," in *The British General Elections of 1997,* ed. D. Butler and D. Kavanagh. London: Macmillan.

Schattschneider, E. E. 1960. *The Semi-Sovereign People.* New York: Holt, Reinhardt and Winston.

———. 1975. *The Semisovereign People: A Realist's View of Democracy in America.* Hinsdale, Ill.: Dreyden.

Scheppele, Kim Lane. 1996. "Constitutionalizing Abortion," in *Abortion Politics,* ed. Marianne Githens and Dorothy McBride Stetson. New York: Routledge.

Schneider, Mark, and Paul Teske with Michael Mintrom. 1995. *Public Entrepreneurs: Agents for Change in American Government.* Princeton, N.J.: Princeton University Press.

Schroedel, Jean Reith, and Pamela Fiber. 1998. "Fetal Personhood: A Moral and Legal Quagmire." Paper presented at the annual meeting of the American Political Science Association, Boston.

Schumach, Murray. 1964. *Faces on the Cutting Room Floor: The Story of Movie and Television Censorship.* New York: William Morrow.

Schwartz, Mildred A. 1981. "Politics and Moral Causes in Canada and the United States." *Comparative Social Research* 4:65–90.

Schwed, Roger. 1983. *Abolition and Capital Punishment.* New York: AMS Press.

Scott, Joseph E., and Steven J. Cuvelier. 1993. "Violence and Sexual Violence in Pornography: Is It Really Increasing?" *Archives of Sexual Behavior* 22:357–371.

Scott, W. J. 1985. "The Equal Rights Amendment as Status Politics." *Social Forces* 64:499–506.

Seelig, Michael Y., and Julie H. Seelig. 1998. " 'Place Your Bets!' On Gambling, Government and Society." *Canadian Public Policy* 24:91–106.

Seltzer, Richard. 1993. "AIDS, Homosexuality, Public Opinion, and Changing Correlates over Time." *Journal of Homosexuality* 26:85–97.

Sharkansky, Ira. 1969. "The Utility of Elazar's Political Culture." *Polity* 2:66–83.

Sharp, Elaine B. 1992. "Interest Groups and Symbolic Policy Formation: The Case of Anti-Drug Policy." Lawrence: University of Kansas. Typescript.

———. 1994. "The Dynamics of Issue Expansion: Cases from Disability Rights and Fetal Research Controversy." *Journal of Politics* 56:919–39.

———. 1997. "A Comparative Anatomy of Urban Social Conflict." *Political Research Quarterly* 50:261–80.

Short, E. 1989. *Whip to Wilson.* London: MacDonald.

Sigelman, Lee, Phillip W. Roeder, and Carol Sigelman. 1981. "Social Service Innovation in the American States." *Social Science Quarterly* 62:503–15.

Simon, Herbert A. 1958. *Administrative Behavior.* New York: Free Press.

———. 1982. "From Substantive to Procedural Rationality," in *Models of Bounded Rationality. Vol. 2, Behavioral Economics and Business Organization,* ed. Herbert Simon. Cambridge, Mass.: MIT Press.

Sklar, Robert. 1994. *Movie-Made America: The Cultural History of American Movies,* rev. ed. New York: Vintage Books.

Smith, Kimberly K. 1997. "Storytelling, Sympathy, and Moral Judgment in American Abolitionism." Paper presented at the annual meeting of the American Political Science Association, Washington, D.C.

Smith, Richard A. 1995. "Interest Group Influence in the U.S. Congress." *Legislative Studies Quarterly* 20:89–139.

Smith, T. Alexander. 1969. "Toward a Comparative Theory of the Policy Process." *Comparative Politics* 1:498–515.

———. 1975. *The Comparative Policy Process.* Santa Barbara, Calif.: Clio Press.

Smith, Tom W. 1990. "The Sexual Revolution?" *Public Opinion Quarterly* 54:415–35.

Spitzer, Robert J. 1995. *The Politics of Gun Control.* Chatham, N.J.: Chatham House.

Stanley, Harold W., and Richard G. Niemi. 1994. *Vital Statistics on American Politics.* 4th ed. Washington, D.C.: CQ Press.

"States Set to Spend Millions on Abstinence Education." 1997. *USA Today,* 23 July.

Stefanovic, Dragan, and Ruth Ann Strickland. 1998. "Explaining Abortion Clinic Violence in the United States: A State by State Analysis." Paper presented at the annual meeting of the American Political Science Association, Boston.

Steinfels, Peter, and Gustav Niebuhr. 1996. "Shift to Right Looms at Top for U.S. Catholics." *New York Times,* 3 November.

Stimson, James, Michael MacKuen, and Robert Erikson. 1995. "Dynamic Representation." *American Political Science Review* 89:543–66.

Stone, Keith. 1994. "Has U.S. Given Up in War on Porn?" *Los Angeles Daily News,* 11 December.

Strossen, Nadine. 1995. *Defending Pornography: Free Speech, Sex, and the Fight for Women's Rights.* New York: Doubleday.

Studlar, Donley T. 1993. "Ethnic Minority Groups, Agenda Setting, and Policy Borrowing in Britain," in *Minority Group Influence,* ed. Paula D. McClain. New York: Greenwood Press.

———. 1996. *Great Britain: Decline or Renewal?* Boulder, Colo.: Westview Press.

Szymanski, Ann-Marie. 1997. "Dry Compulsions: Prohibition and the Creation of State-Level Enforcement Agencies." Paper presented at the annual meeting of the American Political Science Association, Washington, D.C.

Tatalovich, Raymond. 1995. *Nativism Reborn.* Lexington: University Press of Kentucky.

———. 1997. *The Politics of Abortion in the United States and Canada.* New York: M.E. Sharpe.

———, and Byron W. Daynes. 1981. *The Politics of Abortion: A Study of Community Conflict in Public Policy Making.* New York: Praeger.

———, and Byron W. Daynes, eds. 1988. *Social Regulatory Policy.* Boulder, Colo.: Westview Press.

———, and Byron W. Daynes, eds. 1998. *Moral Controversies in American Politics: Cases in Social Regulatory Policy.* Armonk, N.Y.: M.E. Sharpe.

———, and Byron W. Daynes. 1988. "Conclusion: Social Regulatory Policymaking," in *Social Regulatory Policy: Moral Controversies in American Politics,* ed. Raymond Tatalovich and Byron W. Daynes. Boulder, Colo.: Westview Press.

———, and David Schier. 1993. "The Persistence of Ideological Cleavage in Voting on Abortion Legislation in the House of Representatives, 1973–1988." *American Politics Quarterly* 21:125–39.

———, T. Alexander Smith, and Michael P. Bobic. 1994. "Moral Conflict and the Policy Process." *Policy Currents* 4:1–7.

Tate, C. Neal, and Torbjorn Vallinder, eds. 1995. *The Global Expansion of Judicial Power.* New York: New York University Press.

Thomas, Clive S., and Ronald J. Hrebenar. 1990. "Interest Groups in the States," in *Politics in the American States: Comparative Analysis,* ed. Virginia Gray, Herbert Jacob, and Robert B. Albritton. 5th ed. Glenview, Ill.: Scott, Foresman.

Thompson, Mark, ed. 1994. *The Long Road to Freedom.* New York: St. Martin's Press.

Tribe, Laurence. 1990. *Abortion: The Clash of Absolutes.* New York: Norton.

Truman, David B. 1958. *The Governmental Process.* New York: Alfred A. Knopf.

Tullock, Gordon. 1974. "Does Capital Punishment Deter Crime?" *The Public Interest* 26:108–22.

Tyszka, Tadeusz. 1989. "Preselection, Uncertainty of Preferences, and Information Processing in Human Decision Making," in *Process and Structure in Human Decision Making,* ed. Henry Montgomery and Ola Svenson. New York: Wiley.

U.S. Bureau of the Census. Various years. *Statistical Abstract of the United States.* Washington, D.C.: Government Printing Office.

U.S. Department of Health and Human Services. 1997. "Application Guidance for the Abstinence Education Provision of the 1996 Welfare Law, P.L. 104–193." Rockville, Md.: Maternal and Child Health Bureau.

U.S. House of Representatives. 1977. Committee on Small Business. Subcommittee on Special Small Business Problems. *Movie Ratings and the Independent Producer.* 95th Cong., 1st Sess.

U.S. President. 1994. *Economic Report of the President Transmitted to Congress, 1994.* Washington, D.C.: Government Printing Office.

Valenti, Jack. 1996. "The Voluntary Movie Rating System. How It All Began." Location: www.mpaa.org/ratings.html.

Van Dunk, Emily. 1998. "Handgun Safety and the Making of Controversial Public Policy: An Examination of State Policy Formulation." Paper presented at the annual meeting of the American Political Science Association, Boston.

Vellenga, Jacob J. 1967. "Christianity and the Death Penalty," in *The Death Penalty in America,* ed. Hugh Adam Bedau. Garden City, N.Y.: Anchor.

Verba, Sidney, Kay Lehman Schlozman, and Henry E. Brady. 1995. *Voice and Equality: Civic Volunteerism in American Politics.* Cambridge, Mass.: Harvard University Press.

"Victory at Midnight." 1998. *The Weekend Australian,* 22–23 May.

"Village faces demon drink." 1998. *The Ottawa Citizen,* 9 March.

Vizzard, Jack. 1970. *See No Evil: Life Inside a Hollywood Censor.* New York: Simon & Schuster.

Wainer, Bertram. 1972. *It Isn't Nice.* Sydney: Alpha Books.

Wald, Kenneth D. 1992. *Religion and Politics in the United States.* 2d ed. Washington, D.C.: CQ Press.

———, James W. Button, and Barbara A. Rienzo. 1996. "The Politics of Gay Rights in American Communities: Explaining Antidiscrimination Ordinances and Policies." *American Journal of Political Science* 40:1152–78.

Walker, Alexander. 1968. *Sex in the Movies: The Celluloid Sacrifice.* Baltimore, Md.: Penguin Books.

Walker, Jack L. 1969. "The Diffusion of Innovations Among the American States." *American Political Science Review* 63:880–99.

———. 1973. "Comment: Problems in Research on the Diffusion of Policy Innovations." *American Political Science Review* 67:1186–91.

Walker, Samuel. 1990. *In Defense of Liberties: A History of the American Civil Liberties Union.* New York: Oxford University Press.

Walsh, Frank. 1996. *Sin and Censorship: The Catholic Church and the Motion Picture Industry.* New Haven: Yale University Press.

Warhurst, John, and Vance Merrill. 1982. "The Abortion Issue in Australia: Pressure Politics and Policy." *Australian Quarterly* 54:119–35.

Wasko, Janet. 1994. *Hollywood in the Information Age: Beyond the Silver Screen.* Austin: University of Texas Press.

Wattier, Mark J., and Raymond Tatalovich. 1995. "Senate Voting on Abortion Legislation over Two Decades: Testing a Reconstructed Partisanship Variable." *American Review of Politics* 16:167–83.

Wearing, Joseph. 1998. "Guns, Gays and Gadflies: Party Dissent in the House of Commons under Mulroney and Chretien." Paper presented at the annual meeting of the Canadian Political Science Association, Ottawa.

Wellin, Edward. 1955. "Boiling Water in a Peruvian Town," in *Health, Culture and Community,* ed. Benjamin D. Paul. New York: Russell Sage.

Whiteman, David. 1995. *Communication in Congress: Members, Staff, and the Search for Information.* Lawrence: University of Kansas Press.

Wilcox, Clyde, and Aage Clausen. 1991. "The Dimensionality of Roll-Call Voting Reconsidered." *Legislative Studies Quarterly* 16:393–406.

Wilcox, Clyde. 1992. *God's Warriors.* Baltimore: Johns Hopkins University Press.

Wilson, James Q. 1973. *Political Organizations.* New York: Basic Books.

———. 1989. *Bureaucracy.* New York: Basic Books.

Wilson, Woodrow. 1885. *Congressional Government.* In Wilson, *Papers,* Vol. 4. Princeton, N.J.: Princeton University Press, 6–179.

Winn, Beth M., and Marcia Lynn Whicker. 1989–90. "Indicators of State Lottery Adoptions." *Policy Studies Journal* 18:293–304.

Winneke, Henry. 1970. *Report of the Board of Inquiry into Allegations of Corruption in the Police Force in Connection with Illegal Abortion Practices in the State of Victoria.* Melbourne: Victorian Government Printer.

Wirt, Frederick Marshall. 1956. *State Film Censorship with Particular Reference to Ohio.* Ph.D. dissertation, Ohio State University.

Wlezien, Christopher. 1995. "The Public as Thermostat: Dynamics of Preferences for Spending." *American Journal of Political Science* 39:981–1000.

Wolf, Charles, Jr. 1993. *Markets or Governments: Choosing Between Imperfect Alternatives.* 2d ed. Cambridge, Mass.: MIT Press.

Wolfe, Alan. 1998. *One Nation, After All.* New York: Viking.

Woliver, Laura R. 1998. "Social Movements and Abortion Law," in *Social Movements and American Political Institutions,* ed. Anne N. Costain and Andrew S. McFarland. Lanham, Md.: Rowman & Littlefield.

Woodward, Kenneth L. 1993. "The Rites of Americans." *Newsweek,* 29 November.

"Word 'Unlawful' Is Vital—Defence." 1971. *Sydney Morning Herald,* 21 October.

Wright, John R. 1996. *Interest Groups and Congress: Lobbying, Contributions, and Influence.* Boston, Mass.: Allyn and Bacon.

Wynne, Edward A., and Kevin Ryan. 1993. *Reclaiming Our Schools.* New York: Macmillan.

Yates, Jeffrey L., and Henry R. Glick. 1997. "The Failed Patient Self Determination Act and Policy Alternatives for the Right to Die." *Journal of Aging and Social Policy* 9:29–50.

Zaller, John R. 1992. *The Nature and Origins of Mass Opinion.* New York: Cambridge University Press.

Zimring, Franklin E., and Gordon Hawkins. 1986. *Capital Punishment and the American Agenda.* New York: Cambridge University Press.

Zorza, Joan. 1992. "The Criminal Law of Misdemeanor Domestic Violence, 1970–1990." *Journal of Criminal Law and Criminology* 83:46–72.

Zurcher, Louis A., Jr., R. George Kirkpatrick, Robert G. Cushing, and Charles K. Bowman. 1971. "The Anti-Pornography Campaign: A Symbolic Crusade." *Social Problems* 19:217–38.

Zwier, Robert. 1979. "The Search for Information: Specialists and Non-Specialists in the U.S. House of Representatives." *Legislative Studies Quarterly* 3:31–42.

Name Index

Subject Index

Contributors

RICHARD A. BRISBIN JR. is associate professor of political science at West Virginia University. He won the Franklin L. Burdette Pi Sigma Alpha Award for the best paper presented at the 1996 American Political Science Association meeting. His most recent book is *Justice Antonin Scalia and the Conservative Revival* (The Johns Hopkins University Press, 1997), and he has published in the *American Political Science Review, American Journal of Political Science,* and *Political Science Quarterly.*

PHILIP COWLEY is a lecturer in the Department of Politics at the University of Hull and deputy director of the Centre for Legislative Studies. He is editor of *Conscience and Parliament* (Frank Cass, 1998) and coeditor of the *British Elections and Parties Review* (1998, 1999) and is the author of articles in a range of journals, including the *British Journal of Political Science, Political Studies, Party Politics,* and the *Journal of Legislative Studies.*

PAUL J. FABRIZIO is assistant professor of political science at McMurry University in Abilene, Texas. His research interests include campaigns and elections, as well as religion and politics.

HENRY R. GLICK is professor and chair of political science and research associate in the Pepper Institute on Aging and Public Policy at Florida State University. He teaches and does research on state court systems and judicial policy, including recent work on the right to die. He has written numerous books and journal articles on the courts and judicial process and on right-to-die policy, including *The Right to Die* (Columbia University Press, 1992).

MALCOLM L. GOGGIN is a visiting professor of political science at Michigan State University. His research focuses on abortion politics and the policy processes of implementation, design, and redesign. He is currently cowriting a book on policy change in Michigan in the 1990s and coediting a book on policy design and redesign across nations and time.

DONALD P. HAIDER-MARKEL is assistant professor of political science at the University of Kansas. He has authored and coauthored several articles on gay and lesbian politics, abortion, hate crimes, and citizen militia groups in the *Journal of Politics, Political Research Quarterly, Social Science Quarterly,* and *Demography.* He continues his work on gay and lesbian politics and the role of "outsider" groups in the policy process.

AMY HUTCHINSON is a research associate for Economic Research Services, Inc. (ERS) located in Tallahassee, Florida. ERS is a professional research firm providing a variety of services in economic and statistical analysis. She is also a doctoral candidate in political science at Florida State University.

MEI-HSIEN LEE is assistant professor in the Graduate School of Southeast Asian Studies at National Chi Nan University, Taiwan. She is the author of several articles on U.S. and Southeast Asian politics and is the editor of the *Journal of Southeast Asian Studies.*

KENNETH J. MEIER is the Charles Puryear Professor of Liberal Arts and professor of political science at Texas A&M University. His epistemology reflects the thinking of Flaubert, who advised being neat and orderly in your daily life so you can be violent and creative in your work. Meier is currently cleaning his office.

DONALD E. MILLER is associate professor and chair of mathematics at Saint Mary's College, University of Notre Dame. He is president of the Indiana Section of the Mathematical Association of America and is currently serving on the Education Committee of the Society for Industrial and Applied Mathematics. He has coauthored papers with colleagues in nursing, education, and political science, including an article on the impact of lottery spending.

CHRISTOPHER Z. MOONEY is director of the Illinois Legislative Studies Center at the University of Illinois at Springfield and editor of *State Politics and Policy Quarterly.*

IAN MYLCHREEST has taught at the University of Melbourne, Monash University, the University of Nevada, Las Vegas, and Wells College. He has published articles in the *Journal of Policy History* and *Cultures of the Commonwealth* and is the author of *The Promise of Individual Rights: From Vice Crimes to Victimless Crimes.*

BARBARA NORRANDER is professor of political science at the University of Arizona. She is the author of *Super Tuesday* and the coeditor of *Understanding Public*

Opinion. Some of her articles have appeared in the *American Journal of Political Science* and *Political Research Quarterly.*

PATRICK A. PIERCE is associate professor of political science at Saint Mary's College, the University of Notre Dame. He has published articles on political psychology, the campaigns of women candidates for Congress, and the impact of lotteries on educational spending. He has also worked for the Elections and Survey Unit of CBS News.

KEVIN B. SMITH is associate professor of political science at the University of Nebraska-Lincoln and associate editor of *State Politics and Policy Quarterly.* His research focuses on education, crime, and morality policy.

DONLEY T. STUDLAR is Eberly Family Distinguished Professor of Political Science at West Virginia University. His research on the comparative politics of advanced industrial democracies has been published widely in books and journals. His books include *Great Britain: Decline or Renewal?* (Westview Press, 1996) and an edited volume, *Political Economy: Public Policies in the United States and Britain* (University Press of Mississippi, 1987).

SANDRA VERGARI is assistant professor in the Department of Educational Administration and Policy Studies at SUNY-Albany. Her research focuses on education reform politics and policies.

CLYDE WILCOX is professor of government at Georgetown University. He has written in several areas relating to morality policy, including religion and politics, gender politics, and the politics of abortion.